SAGE was founded in 1965 by Sara Miller McCune to support the dissemination of usable knowledge by publishing innovative and high-quality research and teaching content. Today, we publish over 900 journals, including those of more than 400 learned societies, more than 800 new books per year, and a growing range of library products including archives, data, case studies, reports, and video. SAGE remains majority-owned by our founder, and after Sara's lifetime will become owned by a charitable trust that secures our continued independence.

Los Angeles | London | New Delhi | Singapore | Washington DC | Melbourne

SPORTS LAW IN INDIA

SPORTS LAW IN INDIA
Policy, Regulation
and Commercialisation

Edited by
LOVELY DASGUPTA
SHAMEEK SEN

Los Angeles | London | New Delhi
Singapore | Washington DC | Melbourne

First published in 2018 by

SAGE Publications India Pvt Ltd
B1/I-1 Mohan Cooperative Industrial Area
Mathura Road, New Delhi 110 044, India
www.sagepub.in

SAGE Publications Inc
2455 Teller Road
Thousand Oaks, California 91320, USA

SAGE Publications Ltd
1 Oliver's Yard, 55 City Road
London EC1Y 1SP, United Kingdom

SAGE Publications Asia-Pacific Pte Ltd
3 Church Street
#10-04 Samsung Hub
Singapore 049483

Published by Vivek Mehra for SAGE Publications India Pvt Ltd, typeset in 10.5/13 pt Sabon by Zaza Eunice, Hosur, Tamil Nadu, India and printed at Chaman Enterprises, New Delhi.

Library of Congress Cataloging-in-Publication Data

Names: Dasgupta, Lovely, editor. | Sen, Shameek, editor.
Title: Sports law in India: policy, regulation and commercialisation /
  Edited by Lovely Dasgupta, Shameek Sen.
Description: Thousand Oaks, California: SAGE Publications, 2018. | Includes
  bibliographical references and index.
Identifiers: LCCN 2018013186| ISBN 9789352806782 (print (hardcover) : alk.
  paper) | ISBN 9789352806799 (e pub 2.0) | ISBN 9789352806805 (e book)
Subjects: LCSH: Sports—Law and legislation—India.
Classification: LCC KNS1585 .S66 2018 | DDC 344.54/099—dc23 LC record available at https://
lccn.loc.gov/2018013186

ISBN: 978-93-528-0678-2 (HB)

SAGE Team: Rajesh Dey, Guneet Kaur Gulati and Shobana Paul

*Dedicated to the Barefooted Mohun Bagan Team
of the 1911 IFA Shield Final*

Thank you for choosing a SAGE product!
If you have any comment, observation or feedback,
I would like to personally hear from you.

Please write to me at **contactceo@sagepub.in**

Vivek Mehra, Managing Director and CEO, SAGE India.

Bulk Sales

SAGE India offers special discounts
for purchase of books in bulk.
We also make available special imprints
and excerpts from our books on demand.

For orders and enquiries, write to us at

Marketing Department
SAGE Publications India Pvt Ltd
B1/I-1, Mohan Cooperative Industrial Area
Mathura Road, Post Bag 7
New Delhi 110044, India

E-mail us at **marketing@sagepub.in**

Get to know more about SAGE

Be invited to SAGE events, get on our mailing list.
Write today to **marketing@sagepub.in**

This book is also available as an e-book.

CONTENTS

Foreword by Justice Mukul Mudgal   ix
Preface   xiii
Acknowledgements   xv
Introduction   xvii

I   Constitution and Sports in India   1
Mahendra Pal Singh and Akhilendra P. Singh

II   Impact of Non-profit Laws on Sports in India   19
P. Ishwara Bhat

III   Current Issues Within Sports Law in India   46
Vidushpat Singhania, Nitin Mittal and Gautam Karhadkar

IV   Public Interest Litigation and Sports in India   83
Shivam Singh and Shreeyash Uday Lalit

V   Privacy Issues and Sports in India   100
Agnidipto Tarafder and Carmel Sharma

VI   Doping and Sports in India   121
Richa R. Mulchandani

VII   Religious Dictates and Sports in India   142
Saurabh Mishra and Shreya Mishra

VIII   Arbitration and Sports Disputes in India   156
Daniel Mathew

IX   Image Rights and Sports in India   177
David McArdle

X   Broadcasting of Sports in India   192
Saurabh Bhattacharjee

XI   Commercialisation of Sports and Indian Franchise Leagues   221
     Shameek Sen

XII Way Forward for Sports in India   241
     Lovely Dasgupta

     About the Editors and Contributors   249
     Index   257

FOREWORD

It is an honour to be requested by West Bengal National University of Juridical Sciences (NUJS), Kolkata, and its esteemed professors Dr Lovely Dasgupta and Dr Shameek Sen to write a foreword for the book *Sports Law in India: Policy, Regulation and Commercialisation* on a subject that is extremely dear to me. India has moved from being in the nascent phase of sports law to a developing phase. I am glad that other experts in the field Professor M. P. Singh, Vidushpat Singhania and Professor David McArdle have also contributed to this book.

The culmination of various leagues across sports varying from cricket to bridge, the disputes before authorities and the efforts of the government to legislate on sports have given impetus to this developing field of sports law. India is developing expertise and capability by hosting major sports events such as the FIFA U-17 World Cup 2017, Lusophony Games 2014 and South Asian Games 2016. Each of these major events besides the main attraction of sport at the event has to address manifold facets while administering them. The role of a person who understands sports law is critical in order to successfully administer and effectively deliver glitch-free games. It is better to learn from the experience from other games which have been hosted worldwide and understand the issues that they faced, so that the mistakes made can be avoided and challenges can be foreseen and tackled.

India unfortunately has been determined to be third from among countries worldwide for anti-doping violations. This is both a concern that we have so many sports-persons who are taking prohibited substance and a reflection of our anti-doping administration, which while effectively detecting the prohibited substance in samples is not being able to provide effective education to the sports-persons and the support personnel in Indian sport ecosystem. The Government of India is contemplating a robust system of detection of doping by introducing athletes' biological passport within the ambit, proposing a legislation to govern anti-doping as well as exploring tie-ups with the Food Safety and Standards Authority of India and National Pharmaceutical Pricing Authority of India.

The successful bid of Star India in procuring the commercial rights pertaining to broadcast the Indian Premier League for the years 2018–2022, for a whopping ₹16,000 crores, stresses upon the known fact that sport is no longer only a hobby but also a robust industry. As any industry grows, be it the petroleum industry, the steel industry, the broadcasting industry, the telecommunication industry etc., it develops its own set of regulations and expertise. Sports in India is undergoing such a transformation in India.

A key area of development for sports law is also facilitating effective governance of sports organisations. Earlier sports were pursued as a hobby. With the increase of spectator interaction and revenue from sponsorships and endorsements, some sports-persons started getting paid to participate in sports events. Most international federations prohibited professional sports-persons from participation within their folds earlier. However, most sport federations are now embracing commercial leagues and are promoting professional sports-persons. At the national level, the Supreme Court of India, accepting the recommendations of Justice Lodha Committee and of the earlier IPL Probe Committee chaired by me, has lent judicial support to the process of reformation of sports governance. There are efforts being made to issue an improved version of the National Sports Code which is likely to consider the international expertise that has developed in governance of sports whilst taking into account the issues and uniqueness of India. The formation of the All India Council of Sports as a policy advisory body to the government and sports at large in India is also a welcome step. International federations such as Fédération Internationale de Football Association (FIFA) and International Cricket Council (ICC), which have a worldwide presence and are radically commercialised, are looking within to improve their governance structure, so that robust models can be developed for long-term sustenance and growth. Indian federations may be heading down this path if they seek to avoid regulations and standards being imposed upon them.

Justice Mukul Mudgal

PREFACE

Sport has the power to change the world. It has the power to inspire. It has the power to unite people in a way that little else does. It speaks to youth in a language they understand. Sport can create hope where once there was only despair. It is more powerful than government in breaking down racial barriers.

—Nelson Mandela

Indeed, sport is probably one of the greatest instruments of social cohesion in today's conflict-stricken world. The sheer joy of watching sporting icons display their sporting bravado makes people forget their pains and sorrows, and transports them into a state of blissful oblivion.

However, sport has, over the years, become more and more professional, and commercially motivated. Puritans often rue the loss of the simplicity in the different sporting disciplines, in view of the insane urge to win at any costs. This insatiable desire towards achievement of success often provokes sports-persons to adopt unfair means. And, this is one area where the interplay of sports with the legal system becomes an absolute inevitability. Moreover, issues of governance and management of sports by the sporting federations and their engagement with the basic rights of the sports-persons, on the one hand, and with the state, on the other, become a typical public law topic of discussion. Similarly, commercialisation of sports has led to several vistas where an active construction of both public and private laws becomes necessary. This interplay of sports and law has led to the emergence of this discourse called 'sports law' in the Western legal scholarship, and this has become a very important upcoming legal discipline in the Indian context as well in the recent times. Today, there are specialised law firms and policy research centres debating on sports law.

Hence, the idea of writing a book on sports law is a logical outcome. It is to be noted that in the Indian context, there is an imminent need for such scholarship in sports law, more so in light of the fact that in recent times, judicial interventions have led to large-scale reforms within sports governing bodies. Additionally, broadcasting rights, especially in the context of cricket, are being sold at astronomical rates. Moreover, sporting achievements of the Indian athletes are being highlighted, both by the media and by the State, like never before. To add to this is the fact that an increasing number of lawyers and academicians are taking immense interest in sports and its interplay with law and policy. It is this background that convinced us to write the book.

However, since the objective was to map the most relevant topics currently being debated within the realm of sports law, two persons' co-authorship would not have done complete justice to the entire spectrum of issues involved. Hence came the inspiration of bringing on board a group of experts of unquestionable eminence, renowned in their respective fields. Accordingly, this book is a collage of multiple opinions and reflects varied personalities. Each chapter is a conversation and gives insight into specific debates that are relevant in the present context. The reader, while reading the book, would be able to notice the rapid developments taking place within the Indian sports. Importantly, the growing professionalism of the Indian sports is pushing its boundaries to levels comparable with standards within international sports. The authors bring in their life experiences, and hence the reader has the benefit of different viewpoints, not only from India but also from other parts of the world. The focus though, while reading the book, has to be essentially the Indian perspective. Hence, specific examples from the Indian context are put forth in order to reflect on the issues, which would help the readers immediately identify these issues while exploring the legal complexities involved.

ACKNOWLEDGEMENTS

We sincerely acknowledge, in equal measures, all our contributors for their cooperation. The fact that they believed in us and agreed to contribute to the book is a gesture we shall forever remember fondly. We hope that we have been able to do justice to the faith they had reposed on us and have been able to live up to their expectations. We thank Professor P. Ishwara Bhat, vice chancellor, NUJS, for inspiring and encouraging us to take up the project and go ahead with it. He assured all guidance and gave ideas, including authoring a chapter himself, enabling us to make the book a reality. We thank Professor M. P. Singh, our teacher and former vice chancellor of NUJS, who enthusiastically supported us towards the completion of this book, and also readily agreed to contribute a chapter. At the end, we acknowledge each one of our sports-persons, whose achievements in the field are the real motivator for this book. Their difficulties and struggles served as a constant reminder when we were conceptualising and envisaging this book. We hope we have been able to do a sincere work which will help improve the sports law interventions, making Indian sports-persons achieve greater laurels.

INTRODUCTION

Sport, as per sociologists, is different from play, which is essentially an act in leisure, indulged in to relax, and is informal. Play does not entail formal rules or codes of regulation. There are no institutions governing play since its run is governed and determined by the participants. On the other hand, sport is formal and codified. It has rules and institutions implementing those rules. Since sport is rule based, it is aimed to serve multiple purposes for those who participate in the process. One aim of sports is cultural, since the rules and codes are often meant to further the cultural ethos of the community and the concerned society. There are thus, for example, traditional sports in India such as kho-kho and gilli-danda, which have their roots in the Indian cultural context. Similarly, other countries also have their traditional sports. These sports are competitive in nature and do encourage the idea of winning. However, the fundamental difference is that neither the traditional sports are dictated by rules of international federations nor does a mandate exists to comply with international standards. Further, the traditional sports are essentially played with the idea of participation and are rarely seen as a source of livelihood. Thus, the traditional sports support the philosophy of sports as a culture. On the other hand, sports that are governed by a hierarchy-based structure with a top-down approach are geared towards a different level of competition. Such kind of sports are more concerned with the rules and regulations and hence have the potential of giving rise to conflict. There is conflict, for example, with respect to the correct interpretation of the phrase 'spirit of sport', as gathered from the different sporting codes of conduct.

Since the participants are expected to comply with the rules, legalisation of sports takes place almost automatically. The contractual aspect of compliance gives rise to a cause of action. Further, the sports governing bodies have enough power to ensure that athletes are penalised for non-compliance. This power is derived from the lack of choice of an athlete, since practising a sport means an inevitable adherence to rules and codes. The powers of the sports governing bodies originate from the mandate to determine the status of an athlete. An amateur athlete is barred from using sport as a means of livelihood. This does definitely deprive a skilled athlete from financial security and has the danger of pushing the athlete to penury. The ethos of amateurism has been propagated by the major and dominant international federations. Additionally, the amateurism agenda has been highlighted and codified by the International Olympic Committee (IOC). The concept of amateurism is based on the ideals of fair play and participation in sports for the sake of establishing a model code of conduct. The exploitation of sports for earning livelihood or profit has been severely frowned upon by the IOC. Its philosophy of not-for-profit participation, however, does not fit in with the realities of modern sport. Furthermore, there are deep-rooted contradictions that the IOC itself is responsible for. The motto of IOC is *Citius–Altius–Fortius* which means faster–higher–stronger. The focus, therefore, is not merely on participation and fair play but also on winning. The celebration is of the winner and iconisation of the winning athlete.

This approach of the IOC fits in with the concept of modern sport which is primarily defined, among others, in terms of records. The celebration of sports-persons' achievement is measured in terms of records set. This iconisation is further underlined by the number of records owned by an individual athlete. Against this background, the insistence on amateurism is problematic, since the amateur sportsperson has been traditionally expected to be a detached soul, interested only in participation and not on any larger glory. Further, the creation of records means that the individual is expected to spend time in training but not earn from the investment to access more sophisticated training and nutrition dietary plan. Thus, amateurism takes sports idolisation to a level where sports-persons are expected to behave equivalent to ascetics.

This clearly goes on to show that the IOC clearly has undermined human frailties and desires. It is these aspects of human nature that lead the athlete to surreptitiously move towards professionalism. The fallout has been tremendous, with international federations forced to acknowledge the reality of professionalism. Hence, the IOC-sponsored rule of amateurism has withered away in view of the demand of professionalism. And with professionalism came more problems since the zeal to earn money has gone beyond livelihood issues. The international as well as national sports governing bodies have joined in to exploit sports to gain commercial advantage and maximise profits. Commodification of sports has also commodified the sports-persons, who are being auctioned off, as the phenomenon of franchise leagues, something that has captured the fascination of the sporting bodies, investors and the general public alike, has adequately shown in the recent times. The branding of sports teams, clubs and even stadiums has become the norm, and private leagues are equally prolific. Commodification of sports thus threatens and to a large extent dilutes the idea of sports as culture.

The other fallout of commodification of sports has been the growing intervention of law, since, quite expectedly, commercialisation goes hand in hand with dispute. This also leads to difficulties in handling the demands of different stakeholders. On the one hand are the growing wages/payout to the players; on the other hand are the increasing prices of the tickets. Further, the selling of sports as a content has also led to disputes. Another fallout has been the demand of players to be indemnified by the clubs or federations. The context of sports, thus, has undergone a sea change. Traditional court systems are grappling with sports-related disputes, but the demand is growing for sports-specific arbitrations and dispute resolutions in a specialised format. Moreover, the application of general law of the land requires taking into account the sporting context. The challenge is to balance the application of general principles of law against the specific nature of sports. Be it criminal law or competition law, all are arguably subsumed to the specific context of sports. Thus, commercialised and commodified sports are taking us to an era of more nuanced conflict resolution. Further, demand from the athletes to have more control over their career choices means that they are not willing to adhere to restrictive norms of the sports governing bodies. Here too, the unique features of sport vis-à-vis the free agency of sports-persons are matters of dispute, where general principles of law are often helpful. The roles of television in general and broadcasting media in particular have been the other most significant drivers of commercialisation of sports.

The symbiotic relationship of broadcasting and sports though has given rise to equally important issues pertaining to property rights and profit-sharing. Additionally, varied questions such as image rights of the sports-persons and ambush marketing are some of the issues that have cropped up over the years. All these disputes are being dealt with by the application of the law through processes both within and outside the sports field. Similarly, issues pertaining to intellectual property rights (IPRs) are a major point of debate in sports. Rights over logos to team names to use of players' names to colour of jerseys are some of the numerous ways in which IPR laws are interacting with sports and giving rise to sports law jurisprudence on the issues. Additionally, more serious issues such as doping and privacy rights as well as gender justice and human rights have also become the topic of discussion among the various stakeholders in the field of sports. The topics range from transgender rights to whereabouts clauses. The larger question is the excessive level of scrutiny of athletes and the complete breakdown of trust between the sports-persons and the sports governing bodies. Additionally, the rationale of the existing regime to deal with doping or hyperandrogenism continues to be matter of great concern, and the solutions are sought to be based on accepted legal principles of equality and transparency. However, the justification for intrusions into an athlete's privacy, in the context of both doping and gender, is unique and depicts the longstanding argument of sports being equal and everyone is entitled to equal opportunity. The intervention of law in this field is thus used to maintain the stranglehold of the sports governing bodies on the sports-persons and their right to livelihood.

Sport is also an important tool in propagating the political ideology of the State and its politics. Hence, laws and policies are framed to ensure that sporting performances can be used to affirm the superiority of the State's decisions. In this context, the impact of the State's obsession with sporting performances can have a devastating impact on the sports-persons. The recent scandal involving Russia is just an example of State-sponsored doping. State uses its machinery to exploit the sportspersons' frailties and ensure that they obey the diktat. Similarly, in terms of training and other facilities being made available to sports-persons, the agenda of the State has an important role to play. All these are matters of discussion and on each of the previously referred issues, a book can be written.

This book, however, tries to address a cross section of these various issues, rather than putting particular emphasis on one or two of them. It is written primarily from Indian perspective, with sprinkling of international flavour, wherever necessary. Hence, it was important for the editors to key in on issues that were the most relevant of all the issues impacting sports law. As has been mentioned earlier, the editors' job was made easy by the expertise of the contributors. The contributors applied their experiences to suitably highlight the relevant topics. Accordingly, this book seeks to cover a plethora of relevant issues pertaining to the legal regulation of sports in the Indian context against the developments in the global arena. One of the primary reasons to focus on India is the fact that commercialisation of sports has changed the perception within India. There is a growing interest in not only watching sports but also pursuing sports as a profession. The consequence of the same is that there is a growing demand for accountability and transparency in the governance of sports within India. The key driver for the changing landscape of sports in India has been cricket, which has not only been the first sport to openly embrace commercialisation but also been subject to extensive public scrutiny. Quite naturally, therefore, there are essays in this book which focus around different areas of inter-play of the legal system with the game of cricket—be it about the constitutional status of the Board of Control for Cricket in India

(BCCI) or the controversies surrounding the broadcasting of the cricket matches in the public broadcasting platforms.

The ideological conflict between the cultural notions of sports as against commercialisation of sports is quite significantly responsible for the ongoing debates. The current debates within sports law in India thus range from the demand for judicial review to interventions by the Competition Commission of India. This book aims to introduce to the reader the diverse opinions on the challenges that sports in India are faced with. The opinions range from those of eminent constitutional law experts to leading sports lawyers. The book is aimed at being more than a textbook. It flags off the key issues and puts forth concrete suggestions on the future roadmap. That there is a dearth of research on sports law and policy in India is a given reality. This book is a one of its kind endeavour which aims to fill in the scholarship vacuum that currently exists in this area. Being an edited volume, it has the advantage of collating the opinions of experts responsible for establishing a distinct discipline of study called sports law. The book, it is hoped, will be key in furthering the cause of sports law in India. Importantly, for all future sports lawyers, the book will be the one of the first and foremost points of reference.

The book deals with a detailed analysis of the constitutional jurisprudence with respect to sports that has undergone some significant evolution recently in the context of sporting federations, more particularly the BCCI. The concerns and the debate generated by the Supreme Court have raised intriguing questions about the extent of State intervention within the field of sports. How far should the State control policy decision of the sports federation is a question that Chapter 1 addresses.

Related to the issue of governance in sports is the amenability of the sports federation under the non-profit organisations (NPOs) law. This is an interesting analysis considering that officially all sports federations including the BCCI are regarded as not-for-profit organisations. The paradox is that the sports federations are, as much as there has been a non-profit motivation behind their constitution, steadfastly engaging themselves into commercialising sports. Hence, the question is, can they legitimately be called not-for-profit organisations and, if so, how should they be regulated?

The book discusses at length the different judicial interventions on different aspects of sports, including, but not limited to, concerns of good governance, gender discrimination, doping, match-fixing, etc. Interventions in the conventional modes involving aggrieved litigants and in the form of public interest litigations are highlighted in some detail.

The book also focuses on the rights of athletes and the gravest concerns pertaining to privacy rights. With the emergence of right to privacy as a fundamental right, the status of athletes and their respective rights to privacy needs further evaluation. Privacy right concerns arise from the range of compliance requirements vis-à-vis an athlete. The sample testing and whereabouts clause as part of doping regulation, gender testing as part of performance qualifications, etc. are some of the issues that give rise to concerns of privacy. Hence, Chapter 5 raises the question as to how far domestic regulation can override the mandate of international sports law on the issue of privacy.

The other issue where athletes need to be taken into confidence is anti-doping advocacy programmes. Since the athletes are most affected by anti-doping regulation, they are also the most vulnerable group. Lack of education hinders their compliance ability and lead to detrimental consequences. These issues are highlighted through empirical evidence.

Another issue that is discussed in this context is the issue of sports and religion, putting specific focus on the restriction of headgears in basketball, which had been the bone of contention for multiple reasons. This issue is highly relevant in a country like India where the diversity of religions and religious rituals percolate down to every aspect of our societal lives, and sport is definitely no exception.

Corruption in sports is another area which is discussed by the authors in the context of sports governance. Specific issues include, but are not limited to, doping, match-fixing, etc. A key feature of sports governance is the resolution of dispute. In this context, the role of Court of Arbitration for Sport (CAS) is discussed in great depth.

The book also deals with debates arising due to commercialisation and commodification of sports. An important area that is in focus in the context of commercialisation and commodification of sports is the broadcasting rights of sporting events. The judicial response over the years to the sale of broadcasting rights of sports events raises many interesting questions. This issue has been dealt with in the backdrop of the developments in the international arena. A related issue arising from commercialisation of sport is the regulation of pertaining to the recent phenomenon of franchise leagues. Especially in the field of cricket, the Indian Premier League has set new benchmarks and explored newer methods of maximising profits. However, the impact of private league on Indian football is leading to a lot of discussion and dilemma, in view of the clear conflicts between the cultural aspects of Indian football, which has a distinct socio-political context. The argument is that privatisation need not necessarily benefit the traditional structure within the sport, especially when the traditional structure is losing out in terms of finances. The problem is of ensuring the viability of the traditional football structure in view of the onslaught of such commercially lucrative private leagues.

The book, while discussing issues emanating out of commercialisation, also puts forth an international perspective on the key issue of image rights of sports-persons. The points raised therein are also important from Indian perspective due to the growing professionalism among our sports-persons. Indian sports-persons are gradually branding themselves and image right is a significant part of this branding. The discussion on the ongoing debates in the international arena makes an important read for it adds relevant nuances to the topic.

The primary focus of this book is to acquaint the reader to the fast emerging area called sports law, from both public law and private law perspectives. The different chapters explore the numerous legal issues that have arisen and are most likely to arise with respect to sports in the context of India. The comparison with the developments within the international sports law helps in a better understanding of these issues. This book seeks to act as a compendium and a reference material insofar as issues of sports law and governance are concerned, especially in view of the fact that there is a significant dearth of authentic and quality literature available on sports law in India that covers such a wide spectrum of issues in relation to the interface of sports and law.

In accordance with the objective, stated previously, the first chapter titled 'Constitution and Sports in India' by Professor M. P. Singh and Akhilendra P. Singh is written keeping in view the contemporary significance of sports which is much more than being a pastime and recreational activity. The authors have sought to locate the issues of sports governance and administrative within the larger constitutional fabric, especially in the context of the amenability of the sports federations to the writ jurisdiction of the courts, in light of contemporary constitutional developments. The authors have also laid emphasis on the evolution of the Article 12 jurisprudence, and the scope of horizontal enforcement of fundamental rights in the context of sports. The chapter acknowledges that sports have been transformed into organised activities coupled with enormous professionalism and affecting almost every area of public life, be it social, political or economic. Although the pace of this transformation was slow during the nineteenth and most part of the twentieth century, it has been boosted enormously in the past few decades owing to globalisation of technology and commerce.

The other way of enforcing accountability is through the application of the NPO law. Professor (Dr) Ishwara Bhat nuances the ways in which NPO law can be used to make the sports governing bodies in India accountable in the chapter titled 'Impact of Non-profit Laws on Sports in India'. This is an interesting take considering that the governance of sports in India is getting increasingly intertwined with commercialisation and profit-making. Application of the NPO laws can help in instilling accountability within the sports governing bodies. Professor Bhat nuances the debate between commercial sports and sports for all, essentially the argument being that professionalism in sports need not be necessarily at the expense of purity of sports.

In the third chapter titled 'Current Issues Within Sports Law in India', Vidushpat Singhania, Nitin Mittal and Gautam Karhadkar give an overview of the effect of commercialisation of sports by highlighting a range of issues including spot-fixing and match-fixing. The chapter collates several incidents in the recent past and how the Indian sports federations, and the Indian judiciary, have been dealing with the same. The analysis of the juristic developments on the various issues also takes the reader into an exploratory journey into the evolution of the Indian sports law jurisprudence. It also allows the reader to reflect upon the current trends and the future discourse. The vibrancy of sports law in India as a subject area of research also gets reflected through the arguments given in this chapter.

Shivam Singh and Shreeyash Uday Lalit write about the role of public interest litigation in governance of sport in their chapter titled 'Public Interest Litigation and Sports in India', which is the fourth chapter of the book. The aim is to find ways to make the sports governing bodies accountable and transparent in their functions. Usage of constitutional law principles are thus proposed by the authors to be a better way to ensure accountability. Sports law is getting immensely benefited through the use of public interest litigation in India. Further, public interest litigation is an alternative available to the sports-persons and stakeholders alike. The chapter nuances the ways and means in which public interest litigation is adding to the existing debates on sports law, policy and commercialisation.

In the chapter titled 'Privacy Issues and Sports in India', which is the fifth chapter of the book, Agnidipto Tarafder and Carmel

Sharma debate on the implications of the right to privacy in the context of sports-persons. They evaluate the topic, keeping in view the enormous amount of concessions on this universally guaranteed right that athletes are forced to make in complying with the requirements of World Anti-Doping Agency (WADA). Impact on Indian sports-persons due to WADA compliances are issues that the authors deal with in detail. Importantly, from a developing country perspective, privacy issues are crucial. With poverty and illiteracy, the athletes are in the most precarious position. The authors highlight the plight of the developing country athletes.

Dr Richa R. Mulchandani in her chapter titled 'Doping and Sports in India', which is the sixth chapter of the book, deals with advocacy issues within anti-doping regulations. She goes into the current state of advocacy programmes within the Indian sports administration. The sensitisation of the athletes and their support staff about the World Anti-Doping Code and its compliances is studied with a comparative perspective. The lack of information on the part of Indian athletes is a major issue. And the lack of access to information causes inadvertent doping.

Saurabh Mishra and Shreya Mishra, in the seventh chapter titled 'Religious Dictates and Sports in India', deal with the important issues of sports and religion and the approach of the sports governing bodies. The issues flagged and concerns raised by the authors in their chapter are particularly pertinent for a pluralistic country like India, where religion plays a very significant role in many spheres of our personal and professional life, and restrictions on religious practices of sports-persons can prove to be a really touchy issue. Both have brought out the existing disputes pertaining to the use of headgear within sports and its religious connotation from the developing country perspective.

The eighth chapter is written by Daniel Mathew and is titled 'Arbitration and Sports Disputes in India'. It is an exhaustive analysis of the role of domestic law in enforcing sports arbitral awards that are handed down by the CAS. As in all matters, disputes remain a silent yet potent possibility in sports. Given the high stakes in terms of athletes' career, technicalities and pressures of time that are involved, over the years enormous investment has gone into structuring dispute resolution mechanisms to resolve sports disputes. These mechanisms are highly customised and continuously fine-tuned to, among other things, respect the confidentiality and yet render, given the duration of sporting events, a timely award that remains relevant within the broader context. The chapter aims to delve deeper into issues surrounding utilisation on one specific method of dispute resolution, namely arbitration in resolving sports disputes. Over the years, arbitration has emerged as the method of choice for resolving sports-related disputes, with CAS being a widely acclaimed success story. However, for arbitration to operationalise, especially in disputes with a cross-border dimension, presence of certain core ideas such as existence of valid arbitration agreement and jurisdictional competence remains crucial. Of further interest would be the manner in which outcome of sports arbitration would be enforced and the roles that courts in a domestic jurisdiction play in sports arbitration. In addition to looking at these issues in an international context, the chapter, in particular, attempts to explore and understand these issues in light of the prevailing arbitration law in India, namely the Arbitration and Conciliation Act, 1996.

The ninth chapter deals with image rights and their impact on sports-persons. Titled 'Image Rights and Sports in India', this chapter authored by David McArdle presents an international perspective on the issues of commercialisation of sports and their impact on athletes. The context, as the title indicates, is the IPRs of the athletes which are distinct from the rights of the sports governing bodies. It also envisions the impact of the developments at the global level on sports within India. Especially, the author looks at the Indian law on image rights and gives a comparative perspective of the same.

'Broadcasting of Sports in India' by Saurabh Bhattacharjee is the tenth chapter, highlighting the disputes pertaining to sports and broadcasting. The chapter highlights the fallout of commercialisation in the Indian context. Further, the chapter investigates ways and means to balance the interest of the broadcaster as against other stakeholders, including the spectators.

The eleventh chapter titled 'Commercialisation of Sports and Indian Franchise Leagues' is written by Dr Shameek Sen who exclusively deals with the issue of corporatisation of sports in the context of franchise leagues. The focus of this chapter is the impact of this development on sports in India. His concern primarily is the effect of the private football league on traditional football clubs such as Mohun Bagan and East Bengal, which occupy prominent places in the history of Indian sports and cultural traditions and are currently standing on the cusp of extinction, with the onslaught of the more commercially lucrative franchise leagues. The chapter, therefore, presents a cross section of cultural and legal concern.

The concluding Chapter 12 amalgamates the thoughts on the issues presented within the book and investigates the future possibilities. It looks into possible ways of resolving the current conflict within sports in India. It compares the different models of sports governance present across the world especially in USA. The chapter ends with specific suggestions to make sports in India truly global and effective as a tool of achievement and National glory.

The main readership for this book will be students of sports law and management, at both graduate and postgraduate levels. Apart from them, sporting professionals and administrators, journalists, etc. will also get equally benefited by this book. In addition, any sporting enthusiast can refer to this book as their primary reference point, insofar as understanding and appreciating relevant sporting issues are concerned. The book is equally relevant for the judiciary, helping them in keeping the required perspective while determining the sports disputes. The book, though not intending to be an answer to all the questions generally arising within the domain of sports law, definitely aims at taking a specialised approach to sports law disputes that are debated in detail. Hence, unlike the existing literature on Indian sports law, this is neither intended to be a textbook nor a case material series. It is an attempt at delving into issues that are topical and need an in-depth analysis. Importantly, it aspires to be a worthwhile addition to the existing literature, since the perspective in this book is predominantly Indian, suitably garnished with an international flavour. It is also reflective of the attempt by the legal fraternity at pointing out key areas of concern that need immediate attention. Importantly, the roles played by the national law schools such as NUJS, Gujarat National Law University (GNLU) and National Law University, Delhi (NLUD) are relevant in developing the field of sports law within India. The book aims at setting the tone for further development.

Constitution and Sports in India

Mahendra Pal Singh and Akhilendra P. Singh

Introduction

Contemporary significance of sports is much more than being a pastime and recreational activity. They have been transformed into organised activities coupled with enormous professionalism and affecting almost every area of public life, may it be social, political or economic. Although the pace of this transformation was slow during the nineteenth and most part of the twentieth century, it has boosted enormously in the past few decades owing to globalisation of technology and commerce.[1] Commenting on the importance which sports have assumed in contemporary times, Blake observes:

> Sports is very much part of the popular culture. Many people participate in it, either as amateurs or professionals, and many people observe it as spectators inside stadia or by listening to the radio or watching television. At any rate, sport is continuously visible

[1] Saurabh Bhattacharjee, *Private and Yet Public: The Schizophrenia of Modern Sports and Judicial Review*, 8 NUJS L. REV. 153 (2015).

everywhere in the world [and has become]... a crucial component of contemporary society....[2]

Such immense significance has, among other things, encouraged the academic study of sports, making it the focus of several historical, scientific, philosophical and sociological enquiries.[3] The importance of such studies is beyond question. But owing to increased commercialisation of sports, currently the economic dimension of sports has assumed utmost significance.[4] Statistically, organised sports are a multibillion-dollar industry with a global worth ranging between 350 billion and 450 billion ($480–$620 billion).[5] A 2006 report estimated that macroeconomic impact of sports in the European Union (EU) accounted for 3.7 per cent of EU GDP, providing employment to 5.4 per cent of the entire labour force.[6] Such all-round significance of sports in public life necessitates law to play a major role in order to regulate it in a better manner.

Another reason why the role of law becomes excessively important is that regulation of sports has largely been internal, that is, done through newly emerging sports governing bodies, at both international and national levels.[7] These bodies, which generally possess institutional and legal structures and interests of private associations, not only enjoy a great level of autonomy with respect to deciding the rules of the particular sports they govern but are also engaged in licensing of playing facilities, employment relationships, commercial transactions, regulation

---

[2] ANDREW BLAKE, THE BODY LANGUAGE: THE MEANING OF MODERN SPORT (1996). Cited from SIMON GARDINER ET AL., SPORTS LAW 24 (2012).

[3] *See, e.g.*, JOHN HARGREAVES, SPORT, POWER AND CULTURE: A SOCIAL AND HISTORICAL ANALYSIS OF POPULAR SPORTS IN BRITAIN (1986); JOHN BALE & MIKE CRONIN, SPORT AND POSTCOLONIALISM (2003); DEREK BIRLEY, SPORT AND THE MAKING OF BRITAIN (1993).

[4] JACK ANDERSON, MODERN SPORTS LAW: A TEXTBOOK 1–2 (2010).

[5] The figure is taken from https://www.atkearney.com/en_GB/paper/-/asset_publisher/dVxv4Hz2h8bS/content/the-sports-market/10192

[6] ANDERSON, *supra* note 4, at 1.

[7] BHATTACHARJEE, *supra* note 1.

of corruption and cheating, and many more important functions. Several of these functions are those that are generally performed by the State or its agents, and are crucial from the viewpoint of fundamental rights (FRs) of the individuals.[8] Therefore, the questions whether the State should intervene in the regulation of sports and should the courts have the power to review the decisions of such governing bodies become extremely relevant in view of the contemporary significance of sports.

The Indian scenario of sports is quite similar to this. Sports regulatory bodies, such as Indian Olympic Association, Hockey India and the Board of Control for Cricket in India (BCCI), are autonomous to a great extent. Nevertheless, it seems pertinent to mention at the outset that autonomy of such sports bodies is not absolute. This is because sports are specifically included in the Seventh Schedule of the Constitution.[9] Moreover, the sports bodies which are concerned with the management and regulation of different sporting activities in the country are generally registered as societies or associations in different states of India and, therefore, fall under the jurisdiction of states.[10] Therefore, sporting activities and bodies by which they are regulated fall within the jurisdiction of the states.

However, in light of the liberal economic policy that supports privatisation of economic activities and keeping in mind the economic significance of sports, it seems prudent that there is minimum State intervention in sporting activities. At the same time, it would be fallacious to presume that sporting activities and sports regulatory bodies are beyond the reach of law, particularly when they are in conflict with FRs guaranteed under Part III of the Indian Constitution. Engaging with this particular issue in this chapter, we argue that although the sports regulatory bodies in

[8] GARDINER ET AL., *supra* note 2, at 89–90.

[9] Entry 33, List II, Seventh Schedule, The Constitution of India (1950). It runs as follows: 'Theatres and dramatic performances; cinemas subject to the provisions of entry 60 of List I; sports, entertainments and amusements'.

[10] *Id.*, Entry 32.

India enjoy high degree of administrative, financial and functional autonomy, they are subject to the discipline of FRs under Part III of the Constitution.

Since the sports jurisprudence in India has been revolving around two central issues: first, do sports regulating bodies fall within the definition of 'the State' as mentioned in Article 12 of the Constitution, and second, are such bodies amenable to writ jurisdiction of various High Courts (HCs) of the country, this chapter proceeds in the following manner. In the second part of this chapter, we provide an overview of the judicial developments with regard to the definition of 'the State' in Article 12 of the Constitution, focusing specifically on the legal status of registered societies and associations. It does so because sports regulatory bodies are generally registered societies and associations under different State Acts of the country. Thereafter, in the third part, in light of broadening scope of FRs and their horizontal application, it is argued that regardless of whether the sports regulating bodies are 'the State' within the meaning of Article 12, they are subject to the FRs, and hence, their actions are subject to judicial review powers of the HCs under Article 226.

Definition of 'the State' under the Indian Constitution

Definition of 'the State' is provided in Article 12 of the Indian Constitution which reads as follows:

> 'The State' includes the Government and Parliament of India and the Government and the Legislature of each of the States and all local or other authorities within the territory of India or under the control of the Government of India.[11]

Although the chapter specifically lists the institutions which fall under the purview of the definition of the State, the definition is

---

[11] The Constitution of India (1950), Article 12.

not exclusive. This is primarily because of the expression 'other authorities' appearing in the definition. During the starting years of the Constitution, some HCs held that because the expression appears after 'government' and 'Parliament of India', it would be reasonable to apply the ejusdem generis rule while interpreting it.[12] However, the Supreme Court (SC) in *Rajasthan State Electricity Board* v. *Mohan Lal*[13] rejected this view by forwarding the reasoning that ejusdem generis rule could be applied for interpreting the expression 'other authorities' appearing within the definition of 'the State', only when the bodies preceding it constitute a distinct genus, which was not the case with Article 12. In addition to this, the SC also held that 'other authorities' included all authorities created by the Constitution or statute, irrespective of the fact of performing government functions.[14] Therefore, relying on the legal personality—Rajasthan State Electricity Board being a statutory body—of the body in question, the Court held it to fall within the definition of 'the State' under Article 12.[15]

In *Sukhdev Singh* v. *Bhagatram Sardar Singh Raghuvanshi*,[16] the SC held that the statutory corporations, such as Industrial Finance Corporation (IFC), Life Insurance Corporation (LIC) and Oil and Natural Gas Corporation Limited (ONGC), created by the Industrial Finance Corporation Act, 1948; the Life Insurance Corporation Act, 1956; and the Oil and Natural Gas Commission Act, 1959, respectively, would fall within the State as they were

[12] *See, e.g., University of Madras* v. *Shantha Bai*, AIR 1954 Mad 67; *B. W. Devadas* v. *Karnataka Regional Engineering College* AIR 1954 Mys 6; *Krishna Gopal Ram Chandra Sharma* v. *Punjab University*, AIR 1966 Punj 34.

[13] *Rajasthan State Electricity Board* v. *Mohan Lal*, AIR 1967 SC 1857.

[14] See M. P. SINGH, VN SHUKLA'S CONSTITUTION OF INDIA 27 (12th ed. 2013).

[15] ANANTH PADMANABHAN, *Rights: Breadth, Scope, and Applicability* IN THE OXFORD HANDBOOK OF THE INDIAN CONSTITUTION 585 (S. Choudhry, M. Khosla & P. B. Mehta ed., 2016).

[16] *Sukhdev Singh* v. *Bhagatram Sardar Singh Raghuvanshi*, AIR 1975 SC 1331.

acting as an 'agency or instrumentality' of the State,[17]although the majority following the rationale of *Rajasthan Electricity Board*[18] in *Sukhdev Singh*[19] relied upon the legal personality of the bodies in question to hold them 'agency or instrumentality' of the State. But Mathew J. took a different approach to reach the same conclusion. Rather focusing upon the legal personality of the body in question, he stressed upon the nature of 'function' carried on by the body. Therefore, in his view, even private bodies whose actions could be attributed to 'the State' could be included under Article 12.[20]

Carrying forward the agency or instrumentality test, the SC in *Ajay Hasia* v. *Khalid Mujib Sehravardi*[21] laid down the following factors for determining whether a body is an instrumentality or agency of the State:

1. If the entire share capital of the body in question is held by government, or where the financial assistance of the State is so much as to meet almost entire expenditure of the body.
2. If the body enjoys a monopoly status which is State conferred or State protected.
3. Existence of deep and pervasive State control in the affairs of the body.
4. If the functions of the body are of public importance and closely related to the functions of the government.

Although these and some other cases[22] clarified to a great extent the ambiguity with respect to the expression 'other authorities'

---

[17] SINGH, *supra* note 14, at 28.
[18] Rajasthan State Electricity Board v. Mohan Lal, AIR 1967 SC 1857.
[19] Sukhdev Singh v. Bhagatram Sardar Singh Raghuvanshi, AIR 1975 SC 1331.
[20] For more on this point, *see* PADMANABHAN, *supra* note 15, at 585.
[21] Ajay Hasia v. Khalid Mujib Sehravardi, AIR 1981 SC 487.
[22] *See, e.g.*, Ramana Dayaram Shetty v. International Airport Authority of India, AIR 1979 SC 1628; Som Prakash Rekhi v. Union of India, AIR 1981 SC 212; M. C. Mehta v. Union of India, (1987) 1 SCC 395.

by applying the 'agency or instrumentality' test, the Court also said that these tests were not conclusive, as it is not possible to bring every autonomous body having some governmental nexus under the ambit of the definition of the State.[23] One of the effects of *Ajay Hasia*[24] on the definition of 'the State' in Article 12 was that '[it] replaced Mathew J's functional approach... with a structuralist approach that took into account a few more factors than the narrow one advocated in [Rajasthan State Electricity Board case]'.[25]

Engaging further with this issue so as to determine whether registered societies would fall in the domain of the State under Article 12, the Court in *Sabhajit Tewary* v. *Union of India*[26] held that the Council of Scientific and Industrial Research, a non-statutory body registered under the Societies Registration Act, 1860, and having dominant government control, was not 'the State'. Later, in *Pradeep Kumar Biswas* v. *Indian Institute of Chemical Biology*,[27] the Court by a majority of 5:2 overruled its decision in *Sabhajit Tewary*.[28] However, the Court also said that if the government control on such registered societies is merely regulatory, whether under statute or otherwise, then it would not be deemed to fall within the ambit of the definition of 'the State'.[29] It further held that a body would be considered as 'the State' only if it is 'financially, functionally and administratively' dominated by or under the control of the government, and such control must

[23] SINGH, *supra* note 14, at 29.

[24] Ajay Hasia v. Khalid Mujib Sehravardi, AIR 1981 SC 487.

[25] For more effects of Ajay Hasia on the interpretation of Article 12, *see* PADMANABHAN, *supra* note 15, at 589. Moreover, the focus on structuralism is clear from the four points which the Court notes in Ajay Hasia v. Khalid Mujib for deciding whether a body in question is the State or not. Three of the points hint at the structural characteristic, whereas only one hints at the functional aspect.

[26] Sabhajit Tewary v. Union of India, AIR 1975 SC 1329.

[27] Pradeep Kumar Biswas v. Indian Institute of Chemical Biology, (2002) 5 SCC 111, para 66.

[28] Sabhajit Tewary v. Union of India, AIR 1975 SC 1329.

[29] *Supra* note 27, paras 27 and 40.

be pervasive.[30] In saying so, the SC further narrowed the 'agency or instrumentality' test by not only making functional aspect of the body as one of the three prongs that were required to hold a body as 'the State' but also shifting the weight of the balance towards the structure of the body in question—financial and administrative aspect of a body are structural issues.[31]

As the purpose of this section is to shed light on the legal status of sports regulating bodies which are generally registered as societies under different State Acts, the SC judgement in *Zee Telefilms* v. *Union of India*[32] is most important for our purpose. In this case, the Court held that BCCI, a society registered under the Tamil Nadu Societies Registration Act, 1975, and enjoying extensive powers in relation to the sport of cricket in India, was not 'the State' under Article 12. Deciding on the lines of *Pradeep Kumar Biswas*,[33] the majority concluded that BCCI did not fulfil the criteria of being 'financially, functionally and administratively' under the governmental control. However, Sinha J. in his dissenting opinion stressed on the functions test and pointed that meaning of 'the State' under Article 12 was not confined to entities controlled by the government.[34]

Although *Pradeep Kumar Biswas*[35] holds the authority with respect to evaluating whether a body is 'the State' under Article 12 until now, and has upheld its decision in *Zee Telefilms* of excluding sports bodies from falling within the definition of 'the State' on the basis of lack of pervasive financial, functional and administrative government control,[36] it would not be wrong to

---

[30] *Id.*

[31] PADMANABHAN, *supra* note 15, at 593.

[32] Zee Telefilms v. Union of India, (2005) 4 SCC 649.

[33] *Supra* note 27.

[34] *See generally*, SINGH, *supra* note 14, at 32. For a critical comment on this case, *see* M. P. Singh, *Fundamental Rights, State Action and Cricket in India*, 13 ASIA PAC. L. REV. 203 (2005).

[35] *Supra* note 27.

[36] *See* A. C. Muthiah v. BCCI, (2011) 6 SCC 617; BCCI v. Cricket Association of Bihar, (2015) 3 SCC 251.

say that the Court's interpretation of Article 12 has been considerably incoherent. The incoherence of it comes out more clearly from its judgements concerning interpretation of registered societies and associations' vis-à-vis Article 12. On the one hand, the SC by focusing on the nature of function the body in question performs has held registered societies to be falling within the definition of 'the State' such as in *Ajay Hasia* v. *Khalid Mujib*,[37] the Court held that the Regional Engineering College, Srinagar, established under the Jammu & Kashmir Registration of Societies Act, 1898, was 'the State' within the meaning of Article 12. Again, in *S. M. Ilyas* v. *Indian Council of Agricultural Research*,[38] the SC held that Indian Council of Agricultural Research, a body registered under the Societies Registration Act, 1860, was 'the State'. On the other hand, it has held that the Institute of Constitutional and Parliamentary Studies,[39] the National Council of Educational Research and Training[40] and the State Councils of Educational Research and Training[41] are registered societies but not 'the State' within the meaning of Article 12.[42] On similar lines, sports regulatory bodies which are generally registered societies or associations have also been held to fall outside the scope of Article 12.[43]

Although there is a high probability that the question of the sports falling within 'the State' may be taken up by a larger bench of the Court any day in the future which may come up with some new or a conceptually more clearer version of 'agency or instrumentality' test, the more important question which is directly relevant for the purpose of this chapter is whether such bodies which do not fall within the definition of 'the State', which includes sports regulatory bodies, are subject to the discipline

[37] Ajay Hasia v. Khalid Mujib, (1981) 1 SCC 722: AIR 1981 SC 487.
[38] S. M. Ilyas v. Indian Council of Agricultural Research, (1993) 1 SCC 182: AIR 1993 SC 384.
[39] Tekraj Vasandi v. Union of India, (1988) 1 SCC 236.
[40] Chander Mohan Khanna v. NCERT, (1991) 4 SCC 578.
[41] Lt. Governor Delhi v. V. K. Sodhi, AIR 2007 SC 2885.
[42] SINGH, *supra* note 14, at 32.
[43] *See supra* note 32; *supra* note 36.

of FRs guaranteed under the Indian Constitution. The following section analyses this issue from the viewpoint of horizontal application of FRs.

Horizontal Application of FRs

The idea of rights, particularly since the Second World War, has been a dominant strand of public law discourse.[44] Speaking on similar lines, Loughlin says, 'The modern system of government exists to protect the interests of the right-bearing individuals... through the constitutional arrangements of the modern state.'[45] Therefore, securing the fundamental human rights is considered as one of the basic roles of modern constitutions. The Indian Constitution, falling among the most liberal and progressive constitutions of the world, also recognises these basic human rights. Referred to as 'FRs', these are placed in Part III of the Constitution, and unlike the Directive Principles of State Policy under Part IV of the Constitution, these are justiciable and can be enforced in courts of law. However, the question as to whom do the FRs bind or constrain has generally been answered in light of the definition of 'the State'.[46] Undoubtedly, such a view regarding the scope of application of FRs is problematic, as they face an equal threat from non-State actors as they do from State actors. Thus, in order to provide wider protection to FRs of the individuals, a distinction is made with respect to their 'vertical' and 'horizontal' application. Vertical application of FRs is solely

---

[44] M. P. SINGH, *Constitutionalization and Realization of Human Rights*, IN HUMAN RIGHTS, JUSTICE, & CONSTITUTIONAL EMPOWERMENT 26 (C. Rajkumar & K. Chockalingam ed., 2007).

[45] MARTIN LOUGHLIN, FOUNDATIONS OF PUBLIC LAW 342–343 (2010). For the impact of rights discourse on contemporary public law, *see* MARTIN LOUGHLIN, THE IDEA OF PUBLIC LAW 114–130 (2003). For a historical and philosophical overview regarding the idea of rights vis-à-vis constitutional theory, *see* CARL SCHMITT, CONSTITUTIONAL THEORY 197–219 (Jeffrey Seitzer trans. & ed., 2008).

[46] *See* Singh, *supra* note 34.

concerned with the conduct of State actors in their dealings with private individuals, while horizontal application concerns the relations between private individuals.[47]

The architects of the Indian Constitution were well aware of the fact that FRs faced an equal threat from non-State actors as they did from State action. This is why some of the FRs mentioned in the Indian Constitution are available not only against the State but also against anyone. Furthermore, bestowed upon with the responsibility for constitutional interpretation as well as the duty to protect the FRs of the individuals, the Indian judiciary has been proactive in its job and has provided wider protection to FRs. Therefore, in this section, we first provide an overview of the constitutional provisions which allow horizontal application of FRs. Thereafter, we proceed to trace the judicial approach in this regard. Finally, in light of the foregoing discussion and focusing on sports bodies, we argue that regardless of whether a body is or is not 'the State' under Article 12, it is subject to the discipline of FR's guaranteed by the Constitution.

Constitutional Provisions

As an aid in the interpretation of statutes, certain terms are generally defined at the beginning of a statute to help in understanding

[47] Stephen Gardbaum, *The 'Horizontal Effect' of Constitutional Rights*, 102 MICH. L. REV. 387 (2003), *available at* http://www.jstor. org/stable/pdf/3595366.pdf?retreqid=excelsior:50d20956384d3dfc0 63c597582866173; for the Indian context, *see* M. P. SINGH, *Protection of Human Rights against State and Non-State Action*, IN HUMAN RIGHTS AND THE PRIVATE SPHERE: A COMPARATIVE STUDY (Dawn Oliver & Jörg Fedtke ed., 2007). *See also* STEPHEN GARDBAUM, *Horizontal Effects*, IN THE OXFORD HANDBOOK OF THE INDIAN CONSTITUTION 600 (S. Choudhry, M. Khosla & P. B. Mehta ed., 2016); SUDHIR KRISHNASWAMY, *Horizontal Application of Fundamental Rights and State Action in India*, IN HUMAN RIGHTS, JUSTICE, & CONSTITUTIONAL EMPOWERMENT (C. Rajkumar & K. Chockalingam ed., 2007); Ashis Chugh, *Fundamental Rights—Vertical or Horizontal?*, (2005) 7 SCC (J) 9.

the meaning of that term wherever it occurs in subsequent pro-visions of the statute.[48] On similar lines, the FRs in the Indian Constitution have generally been interpreted in the light of the definition of 'the State'. However, on a plain reading of the FRs it can be easily realised that not all FRs are addressed to 'the State' and therefore can be applied against non-State actors too. For example, FRs in Articles 15(2), 17, 21, 23 and 24, 25, 26, 29(1) and 30(1) are not expressly addressed to 'the State'.[49] Therefore, they may apply as much against private parties as against the State.[50] Furthermore, the 'right to constitutional remedies' in Article 32 as well as the 'power of the High Courts to issue cer-tain writs' under Article 226 can be used by any individual to approach the SC or HCs for enforcement of their FRs regardless of whether violation of FRs has been done by the State or non-State actor. Although the makers of the Constitution should be appreciated for recognising the horizontal application of FRs so as to give them wider protection, the role of Indian judiciary is more prominent in this regard.

The Judicial Approach

Being one of the most active judiciaries in the world and commit-ted to protection of human rights, the Indian SC has been cogni-zant of the developments with regard to the scope of application of FRs, and has thus engaged at length with their horizontal application. On the one hand, the SC has adhered to the tradi-tional approach of FRs being available only against 'the State' on the basis that certain articles contained in the FRs chapter such as Articles 14, 15(1), 16(1) and 21A are addressed to 'the State'.[51] On the other hand, it has held that provisions such as

---

[48] Singh, *supra* note 34.

[49] The Constitution of India (1950), Articles 25, 26, 29(1) and 30(1).

[50] SINGH, *supra* note 47, at 183. *See also* N. Adityan v. Travancore Devaswom Board, (2002) 8 SCC 106; Rev Stainislaus v. State of MP, AIR 1977 SC 908.

[51] *Supra* note 32. *See also* Gardbaum, *supra* note 47, at 602–603.

Articles 15(2), 17, 21, 23 and 24, which are generally addressed, are enforceable against everyone.[52] Therefore, the Court expressly recognised the 'vertical' and 'horizontal' application of FRs on the basis of their nature and phrasing.[53]

Moving beyond the traditional distinction and recognising further distinction within horizontal application of FRs based on the 'direct' and 'indirect' effects,[54] the SC in *People's Union of Democratic Rights* v. *Union of India*[55] said:

> Whenever any fundamental right which is enforceable against private individuals such as, for example, a fundamental right enacted in Article 17 or 23 or 24 is being violated, it is the constitutional obligation of the State to take the necessary steps for the purpose of interdicting such violation and ensuring observance of the fundamental right by the private individual who is transgressing the same. Of course, the person whose fundamental right has been violated can always approach the court for the purpose of the enforcement of his fundamental right, but that cannot absolve the State from its constitutional obligation to see that there is no violation of fundamental right....[56]

The judicial approach with respect to horizontal application of FRs is more explicit in the SC's engagement with the right to life and personal liberty contained in Article 21 of the Indian Constitution. In *Parmanand Katara* v. *Union of India*,[57] the Court after holding that preservation of life is protected by Article 21 said, 'Every doctor whether at a Government hospital *or otherwise* has the professional obligation to extend his services with

[52] *See, e.g.*, Bandhua Mukti Morcha v. Union of India, AIR 1997 SC 2218; Ram Pal v. Maishi Lal Raj Kumar, (1982) 2 SCC 349; Consumer Education and Research Centre v. Union of India, (1995) 3 SCC 42; M. C. Mehta v. State of Tamil Nadu, (1996) 6 SCC 756.

[53] KRISHNASWAMY, *supra* note 47, at 51–52.

[54] For 'direct' and 'indirect' effect, *see* Gardbaum, *supra* note 47.

[55] People's Union of Democratic Rights v. Union of India, (1982) 3 SCC 235.

[56] *Id.*, para 15.

[57] Parmanand Katara v. Union of India, AIR 1989 SC 2039.

due expertise for protecting life' (emphasis added). In *Consumer Education and Research Centre* v. *Union of India*,[58] the Court while expanding the scope of right to life and including within it the right to health and environment said, under Article 21:

> The State, be it Union or State government or an industry, *public or private*, is enjoined to take all such action which will promote health, strength and vigour of the workman during the period of employment and leisure and health even after retirement as basic essentials to live the life with health and happiness.[59] (Emphasis added)

In *R. Rajagopal* v. *State of Tamil Nadu*,[60] the Court, though adhering to the notion that in cases of right to privacy the State police authority is the sole defendant, suggested that it may apply against private individuals, as right to privacy is implied in the right to life guaranteed under Article 21.

The other way through which the SC has engaged with horizontal application of FRs focusing on their 'indirect' effect is by applying them to private law cases. In *Githa Hariharan* v. *Reserve Bank of India*,[61] the SC held that Section 6 of the Hindu Minority and Guardianship Act, 1956, which stated that 'the natural guardians of a Hindu minor... are—(a) in the case of a boy or unmarried girl—the father, and after him, the mother...', could be interpreted to mean that the mother could become the guardian not only after the death of the father but also in his absence or because he was indifferent towards the child, or due to lack of understanding between the mother and father. Therefore, rather than invalidating the relevant section on the basis of sexual discrimination prohibited under Article 15(1), the Court interpreted the Hindu Minority and Guardianship Act, 1956—a private law statute—consistently with the right to equality. In doing so, the

---

[58] Consumer Education and Research Centre v. Union of India, (1995) 3 SCC 42.

[59] *Id.*, para 24.

[60] R. Rajagopal v. State of Tamil Nadu, (1994) 6 SCC 632.

[61] Githa Hariharan v. Reserve Bank of India, (1999) 2 SCC 228.

SC applied Article 15(1) to a private law case, thereby not only impacting and regulating the action of private individuals but also recognising the 'indirect horizontal effect' of FRs.[62] In *Mohini Jain* v. *State of Karnataka*,[63] the SC entertained a writ petition in context of a private law issue concerning admission to private medical colleges on the payment of a capitation fee and held that 'it is not permissible under law for any educational institution to charge capitation fee as a consideration for admission...'.[64]

This brief discussion suggests that though the Indian Constitution provides protection to some of the FRs by making them available against private actors, the judicial approach has been more expansive. This is because the courts have not only recognised the traditional distinction of 'vertical' and 'horizontal' application of FRs but also moved beyond it to recognise 'direct' and 'indirect' effects of horizontal application of FRs. In doing so, the courts besides imposing affirmative duties on the State to protect individuals from certain types of private action and applying the FRs in private law cases has also blurred the public–private dichotomy.

Having discussed the horizontal application of FRs and the expansive judicial attitude towards protection of FRs, it now seems pertinent to engage with the primary issue of this chapter, that is, whether the bodies which do not fall within the definition of 'the State', particularly the sports regulating bodies, are subject to the discipline of FRs. The following section provides in brief the position of sports bodies vis-à-vis FRs.

Judicial Review and Sports Bodies

Although, giving more weight to structure rather than function, the Court has upheld its decision in *Zee Telefilms* of excluding sports bodies from falling within the definition of

[62] *See* Gardbaum, supra note 47, at 608–609.
[63] Mohini Jain v. State of Karnataka, (1992) 3 SCC 666.
[64] *Id.*, para 29.

'the State' on the basis of lack of pervasive 'financial, functional and administrative' government control,[65] it has not completely ignored the fact that the functions of such sports bodies are such that they may at times adversely affect the FRs of the individuals. Therefore, the Court has held that relief against such bodies is available in the HCs under Article 226 of the Constitution.[66]

Speaking with reference to BCCI, the SC observed:

> The rationale underlying the view [that decision of BCCI is amenable to writ jurisdiction of the High Courts under Article 226 even when it is not 'the State' within the meaning of Article 12] lies in the nature of duties and functions which BCCI performs.[67]

The Court further observed:

> Any organization or entity that has such pervasive control over the game and its affairs and such powers... cannot be said to be undertaking private functions... if the Government not only allows an autonomous/private body to discharge functions which it could in law take over or regulate but even lends its assistance to such non-government body to undertake such functions which by their very nature are public functions, it cannot be said that the functions are not public functions or that entity discharging the same is not answerable on the standards generally applicable to judicial review of State action.[68]

These statements of the Court besides highlighting the inadequacy of the narrow structural approach in interpretation of Article 12 also point towards the 'functionality' approach as suggested by Mathew J. in *Sukhdev Singh*. However, the Court has without going into the question whether sports bodies are 'the State'

[65] *See* A. C. Muthiah v. BCCI, (2011) 6 SCC 617; BCCI v. Cricket Association of Bihar, (2015) 3 SCC 251.

[66] *See* BCCI v. Cricket Assn. of Bihar, (2015) 3 SCC 251, paras 22, 33, 34, 35, 74 and 84.

[67] *Id.*, para 33.

[68] *Id.*, paras 33, 34 and 35.

within the meaning of Article 12 has subjected them to judicial review.

In support of this proposition, we may mention some of the decisions of the HCs under Article 226. In *Ajay Jadeja* v. *Union of India*,[69] the Delhi High Court, while focusing on the central nature of BCCI with respect to the sport of cricket in India, held that it would be amenable to writ jurisdiction of the HC.[70] It took the same position in *Rahul Mehra* v. *Union of India*.[71] The principle that sports governing bodies are amenable to writ jurisdiction has also been adhered to in the context of other sports. For instance, in *Narinder Batra* v. *Union of India*,[72] the Delhi High Court held that the Indian Hockey Federation (now Hockey India) was amenable to writ jurisdiction. In *Amit Kumar Dhankhar* v. *Union of India*,[73] it was held that a writ of mandamus could be issued for holding selection trials for the Asian Games.

Conclusion

The modern understanding of rights and their application has extended beyond the concept of the State action, making them applicable against private parties also. Therefore, FRs cannot be viewed merely as a guarantee against 'the State' only. The FRs are not a plaything and can be left by the State in private hands by transferring its powers or responsibilities to bodies that wield as wide powers over the individual as the State in denying him/her participation in public activities of immense interest or dimensions. Therefore, whether a body is 'the State' within Article 12 may be relevant where a FR specifically so requires against a sort of very small private body based on closely knit private relations

---

[69] Ajay Jadeja v. Union of India, 2001 SCC OnLine Del 1024.
[70] *Id.*, para 32.
[71] Rahul Mehra v. Union of India, 2004 SCC OnLine Del 837.
[72] Narinder Batra v. Union of India, 2009 SCC OnLine Del 480.
[73] Amit Kumar Dhankhar v. Union of India, 2014 SCC OnLine Del 3451.

such as family but cannot be extended to bodies which affect the interests of such large sections of society as the ones regulating or controlling popular sports or events in which large sections of the society have interest.

Definitely, therefore, sports regulatory bodies enjoying great degree of autonomy are also subject to the discipline of FRs in the Constitution. It is a matter of some satisfaction that the Court without finally going into the question of deciding the position of sports bodies under Article 12 have subjected them to judicial remedy under Article 226, which is even more easily accessible than approaching the SC directly. Let us hope that in course of time, further clarity will be given by the courts in this regard.

Impact of Non-profit Laws on Sports in India

P. Ishwara Bhat

Introduction

Sports associations (SAs), as voluntary organisations for facilitating and promoting sports and games, play a cardinal role in the sports life of any nation. Belonging to a sphere other than State and market, but always getting support and radiation from these sectors, the non-profit SAs have real driving energy in the community power of sporting activity in which vast number of players, viewers, organisers and media intensively participate and immensely contribute to the successful organisation of sporting event or sustaining the sporting tradition. Huge generation and flow of funds, use and production of substantive properties, and the emerging socio-political power attached to the sports events challenge the character of non-profit legal status of SAs. A question arises, whether the giant corporate activities of some of the SAs have potentiality of undermining the feeble controls of non-profit laws which believe in adequacy of inner democratic control, accountability through purpose compliance principle and transparency in policy-making and implementation, whereas local-level sporting bodies and not-so-popular sporting activities, which attract less attention and money power, experience perpetual fund crunch and social lags? The laws on society reg-istration (SR), trusts and non-profit companies (NPCs) are the governance laws within which the inner rules of SAs in the form of bye-laws, memorandum or articles of associations, charter or trust deed norms are operating upon SAs and shape their gov-ernance structure. Tax exemption laws, constitutional remedies against bodies of semi-State character, application of funda-mental human rights and law of corporate social responsibility (CSR) also wield great influence on their functioning. Whether these laws—protective, facilitative and regulative—are power-ful enough to control the strong and support the weak so that level playing field in this area would bring justice to the domain of sporting world is a question addressed in this chapter. In the context of ongoing debate on controls on Board of Control for Cricket in India (BCCI) and other developments, the discussion gains importance. The human rights parameters, good govern-ance objectives, gender justice and social happiness constitute the criterion for testing the propriety of the direction of legal development in this regard. The roadmap of the chapter consists in discussing the importance and limits of associational freedom in the background of human rights aspects of sports law and historic developments, the analysis of legal controls under the non-profit laws and critical discussion of the legal development. The chapter argues that protection against pilferage, waste and corruption in rich games and siphoning of surplus and canalising the resources through CSR to the dry fields of local sports and non-popular games go a long way to subserve the common good, which is a paramount constitutional objective.

Historical, Social and Economic Base for Sports Associations (SAs)

The communitarian forum of SAs has roots in the traditional experience, social practice and collective economic involvement. It is a natural attribute of every human being to play. But s/he can play only with others, either singly or in teams. Bowling alone is not a possibility in popular games or in a nation of joiners.[1] The sportsperson expects to be watched and recognised by others as either an individual or a team in a competitive world. Training of players or sports-persons, organisation of competition at various levels and fair conducting of the event with its adequate media display for viewers' watching have wider dimensions of associational acts. Hence, sporting is essentially a social activity having vast cultural dimension. Playing in the context of religious, local or social festival, as part of educational activity or seasonal fair or as ethnic ritual, provides linkage with sociocultural community power.[2] As Hargreeves writes, 'Cultures in this sense are profound source of power, reproducing social division here, challenging and rebelling against them there, while in many ways accommodating subordinate groups to social order.'[3] Coakley brings out the sociological aspects of sport by referring to critical theory which states that 'sports are connected with social relations in complex and diverse ways and that sports change as power and resources shift and as there are changes in social, political and economic relations in society'.[4] In all these matters, SAs play a cardinal role and supply the much needed group energy and integration of social force.

The idea of sports for all requires that all eligible and interested persons should have an opportunity to participate at the level available to his/her competence. Denial of opportunity on

---

[1] Robert Putnam in his book refers to the revival of social capital in American society which experienced the need for enhanced social engagement. See ROBERT PUTNAM, BOWLING ALONE (2000).

[2] This is a long-standing social tradition in both urban and rural India. Dasara sports, games and wrestling in Mysore of Karnataka are some examples in India. For similar practices in Canada, *see* J. BARNES, SPORTS AND THE LAW IN CANADA 4–7 (1996) cited in SIMON GARDINER ET AL., SPORTS LAW 22 (4th ed. 2012).

[3] J. HARGREEVES, SPORT, POWER AND CULTURE: A SOCIAL AND HISTORICAL ANALYSIS OF POPULAR SPORTS IN BRITAIN 9–10 (1986) cited in SIMON GARDINER ET AL., SPORTS LAW 25 (4th ed. 2012).

[4] J. COAKLEY, SPORT IN SOCIETY: ISSUES AND CONTROVERSIES 49–50 (1976) cited in GARDINER ET AL., *supra* note 3, at 26.

grounds of race, religion, caste, region and sex is an insult to human dignity and has the effect of heartburn and disappointment. Application of organisational ability linked with human rights approach is an antidote to such undersides. A leaf from a subaltern story of Koti Chennaya in Tulu folklore from coastal Karnataka which dates back to the sixteenth century AD demonstrates this proposition as follows: in response to caste-based denial of opportunity to play country football, the brave twins belonging to backward caste challenged and won the game and were about to keep the ball as trophy; when the ball was snatched by the village headman, the father of the brave twins said, 'Keep the ball safe and we will recover with our strong hands in future', a vow they kept by valour in due course; when driven away from training for wrestling in *garadi* (gymnasium) on account of caste, they learnt the art from a socially backward person and went on establishing number of garadis at length and breadth of the region for youngsters to have the coaching of wrestling and physical exercise without any discrimination.[5] The moral of the story is validity and significance of power of organisation and the imperative for its use with benevolence and sense of justice and equity. There are also epic stories of unsuccessful poisoning of a chivalrous boy, of punishing the stealthy learners of archery and of the deceitful dice which brought calamity to perpetrators.[6] The mainstream theme of equal sporting opportunities in chariot racing and boxing for men and women during Vedic period; equality in access to varieties of games at the campuses of Nalanda and Takshila; fair play in polo, fencing and wrestling during Mughal period; and equality of opportunity in various Indian games and sports—kabaddi, kho-kho, gilli-danda—which are cheap, simple and accessible to all speaks about collectivism's concern for equality in sports in the long run.[7]

---

[5] http://wikieducator.org/Introducing_the_Koti-Chennayya_and_the_The_Shri_Brahma_Baidarkala_Samskritika_Adhyayana_Pratishtana_by_S.A._Krishnaiah
[6] The story of Bhima, Ekalavya, Karna and Yudhishthira in Mahabharatha.
[7] Mukul Mudgal, Law and Sports in India 18–21 (2011).

The contribution of organisations to sports and games came to the forefront internationally along with reviving the tradition of Olympics or streamlining of modern popular games. Ancient Greece had organised Olympics for over six centuries until 393 AD.[8] Revival of it by Pierre de Coubertin in 1896 involved use of associational right at the international level. International Olympic Committee's continued efforts and participation by national organisations from Athens (1896) to Rio (2016) made the whole Olympics a great successful enterprise.[9] The Indian Olympic Association founded in 1927 by Sir Dorabjee Tata and Dr A. G. Noehren ushered in a creative role of voluntary organisation in the domain of athletics and games.[10] Formation of Marylebone Cricket Club in England in 1787 became a trend-setter in popularising the game in England and its colonies, and after the decolonisation amidst the Commonwealth nations.[11] Establishment of International Cricket Council (ICC) and various national cricket committees which federated into the former became a strong structure in cricket. BCCI is one such organisation that came into existence in 1929 by registering itself under the Tamil Nadu Societies Registration Act. Its flourish through commercialisation with varieties of cricket is a roaring success but is a big challenge to the non-profit organisations (NPO) law's control mechanism, an analysis that will be undertaken later. While historical traces of hockey can be found in ancient civilisations, its formal start took place when seven London clubs formed Hockey Association in 1886 in Cambridge. When the game became popular in the continent, the French led by Paul Léautey constituted Federation Internationale de Hockey (FIH) in 1924 to popularise the game internationally and make it a regular feature of Olympics.[12] India's golden days in hockey in 1932–1956 and in 1964–1980 are traceable to Indian Hockey

---

[8] GARDINER ET AL., *supra* note 3, at 13.
[9] MUDGAL, *supra* note 7, at 9.
[10] *Id.* at 42.
[11] *Id.* at 10.
[12] *Id.* at 12.

Federation established in 1928 at Gwalior, which had provided affiliation to regional hockey associations. After its suspension from FIH, Hockey India with more than 40 regional hockey associations attached to it manages Indian hockey. In the field of football, Federation Internationale de Football Association (FIFA), an international association formed in 1904 by leading European countries playing football, provides international forum for managing the international competitions like World Cup.[13] National football associations get affiliation from it and accommodate regional associations within themselves. One common feature amidst these bodies is that pyramid type of structure starting from regional associations at the bottom, national associations at the middle level and international associations at the top provide for hierarchical governing structure, each being autonomous at its level. Other sporting activities such as tennis, golf, snooker, billiards, chess and kabaddi have both national and international associations to manage the sports events.[14] Maintenance of discipline, purity of game, accountability and adherence to the principle of equality in sporting opportunity is one of the main themes in the legal governance of these associations in order that the purpose of their formation is duly complied. National Sports Policy, 2001, contemplates collaboration of educational institutions, sports federations/associations and sports clubs with various levels of local governments in promoting, organising and encouraging sports.

In England, the post-Industrial Revolution scenario of sports witnessed game-specific federations with hierarchic structure. Sports and Recreation Alliance (SRA; formerly established as the Central Council of Physical Recreation) is an umbrella organisation in the form of non-governmental voluntary organisation funded by private resources.[15] SRA speaks and acts to promote, protect and develop sports at all levels, and provides support and services to those who participate in and administer sports and

---

[13] *Id.* at 12.
[14] *Id.* at 12–16.
[15] GARDINER ET AL., *supra* note 3, at 30.

recreation.[16] It is independent of governmental control, strictly non-party body and has no responsibility for allocating funds. There are also non-profit voluntary organisations (NPVOs) such as Sports Coach UK and British Olympic Association. Sport England and UK Sport are governmental agencies having liaison with community organisations for sports. State intervention for maintenance of law and order; implementation of sports councils policies and decisions; and promoting sports for women, people with disabilities and countryside people has supported the sport activity.[17]

Economic dimensions of sports activities of SAs are exponentially growing. In the past where sport was only a recreation, medium of maintaining physical fitness, source of entertainment and forum for patriotic feelings, non-profit policy was the dominant approach. But in recent decades, sport is a big industry in some sectors. The worth of global sports industry is estimated to be US$540 billion in 2010 and US$620 billion in 2017, which is inclusive of revenue generated from broadcasting, advertisement, etc.[18] Huge pay hike in the salary of cricketers, football and hockey players and other sports-persons; very high costs involved in establishment of world-class stadiums, playgrounds and well-equipped sports complexes; and diversification of sports facilities in various parts of the country to satisfy the growing population have escalated the cost inputs.[19] The flow of fund to the sports domain is also enormous from various sources, which include sponsoring agencies, Premier League managers, advertisers, franchisees, revenue generated from ticket collection, government's grant or concessions, sale of broadcasting right, etc. The ultimate source for the capital and revenue expenses of the SAs for these purposes accrues from people's spending, government's

---

[16] www.sportandrecreation.org.uk

[17] GARDINER ET AL., *supra* note 3, at 30–32.

[18] https://www.atkearney.com/documents/10192/6f46b880-f8d1-4909-9960-cc605bb1ff34; *see also* MUDGAL, *supra* note 7, at 121.

[19] For example, the salary of chief cricket of Indian team is ₹7 crore per year.

grant, business sector's support and SAs' own resource which was safeguarded over the years. The creation of intellectual property, production of sports materials and goods which have increasing demands and contracts involved in hiring the services of lakhs of people are the ancillary economic acts which keep sporting activity vibrant and involves people. The trickling-down effect of investment is also notable. It can be inferred that as the society is the main stakeholder, the factors of democratic participation, equality in access, accountability, transparency and professional management should gain greatest attention and acceptance.

The communitarian base of SAs has other facets also. Because of the prestige, contact with people, economic power and social recognition, the entry of politicians and their political influences have also been experienced. Corruption in big scale has also frequently taken place. Lack of required level of gender sensitisation in the world of sports has marginalised women or at least discriminated against them. Poverty, tribal background, physical disability and social backwardness have obstructed the percolation of the idea of equal sports for all. Huge surplus in some sports and deep scarcity in other spheres or absence of decentralisation could not be cured by features of voluntarism and collectivism. How NPO law is able to withstand these challenges and deflections is a debatable issue. Its strong inclination to receive and support values of human rights, justice and welfare has to be relied upon for comfortable result.

Parameters of Human Rights, Justice and Welfare in the Sporting World: The Task of SAs

Right to develop one's physical, intellectual and moral powers requires, according to UNESCO International Charter of Physical Education, Physical Activity and Sports, access to physical education and sports as an assured right to all human beings.[20]

---

[20] Preamble of the International Charter of Physical Education and Sports adopted in 1978 by UNESCO.

According to Article 1 of the Charter, the practice of physical education and sport is a fundamental right (FR) of all. International Olympic Charter states that mutual understanding with a spirit of friendship, solidarity and fair play is a prerequisite for practising sports as a fundamental human right of all.[21] Promoting peaceful society preservation of human dignity and harmonious development of man is the goal of Olympism. Rights of children and women and prohibition of child labour become meaningful with availability of right to sport. Article 3 of the European Sport for All Charter states, 'Sport, being an aspect of socio-cultural development, shall be related at local, regional and national levels to other areas of policy making and planning such as education, health, social service, town and country planning, conservation, the arts and leisure services'. European Commission points out five unique functions that sports do as part of community action: (a) educational function for personal development of all, (b) public health function which improves people's health and combats illness, (c) social function by promoting inclusive society by combating intolerance, racial violence, drug abuse, etc., (d) cultural function by creating better understanding and social cohesion and (e) recreational function by providing personal and collective entertainment and good leisure. Potentiality of sports in preventing juvenile crimes is evident from research studies. Because of all these factors, sport is an aspect of human dignity and capability, and reflects intrinsic human worth.[22] Thus, collective bodies like SAs have the task of fulfilling these objectives by organising and facilitating sports and make the facilities available

[21] It also states, 'The practice of sport is a human right. Every individual must have the possibility of practising sport, without discrimination of any kind and in the Olympic spirit, which requires mutual understanding with a spirit of friendship, solidarity and fair play.' *See*, for discussion, report from the UN Inter-Agency Task Force on 'Sport for Development and Peace'.

[22] MARTHA NUSSBAUM, FRONTIERS OF JUSTICE 70 (2006) cited by M. D. A. FREEMAN, LLOYD'S INTRODUCTION TO JURISPRUDENCE 601 (8th ed. 2008); JOHN M. FINNIS, NATURAL LAW AND NATURAL RIGHTS 86 (1980) cited by FREEMAN, at 170; *see also* Fransisco Javier Lopez Frias, *The Sports for All Ideal: A Tool for Enhancing Human Capabilities and Dignity*, 63 PHY. CUL. SPORTS STUD. RES. 20 (2014).

to all and eschew any kind of arbitrariness. While SAs have collective competence right to discipline and regulate the behaviour of individual players by virtue of their associational freedom, the purposive character of SAs compels them to be reasonable. In case of conflict between collective competence right of the group and individual human right (either as member or non-member of the association), the collective participation right, requirement of fair procedure and rule of law provide solution by balancing between the two. In practice, in matters relating to selection of players, coach, etc., or disciplinary action against errant players guilty of match-fixing and other misdeeds, such interplay of human rights brings fair result. SAs have to keep in mind that level playing field between individual and group right is implicit in the relation between human rights. Continuous support to sporting activity, providing of stipends, old-age benefits and medical assistance and such other welfare measures augment the sporting atmosphere. Their efficiency in building strong relations with the network of sports federations is crucial for making human right to sport a meaningful one.

Impact of Constitutional Law upon SAs

Citizens' right to form associations and unions and cooperative societies under Article 19(1)(c) has substantive content of establishing, continuing, identity retaining, merging and closing of the association.[23] Right not to join and right to exclude other persons from becoming members are also within its ambit.[24] The State may, by law, impose reasonable restrictions in the interests of sovereignty and integrity of India, public order and morality, as per Article 19(4). By interpreting that association emerging out of citizens' right has the same level of right as that of citizens and that efficacy of association is not something to be ensured by an additional right like right to strike, judiciary has allowed

[23] Damayanti Naranga v. Union of India, AIR 1971 SC 966.
[24] Tikaramji v. State of Uttar Pradesh, AIR 1956 SC 676.

greater amount of State intervention.[25] This approach has allowed the governments to take over any of the activities and facilities of registered societies through special laws.[26] In another line of development, courts have kept SAs outside the sphere of Article 12 in spite of their public character but without exclusive/substantive state funding.[27] Hence, mandate of right to equality is not operating upon them. This reflects limitation on horizontal application of FRs.[28] However, when an SA performs functions of public importance, and State assistance to the SA is also moderately involved, the judiciary has invoked jurisdiction under Article 226 to supervise its functioning, restructure its organisation by altering its bye-laws and make it more accountable.[29] On the other hand, judiciary has also recognised autonomy of associations in some cases to keep their constitutive laws (bye-laws, charters or memorandum of association) intact even though they might not be conforming to the principle of equality.[30] It is only regarding the cooperative societies that the requirements of voluntary formation, autonomous functioning, democratic control and professional management are operating, which the judiciary has not extended to other organisations.[31] In light of the previously mentioned complex constitutional position, the

[25] All India Bank Employees Association v. National Industrial Tribunal Bank, AIR 1926 SC 171.

[26] L. N. Mishra Institute of Economic Development and Social Change v. State of Bihar, AIR 1988 SC 1136; Dharam Dutt v. Union of India, AIR 2004 SC 1295.

[27] Zee Tele Films Ltd v. Union of India, AIR 2005 SC 2677; Aditya Sondhi, *The Legal Status of BCCI: Unwarranted Ad-hocism, Constitutional Hurdles and the Pressing need for a Cricket-Legislation*, 22 NAT'L L. SCH IND. REV. 111, 111 (2010).

[28] *See generally* Satchit Bhogle, *Amenability of Indian Domestic Sports Governing Bodies to Judicial Review*, 27. MARQ. SPORTS L. REV. 153 (2016).

[29] Anandi Mukta Sadguru Shree Muktajee Vandas Swami Suvarna Jayanti Mahotsav Smarak Trust and Ors v. V. R. Rudani and Ors, 2 SCC 691; AIR 1989 SC 1607.

[30] Zoroastrian Co-operative Housing Society Limited v. District Registrar Co-operative Societies, AIR 2005 SC 2306; (2005) 5 SCC 632.

[31] Article 40-A of the Constitution.

regulative framework of SAs much depends upon NPO laws and other specific sports laws and policies.

In the matter of registration and regulation of societies, associations and cooperative societies, states have exclusive legislative power under Entry 32 of List II of Seventh Schedule to the Constitution. The Societies Registration Act, 1860, and many of the state laws on registration of societies do not specifically mention 'sports, athletics and games' as the purpose for which registered societies could be constituted. This has compelled the SAs to register their organisations as for charitable purpose or for dissemination of knowledge or to go for registration in those states like Tamil Nadu or Karnataka where law mentions 'sports, athletics and games' as the purposes for which registered societies can be formed. Company law including NPCs comes under Entry 44 of List I. Section 8 of the Companies Act provides for incorporation of NPCs for various purposes which, inter alia, include sports. Concurrent power is available to the Union and state governments regarding public trusts. Bombay Public Trusts Act, 1950, provides for formation of public trusts for the purpose of sports and games. Entry 33 of List II vests legislative power upon the states to enact laws on 'sports, entertainments and amusements'. Only the state of Kerala has enacted sports act so far, and has provided for recognition of SAs and accommodated their participation in decision-making process at the levels of sports councils. The regulatory legal framework has not always provided sufficient in-built safeguards and remedial measures against abuses, corruptions, arbitrariness and excessive punishments. There are also instances of challenging constitutionality of legal provisions or administrative actions.[32] All these have given scope for writ remedies under Article 226 and for Supreme Court's intervention as an appellate authority.

The impact of Article 226 jurisdiction on SAs can be briefly discussed with reference to BCCI cases. The Supreme Court has

---

[32] Periyar Self-Respect Propaganda Institution v. State of Tamil Nadu, AIR 1998 SC Mad 27.

declined to treat it on par with commercial bodies in view of the duty of sporting organisations to organise the sports events and employ the best available media for popularising the game.[33] However, it is not 'State' under Article 12 as it is a private organisation regulated and governed by its own rules and regulations without being financially, functionally or administratively dominated by the government, although it gets governmental support in the form of land grant and permission for activities. Since its duties are akin to public duties, BCCI is amenable to actions for remedies under ordinary law or under Article 226 but not Article 32.[34] In the matter of irregularity of conducting election to the office-bearer position of society registered to carry on activities relating to cricket, the Court insisted on strict compliance with the Memorandum of Association, and opined in *Netaji Cricket Club* case[35] that

> In law, there cannot be any dispute that having regard to the enormity of power exercised by it, the Board is bound to follow the doctrine of 'fairness' and 'good faith' in all its activities. Having regard to the fact that it has to fulfil the hopes and aspirations of millions, it has a duty to act reasonably. It cannot act arbitrarily, whimsically or capriciously.

As the Board controls the profession of cricketers, its actions are required to be judged and viewed by higher standards.

When BCCI appointed a probe commission to look into gross malpractices such as match-fixing by officials and cricketers, irregularities in the process of granting franchise rights, bid rigging, allowing of conflict of interests and lack of transparency, the Cricket Association of Bihar moved the High Court of Bombay to nullify the appointment of the probe commission. Although the court nullified the appointment, it did not reconstitute the

[33] Secretary, Ministry of Information and Broad-casting, Govt. of India v. Cricket Association of Bengal, AIR 1995 SC 1236, para 17.

[34] Zee Tele Films Ltd v. Union of India, AIR 2005 SC 2677.

[35] Board of Control for Cricket, India v. Netaji Cricket Club, AIR 2005 SC 592.

commission and left the matter to BCCI. The Supreme Court in exercise of appellate jurisdiction in *Cricket Association of Bihar Case II* appointed Justice Mukul Mudgal Committee to probe into the issue.[36] The committee extensively interacted with officials, players, journalists and stakeholders and held Mr Gurunath Meiyappan guilty of illegal betting and cheating with the connivance of a franchisee. The Justice Mudgal Committee report was considered and accepted by the Supreme Court in its judgement dated January 2015.[37] In order to fix quantum of punishments to the culprits, to complete the process of enquiry and to plan for immediate and long-term reform by bringing necessary changes to the Memorandum of Association in the administration of cricket game, qualifications for membership, conducting of elections and avoidance of conflicts of interests, the Supreme Court constituted Justice Lodha Committee. The committee extensively consulted various stakeholders and recommended several steps and measures that would in its opinion streamline the working of BCCI and possibly prevent any aberrations or controversies in which it has been embroiled in the past. In view of non-representation, under-representation and over-representation of states in the Board, and representation of non-territorial organisations in the Board, the Justice Lodha Committee recommended for 'One State–One Member–One Vote' policy in the structure of the Board and removal of different categories of membership. In bringing the states of Northeast India to the mainstream cricket, such a step was considered as essential. This also has the effect of reducing the number of active associations in Maharashtra and Gujarat from three to one each, and allowing their participation on rotational basis. It recommended for disbursement of funds by BCCI for cricket development equitably in various states, depending on the need, infrastructure and other relevant criteria, to incentivise members to develop the sport. The full members associations were required to provide for democratic management, representation

---

[36] BCCI v. Cricket Association of Bihar I Order dated 8 October 2013, A. K. Patnaik and Justice J. Khehar.

[37] BCCI v. Cricket Association of Bihar II MANU/SC.0069 dated 22 January 2015, CJI T. S. Thakur and Justice F. M. Ibrahim Kalifulla.

of women, representation of international players from the state, limits on tenure of officers, provision for transparency, election officer, ethics officer and ombudsman. The committee suggested for constitution of a nine-member apex council consisting of five elected office-bearers (president, vice-president, secretary, joint secretary and treasurer), two councillors (one male and one female) to be nominated by players' association, one member elected by full members and a nominee of controller and auditor general. It insisted on limited tenure and exclusion of ministers, foreigners and persons aged more than 70. The composition provides for transparency, women's participation, decentralisation and accountability. The committee suggested for a separate governing council for Indian Premier League (IPL); avoidance of conflict of interests; ensuring of transparency, ethics and good governance measures; and mechanisms for dispute settlement and proper financial management. It recommended for bringing legislative changes to ensure right to information against BCCI, punishment for match-fixing, etc. Each state association shall ensure transparency, democratic formation and proper functioning. The Supreme Court in *Cricket Association of Bihar III* upheld the Lodha Committee report and rejected the arguments about violation of freedom of association and principles of natural justice.[38] The Court approached the whole issue from the angle of the need for bringing desirable changes[39] in the functioning of popular game of cricket and cleansing it from abuses, restoring people's confidence in the joyful game and enabling equal access and participation of players from various parts of India without domination by any of the regions, and accepted the report.

In a recent decision, the Kerala High Court has upheld the claim of a cricketer under Article 226 against excessive

[38] BCCI v. Cricket Association of Bihar III judgement dated 18 July 2016 (7) SCALE 143, CJI T. S. Thakur and Justice F. M. Ibrahim Kalifulla.

[39] The opening paragraph in CJI T. S. Thakur's judgement in *Cricket Association of Bihar* case III refers to the inevitability of accommodating changes for good, possible resistances from the vested interests and the need to pursue the matter with rigour.

punishment like lifelong ban for match-fixing.[40] The court lifted the ban on the ground that since the cricketer has already suffered punishment for a period of four years, the continuation of punishment is unjust and disproportionate. Earlier, the Delhi High Court had acquitted the cricketer from all charges except knowledge of cricket betting. But BCCI had imposed lifetime ban. The Kerala High Court judgement vindicates the potentiality of writ remedy to safeguard fundamental human rights of a member against the NPO.

From this, it can be inferred that from the perspective of good governance of SAs and protection of fundamental human rights of various stakeholders, the constitutional impact is towards maintaining equanimity and proper balance in relation to SAs.

Impact of SR Laws

The Societies Registration Act, 1860, has primarily a facilitative policy rather than providing for regulative/regimentation regime.[41] But it does not mention sports, games, gymnastics or indoor play as objects of formation of association. The omission might be due to the then prevalent prejudice in British society that sport is an idler's crime or has an element of gambling. But in course of time, some of the states' amendments as that of Gujarat, Delhi, Uttar Pradesh (UP), etc. have included associations established for these purposes as also eligible for registration. The West Bengal and Tamil Nadu SR laws have provided for inclusive language regarding purposes of registered societies. The SR laws of Tamil Nadu, Karnataka, Meghalaya and Andhra Pradesh have expressly mentioned sport as one of the purposes of societies governed under their SR laws. The Travancore–Cochin Act, 1955, prevalent in Kerala, does not refer to sport as a

[40] http://indianexpress.com/article/sports/cricket/kerala-high-court-lifts-life-ban-on-s-sreesanth-4786853/?gclid=EAIaIQobChMIpPa_0bzz1gIVh5VoCh1P8gMrEAAYASAAEgLZd_D_BwE

[41] P. ISHWARA BHAT, LEGAL ENVIRONMENT GOVERNING THIRD SECTOR: AN ANALYSIS FROM PURPOSE SCRUTINY PERSPECTIVE (2003).

purpose for which society could be registered. Some states have expressly excluded gambling as a purpose of registered society. In those states or where central law is prevalent, formation of SAs as charitable bodies is possible, in case helping the people is its main concern.

The element of non-profit is core character of registered societies as they do not provide for profit distribution amidst members nor allow sharing of resources at the time of dissolution. The residue shall be transferred to another society chosen by the three-fifths of the members voting in the general body meeting which decides about dissolution. SR laws impose the requirement of democratic participation and management and transparency through filing of documents, annual reports and audited account statements. Fairness and periodicity in election to the position of office-bearers is a legal requirement. Promotion of and compliance with the purposes of their origin are insisted by law. Annual general body meeting or special meeting of the general body is the forum for decision-making and choice of leaders for governance. For merger of registered societies, consent of all the merging societies is required.[42] While registration under SR law does not confer corporate legal status, their right to sue and be sued is recognised.[43] The memorandum of association shall not be contrary to the SR law. For example, when the former provides for lifetime tenure as office-bearer of registered society whereas the latter limits the tenure to specific number of years, the former becomes invalid.[44] The registered society has to follow the strict legal procedure for expulsion of any of the members from the society.[45]

---

[42] Vinodkumar M. Malavia v. Maganlal Mangaldas Gameti, AIR 2013 SCW 5782.

[43] Illachi Devi v. Jain Society, Protection of Orphans India, AIR 2003 SC 3397, 3402.

[44] Periyar Self-Respect Propaganda Institution v. State of Tamil Nadu, AIR 1998 SC Mad 27.

[45] T. P. Daver v. Lodge Victoria, AIR 1963 SC 1144; N. R. Murthy v. Bowring Institute, 1967 (1) Mys L.J.521.

State laws contemplate extensive governmental control over registered societies by exercising the powers of enquiry, superseding the governing body of the state-aided society, temporary appointment of administrator and dissolving the society involved in unlawful activity. State intervention in the form of taking over the institution of the registered society by a special law is also within the State's competence.[46] However, taking over the property of minority institution without the authority of law, which ought to comply with the requirement of assent of president of India, is not permissible.[47] Remedy under Section 92 of the Civil Procedure Code is not available in cases of abuse, etc. as it is not an express or constructive public trust.[48] This is too technical an approach that has excluded remediation of grievances through representative suits.

By insisting on democratic management and an in-built system of accountability and transparency, the law of SR amply helps the SAs to operate to fulfil the purposes of origin. In modern times, SAs involve in huge financial transactions, and flow of fund enriches the coffers of many SAs. But law does not provide for compulsory distribution of surplus for the support of financially weaker societies. Because of accumulation of resources in some sectors and inadequacy of funds in other spheres, the very idea of non-profit system is under severe challenge. Corruption is a major issue which causes huge pilferage. Development of one pattern of sport alone has caused imbalance, especially when the community as a whole has extended the economic support. The outcome is hefty income for few players, and lack of care for other sports and games is paralysing the public sport life. The idea of CSR, which is introduced in the corporate sector, may be

---

[46] L. N. Mishra Institute of Economic Development and Social Change v. State of Bihar, AIR 1988 SC 1136; Dharam Dutt v. Union of India, AIR 2004 SC 1295.

[47] Quraish Education Society v. State of Karnataka, AIR 1987 Kar 122.

[48] Abhaya v. State of Kerala, AIR 2005 Ker 233, ILR 2005(2) Kerala 692; P. Ishwara Bhat, *The Parens Patriae Role of the Courts in the Matter of Public Trusts under Section 92 of the Civil Procedure Code: Expectations, Contributions, and Limitations*, 7 (3–4) NUJS L. Rev.215–216 (2014).

employed here to obligate the SAs making profit to transfer the fund to those SAs which are in need of financial support. Another development that has taken place in the non-profit law, especially that of cooperative societies which are meant for supporting economic life of people, to the effect that democratic participation, open membership, accountability and professional management shall be the goals to be effectuated may show the path of reform.

Impact of Public Trust Law

Unlike organisations, foundations or resource endowments in the form of trusts provide reliable and continuous economic support to social and cultural activities. While Indian Trusts Act governs private trusts, charitable and religious trusts are under the governance of state laws. All states do not have public trust law. The Bombay model of public trust law provides for command and control approach where the charity commissioner has a significant role in streamlining, assisting and regulating the activities to suit the requirement of purpose compliance. The Bombay Public Trusts Act, 1950, had originally not included sports, games and recreational acts within the ambit of its governance. It expressly excluded sports from the purview of general public utility, perhaps owing to the then prevalent British practice that unless it is part of promotion of education, sports would not be regarded as an activity of charity. In 1956, the British law underwent change to include recreational charity within the scope of public trust. Indian judiciary mechanically acted ignoring the long-standing social practice of charity supporting wrestling and other recreations. In a case relating to an *akhara* (arena) created by a donor by dedicating it to Mahadeo, Mahabirji and Hazrat Ali by invoking Hindu idol and Muslim *tasweer* (picture) to attract both Hindu and Muslim communities, the Supreme Court declined to recognise existence of public trust.[49] The Court relied on the English cases which denied public trust character to dedication of fund for games. Further, dedication of property partly in the name of

---

[49] Ramchandra Shukla v. Mahadeo Mahabirji, AIR 1970 SC 458.

Hindu god and partly in the name of Muslim saint was held to be deviating from both the Hindu law of endowment and Muslim law of waqf. From the perspective of expansive and multicultural notion of building social harmony and use of endowments in support of it, fulfilment of social expectation would have attained better social result. Holding it as a part of education would have resolved the problem in favour of social capital. An amendment to Section 9 of the Act could bring sports within the governance of public trust law. The development of law is towards pro-sports approach. In view of vast potentiality of foundations coming to the help of sports and recreations, this has great significance and welcome consequence.

Impact of the Law of NPCs

The restrictive approach of not including sports within the permissible objectives of NPCs is visible under both the Companies Act, 1913, and the Companies Act, 1956. Section 26 of the 1913 Act and Section 25 of the 1956 Act used the words 'for promoting commerce, art, science, charity, or any other useful object' and indirectly shut the doors of NPCs to sports and games. It is heartening to note that the Companies Act of 2013 has avoided the restrictive approach. Section 8 of the 2013 Act states that a non-profit-making company is a company which (a) has in its objects the promotion of commerce, art, science, sports, education, research, social welfare, religion, charity, protection of environment or any such other object, (b) intends to apply its profits, if any, or other income in promoting its objects and (c) intends to prohibit the payment of any dividend to its members. Various procedural relaxations such as omission of the word 'limited' in the name of the company, liberty to hold meetings during non-working days or hours, concession in the matter of length of notice for meeting, opportunity to the firms to participate in the activity of NPCs, relaxation from the requirement of minimum paid-up share capital and permission for having less than 15 directors facilitate the smooth functioning of the NPCs. By using the flexibilities from the procedural imbroglio of corporate governance and also by using the facility of effective tools of corporate system, the SAs in the form of NPCs can do significantly well in the domain of sports and games. Considering that it is only since 2013 that SAs have entered into the creative legal personalities of NPCs, there is much in the womb of future for their social contribution.

Impact of the Tax Exemption and Tax Deduction Laws on SAs

Pro-profit actions of some SAs and non-profit actions of other SAs have put the approach of income tax law in the matter of tax exemptions and tax deductions into a complex situation. As tax is the price we pay for civic life, and since all the taxable capacities are to be tapped on equitable basis, the only justification for tax exemptions for NPOs is the welfare activities of the NPOs which benefit the society and substitute the state's public duty of such welfare.[50] Tax being the outcome of the democratic process, any concession from tax obligation should formally come from legal norm as an incentive for helping the society with good work. Do SAs really perform such welfare activity which deserves governmental support tolerating reduction of public revenue is a question around which the issue under this head needs to be discussed.

In the definition of 'charitable purpose' under Section 2(15) of Income Tax Act, 1961, the words 'the advancement of any other object of general public utility' attract SAs for claiming exemption from income tax liability. When the activity has brought benefit to the substantive section of the society, the tax department has

---

[50] Henry Hansmann, *The Rationale for Exempting Nonprofit Organizations from Corporate Income Taxation*, 91 YALE L. J. 54, 72–75 (1981); Karla Simon, *Rule for Not-for-Profit Organizations: A Survey of Practice*. Paper presented at the Conference on Taxes, Civil Society and Law (Wien, 2004).

recognised exemption.[51] But when the objective of encouraging athletic sports and games is mixed with the objective of encouragement to entertainment and promotion of social intercourse among members of the association, the tax department has held a contrary view.[52] The Central Board of Direct Taxes has examined the acceptability of SA claims and has brought out the following circular:[53]

> The Board are advised that the advancement of any object beneficial to the public or section of the public as distinguished from individual or group of individuals would be an object of general public utility. In view thereof, promotion of sports and games is considered to be a charitable purpose within the meaning of section 2 (15). Therefore, an association or institution engaged in promotion of sports and games can claim exemption under Section 11 of the Act....[54]

During scrutiny of the return of association or while granting registration to an association under Section 12A, the revenue department may question the charitable nature of the activities, if the revenue department is of the opinion that the association is trying to avoid tax by carrying out business activities under the garb of charitable activity. For example, in *Mumbai Cricket Association* v. *DIT (Exemption)*,[55] the Mumbai Bench of the

[51] Commissioner of Income Tax Madras II v. Ootacmund Gymkhana Club, (1977) 110 ITR 392 (Mad); Hyderabad Race Club Charitable Trust v. ITO, (1984) 8 ITD 480 (Hyd Trib); Income Tax Officer v. Deccan Gymkhana, 1989 30 ITD 16 (Pune Trib).

[52] South Indian Athletic Association Ltd v. Commissioner of Income Tax, Madras, (1977) 107 ITR (Mad).

[53] Circular No. 395 (F. No. 181 (5) 82/IT (A-I) dated 24 September 1984); N. SURESH, A PRACTICAL APPROACH TO TAXATION AND ACCOUNTING OF CHARITABLE TRUSTS, NGOs AND NPOs 98 (2016).

[54] Section 10(23) which was relating to exemption from tax of SAs and institutions having their objects as the promotion, control, regulation and encouragement of specified sports and games was omitted by the Finance Act, 2002.

[55] Mumbai [TS-590-ITAT-2012- (Mum)]; also, Revenue Department on 9 January 2014 withdrew tax benefit of four cricket bodies—Saurashtra Cricket Association, Baroda Cricket Association, Kerala Cricket Association

Income Tax Appellate Tribunal upheld the cancellation of registration of Mumbai Cricket Association (MCA) under Section 12A of the Income Tax Act, 1961, on the premise that MCA's Indoor Cricket Academy and related facilities were for commercial or profit purpose and were not charitable in nature. However, the tribunal held that the registration could be cancelled only prospectively and not retrospectively. Cancellation of registration provided to Tamil Nadu Cricket Association, which was upheld by the tribunal, was reversed by Madras High Court as it was regarded as contrary to law in the instant case.[56] Similarly, cancellation of registration of Karnataka Golf Association by the tribunal was quashed in appeal.[57] Availability of tax exemption status can be used for receiving donations under Section 80G of the Income Tax Act.

SAs and Control under Competition Act

Possibility of controlling SAs under Competition Act on grounds of abuse of their dominant position is another line of control. On the issue of monopoly and obstruction to economic competition by BCCI, the matter was agitated before the Competition Commission of India (CCI). In *Surinder Singh Barmi*,[58] CCI examined whether BCCI has the position of 'dominance' in the relevant market; whether it is an enterprise as per the Act; and whether BCCI has abused its dominant position in contravention of Section 4 of the Act. Regarding the first question, CCI examined in detail the historical background, the pyramidal structure which exclusively connects BCCI with ICC, the de

---

and Maharashtra Cricket Association—for engaging in certain commercial activities.

[56] Tamil Nadu Cricket Association v. DIT (Exemption), (2014) 360 ITR 0633 (Mad); *see also* Gujarat Cricket Association v. DIT (Exemption) ITA No. 93 (Ahd)/2011; Vidarbha Cricket Association v. CIT Nagpur, ITA No. 3/Nag/10 (30 May 2011).

[57] Karnataka Golf Association v. The Director of Income Tax (Exe.), (2005) 272ITR123 (Bang).

[58] Surinder Singh Barmi v. BCCI, case no. 61/2010, CCI, 8 February 2013.

facto status of monopoly in organising cricket at various levels, the government's indirect support facilitating land, permission for foreign visits and tax exemption, the impact of ICC linkage resulting in disapproval of cricket by alternative agencies and the position that members of ICC are exclusive custodians of cricket, and concluded that BCCI was a de facto regulator of cricket and had the status of dominant position. On the question of 'enterprise', CCI looked into the nature of activities of BCCI, the means and extent of revenue generation, and found that it had entrepreneurial character analogous to business establishments and other sporting associations like All India Chess Federation. In the matter of 'abuse of dominant position', CCI examined how in the different dimensions of relevant market—supply side, demand side and consumer side—BCCI had a dominant position and by excluding the media rights and sponsorship rights for functioning of Indian Cricket League, it had restricted economic competition and abused its dominant position. CCI directed BCCI not to prevent market access for potential competitors in future, cease to exercise its regulatory role and pay a penalty of ₹52 crore. In appeal, the Competition Appellate Tribunal set aside the order of CCI on account of violation of principles of natural justice and inappropriate appreciation of evidences. The development shows the possible impact of competition law to ensure a fair situation.

CSR and SAs

Under Section 135(1) of the Companies Act, 2013, every company with a net worth of ₹500 crore or more, or turnover of ₹1,000 crore or more, or net profit of ₹5 crore or more, during any financial year, shall constitute a CSR committee of the Board consisting of three directors or more, out of which one shall be an independent director. The committee shall formulate and recommend a CSR policy which indicates the activities to be undertaken by the company as specified in Schedule VII, recommend the amount of expenditure to be incurred for the same and monitor the CSR policy of the company from time to time. One such recognised activity is training to promote rural sports, nationally recognised sports, Paralympics and Olympics. The companies may collaborate with SAs for these purposes. Non-profit policy has great potentiality of helping rural and other sports.

Space for SAs in Kerala Sports Act

The Kerala Sports Act, 2000, aiming at sports for all, has contemplated collaboration of recognised sports organisations[59] at the state and district levels and of sports clubs[60] at the municipal, block and village levels with statutory bodies such as state, district, block, village and municipal sports councils in the task of organising, promoting and encouraging sports. Under Section 5(2)(g), the state sports council has the power and function to grant assistance by way of loans or otherwise to any person, educational institutions, sports organisations, clubs or associations with a view to promote sports in general or to promote any particular venture or item of sports. It also has the power of fixing criteria about recognition of SAs including state unit of national sports federations having Central government recognition. There are elaborate provisions about recognition of sports organisations and sports clubs. The sports organisations and sports clubs

[59] 'Recognised sports organisation' means a sports organisation registered with the State Sports Council, in accordance with the provisions of this Act; 'Sports organisation' means an organisation constituted in accordance with law having a written constitution for the promotion of sports and games; 'Sports' shall include such activities organised as outdoor games, athletics, games conducted in open place or country sports, indoor games and aquatic sports and popular games such as equestrian, show jumping, cycling, motor racing, mountaineering, boat racing, rifle shooting, kalaripayattu, fencing, yoga and such other outdoor and indoor sports and games, chess, gymnastics, wrestling, weightlifting, cycle polo and other Olympic disciplines and include other physical activities which the State Government may, by notification in the gazette specify as sports or games on the recommendation of the State Sports Council.

[60] 'Sports club' means a sports organisation registered with the Corporation Council, Municipal Sports Council, Town Sports Council, Block Sports Council or Village Sports Council as the case may be and affiliated to any sports organisation registered with the State Sports Council.

have right of representation at appropriate levels of statutory bodies like sports councils at various levels. National Sports Policy, 2001, has emphasised on role of SAs, federations and clubs. Encouragement to women's sports is also a step towards equality. If all the states provide for meaningful legal framework for coordinating, assisting and collaborating the sports organisations with great initiative and potential to support and promote sporting activity with its grand diversity and enthusiasm with recognition of their important sociocultural roles, that will go a long way in building up the social capital for enduring sporting activity throughout the nation.

Conclusion

'Level playing field' is primarily the grammar of sports. But it is also the spirit of justice in legal world. Logically, sports law has a responsibility of maintaining equanimity amidst different stakeholders and ensuring equal human rights of all. As unfolded in tradition, historical and sociological roots of sports have communitarian basis and the collective spirit has come to surface to protest against discrimination and determine to build social solidarity in the intimate sphere of life, which has immense cultural and human right dimension. Conceding the strong cultural ethos for bottom-up approach and overarching the communities in the love towards sports and games, the impulse of social bonding has put the people together in the joy of sporting. Rich economic resource of sport has also genesis in collective effort. Looked from community perspective and inclination towards sports for all, allowing sports and games to the domain of NPVO rather than to the market or state has greater advantages. But this is not to deny the benefit of state's facilitative, protective and regulative role and flow of fund from commercialisation and corporate assistance. For strengthening their non-profit capacity, the legal environment of NPOs should also be well equipped.

Indian NPO law is on developing stage, and its tendency to include controlling the governance of SAs is in right direction.

In contrast to the past where SAs were explicitly or impliedly excluded from their controlling regime, the present legal position has great merit. The readiness of constitutional remedies, gradual preparedness of laws of SR, trust, NPCs and tax exemption and the potentiality of CSR and state-specific sports law have demonstrated beyond doubt the significant role of NPO law in ensuring good governance of SAs, which constitute the nerve system of the sporting world. Legal development has shown efficacy of arrangement to settle disputes between the SA and its members, between SA and the non-member stakeholders, between SA and state, and among SAs by employing fundamental human rights and legal rights. Level playing field of that sort is a valuable contribution when we look at the impact of various categories of NPO laws.

However, larger dimension of level playing field needs to be achieved in view of bigger challenges faced or posed by SAs. The features such as democratic participation, open membership, accountability, professional management and zero toleration to corruption should be dominant and meaningful characteristics amidst all forms of NPOs. Emphasis on women's sports is adding to the cause of sports for all. When modern sports and games are opening up to the mammoth process and phenomenon of corporatisation and huge flow of funds, the inner strength of democratic participation, accountability and professional management is the indispensable factor that comes to the rescue of SAs and people who love sports. There is also the need to apply CSR principle upon SAs of higher income/property bracket in order that surplus of their income or resources might be used for promotion of other sports and games which have lesser economic resources. Finally, taking a clue from Kerala example, the pyramid of SAs and their well-knit network should be built on sound lines. Accreditation system under income tax law, sports law or SR law will be providing for in-built quality controls and purpose compliance mechanisms.

Current Issues Within Sports Law in India

Vidushpat Singhania, Nitin Mittal and Gautam Karhadkar

Introduction

Sports in India, today, has evolved into a massive public entertainment industry, with a huge boost given to it by the unprecedented growth and reach of media technologies. Internet, television, radio and other satellite technologies have evolved over the years, providing spectators with access to live sporting events taking place all over the world. These myriad of technologies and media streams have brought sports to each and every household in the modern era. Whereas the opportunity of watching sporting events was earlier limited to only the spectators in the stadium, broadcast has multiplied the viewership of a sporting event manifold. This has led to sport's transformation from a largely amateur pursuit to a professional industry providing increased sources of business and profit.

Since the nineteenth century, sport administration has been self-regulated, anchored in their origins as amateur pastimes. However, in the modern landscape, sport is now a multibillion industry, with global audiences and customers—invaluable commodities to be traded and marketed.[1]

The rate at which the sport industry is growing and maturing has seen the capacity of the existing conventional governance structures to deal with modern-day issues come under the scanner, thereby giving rise to a fundamental question: Whether the present model of sport governance is effective or not? Followed by the incidental query raised by a number of fans: What or how much (if any) should be the intervention of the State in governing sports? This chapter seeks to explore all these questions in light of some current issues and controversies and aspires to point out an appropriate model of good governance for administration of sports in India.

Sports Administration and Good Governance Principles

Richard Pound, president of World Anti-Doping Agency (WADA) and vice-president of International Olympic Committee (IOC) said in the 'Play the Game' conference that, 'The right to "autonomy" in the sense of making and administering sport rules must be earned through responsible conduct, not mere assertion of a former and now irrelevant status.'[2]

While media has played an important role in providing the initial impetus to the sports movement, a sustained model of the sports movement would imperatively require the administration of sports to follow the good governance principles:

[1] Ravi Mehta, '*The Future of Sports Governance: Will Sport Sustain in Traditional Mode of Autonomy*', SPORTS LAW BULLETIN (2017), *available at* https://www.sportslawbulletin.org/future-sports-governance-will-sport-sustain-its-traditional-model-autonomy/

[2] Jens Sejer Andersen, *The Year That Killed the Autonomy of Sport*, PLAY THE GAME (2015), *available at* http://www.playthegame.org/news/comments/2015/021_the-year-that-killed-the-autonomy-of-sport/

1. Transparency and public communication
2. Democratic process
3. Checks and balances
4. Solidarity

Transparency and Public Communication

Sport administration particularly at the amateur level relies heavily on the public exchequer's finances. Transparency is closely related to accountability and is seen as a first line of defence against corruption. Accountability requires sports federations to inform their members about their decisions and the grounds on which these decisions are taken. This requires sports federations to implement procedures which shall ensure non-arbitrariness, transparency and flow of information. The sports federations are expected to adhere to stringent disclosure requirements, including but not limited to accurate financial reporting, and adequate communication of their activities to the public.

The sports federations are also accountable to the people because they perform important public functions. These public functions include selection of players for the respective national teams and their efficient management to ensure competitive representation of the country in the international arena. The Hon'ble Supreme Court of India in *Board of Control for Cricket in India & Anr. v. Netaji Cricket Club and Ors*[3] held:

> 80. The Board is a society registered under the Tamil Nadu Societies Registration Act. It enjoys a monopoly status as regards regulation of the sport of cricket in terms of its Memorandum of Association and Articles of Association. It controls the sport of cricket and lays down the law therefor. It inter alia enjoys benefits by way of tax exemption and right to use stadia at nominal annual rent. It earns huge revenue not only by selling tickets to viewers but also selling right to exhibit films live on TV and broadcasting the same. Ordinarily, its full members are the State associations

[3] Board of Control for Cricket in India & Anr. v. Netaji Cricket Club and Ors, (2005) 4 SCC 741.

except Association of Indian Universities, Railway Sports Control Board and Services Sports Control Board. As a member of ICC, it represents the country in the international fora. It exercises enormous public functions. It has the authority to select players, umpires and officials to represent the country in the international fora. It exercises total control over the players, umpires and other officers. The Rules of the Board clearly demonstrate that without its recognition no competitive cricket can be hosted either within or outside the country. Its control over the sport of competitive cricket is deeply pervasive and complete.

In the case of *Ajay Jadeja* v. *UOI and Ors*,[4] it was held that 'the functions of the Board are clearly public functions', including supporting its 'member' state associations and that the Board of Control for Cricket in India (BCCI) would be amenable to writ jurisdiction of the courts in India. BCCI is conducting selection process for the national team, conducting national- and international-level tournaments. When the government stands by and lets a body like BCCI monopolise the game in India, it necessarily imbues BCCI with the responsibility of discharging 'public functions'.

Further in *Pradeep Kumar Biswas* v. *Indian Institute of Chemical Biology and Ors*,[5] the Court stated under Paragraph 29 of the judgement that

29. It was then argued that the Board discharges public duties which are in the nature of State functions. Elaborating on this argument it was pointed out that the Board selects a team to represent India in international matches. The Board makes rules that govern the activities of the cricket players, umpires and other persons involved in the activities of cricket. These, according to the petitioner, are all in the nature of State functions and an entity which discharges such functions can only be an instrumentality of State, therefore, the Board falls within the definition of State for the purpose of Article 12. Assuming that the abovementioned functions of the Board do amount to public duties or State

---

[4] Ajay Jadeja v. UOI and Ors, (2002) 95 DLT 14.
[5] Pradeep Kumar Biswas v. Indian Institute of Chemical Biology and Ors, (2002) 5 SCC 111.

functions, the question for our consideration is: would this be sufficient to hold the Board to be a State for the purpose of Article 12? While considering this aspect of the argument of the petitioner, it should be borne in mind that the State/Union has not chosen the Board to perform these duties nor has it legally authorised the Board to carry out these functions under any law or agreement. It has chosen to leave the activities of cricket to be controlled by private bodies out of such bodies' own volition (self-arrogated). In such circumstances when the actions of the Board are not actions as an authorised representative of the State, can it be said that the Board is discharging State functions? The answer should be no. In the absence of any authorisation, if a private body chooses to discharge any such function which is not prohibited by law then it would be incorrect to hold that such action of the body would make it an instrumentality of the State. The Union of India has tried to make out a case that the Board discharges these functions because of the de facto recognition granted by it to the Board under the guidelines framed by it, but the Board has denied the same. In this regard we must hold that the Union of India has failed to prove that there is any recognition by the Union of India under the guidelines framed by it, and that the Board is discharging these functions on its own as an autonomous body.

Further, in the case of *BCCI* v. *Cricket Association of Bihar*,[6] the Court in Paragraphs 29 and 30 of the judgement held that

> 29. Having said that this Court recognized the fact that the Board was discharging some duties like the Selection of Indian Cricket Team, controlling the activities of the players which activities were akin to public duties or State functions so that if there is any breach of a constitutional or statutory obligation or the rights of other citizens, the aggrieved party shall be entitled to seek redress under the ordinary law or by way of a writ petition under Article 226.

> 30. The majority view thus favours the view that BCCI is amenable to the writ jurisdiction of the High Court under Article 226 even when it is not 'State' within the meaning of Article 12. The rationale underlying that view if we may say with utmost respect lies in

[6] Civil Appeal no. 4235 of 2014 (Arising out of SLP (C) No. 34228 of 2014).

the 'nature of duties and functions' which the BCCI performs. It is common ground that the respondent-Board has a complete sway over the game of cricket in this country. It regulates and controls the game to the exclusion of all others. It formulates rules, regulations norms and standards covering all aspect of the game. It enjoys the power of choosing the members of the national team and the umpires. It exercises the power of disqualifying players which may at times put an end to the sporting career of a person. It spends crores of rupees on building and maintaining infrastructure like stadia, running of cricket academies and Supporting State Associations. It frames pension schemes and incurs expenditure on coaches, trainers etc. It sells broadcast and telecast rights and collects admission fee to venues where the matches are played. All these activities are undertaken with the tacit concurrence of the State Government and the Government of India who are not only fully aware but supportive of the activities of the Board. The State has not chosen to bring any law or taken any other step that would either deprive or dilute the Board's monopoly in the field of cricket. On the contrary, the Government of India have allowed the Board to select the national team which is then recognized by all concerned and applauded by the entire nation including at times by the highest of the dignitaries when they win tournaments and bring laurels home. Those distinguishing themselves in the international arena are conferred highest civilian awards like the Bharat Ratna, Padma Vibhushan, Padma Bhushan and Padma Shri apart from sporting awards instituted by the Government. Such is the passion for this game in this country that cricketers are seen as icons by youngsters, middle aged and the old alike. Any organization or entity that has such pervasive control over the game and its affairs and such powers as can make dreams end up in smoke or come true cannot be said to be undertaking any private activity. The functions of the Board are clearly public functions, which, till such time the State intervenes to take over the same, remain in the nature of public functions, no matter discharged by a society registered under the Registration of Societies Act. Suffice it to say that if the Government not only allows an autonomous/private body to discharge functions which it could in law takeover or regulate but even lends its assistance to such a non-government body to undertake such functions which by their very nature are public functions, it cannot be said that the functions are not public functions or that the entity discharging the same is not answerable on the standards generally applicable to judicial review of State action. Our answer to question No.1, therefore, is in the negative, qua, the first part and affirmative qua the second. BCCI may not be State under Article 12 of the Constitution but is certainly amenable to writ jurisdiction under Article 226 of the Constitution of India.

The dimensions of transparency and accountability can be addressed by the following points:[7]

1. *Establishment of accountability standards*: Clear supervisory and accountability standards should be established by the sports federations for all of their bodies, particularly those which have decision-making powers. This will ensure that the powers conferred upon such bodies and individuals are being exercised responsibly, thereby eliminating any ambiguity and arbitrariness.

2. *Identification of appropriate performance indicators*: In order to promote effective and good governance, key performance measures ought to be set for each level (district, state, national), keeping in mind the size of the sport federation. The performance indicator should not only be linked to the performance of the sports-persons' alone but also to the key activities executed and responsibilities undertaken by the officials among others.

3. *Measures for internal control*: Sport federations should adopt proper, fit and proportionate measures for internal controls, along with strategies for financial management and protection of data. The policies must also be formulated to regulate the grant of finances and formation and/ or execution of agreements/contracts.

4. *Financial reporting*: Stakeholders should have access to audited financial accounts and information which has been disclosed in accordance with the applicable law. The information so disclosed shall be a part of annual report

[7] EU work plan for sport 2011–2014, *Principals of Good Governance in Sports* (September 2013), *available at* http://ec.europa.eu/assets/eac/sport/library/policy_documents/xg-gg-201307-dlvrbl2-sept2013.pdf

presented by the sport federation to maintain trust within the stakeholders and ensure transparency towards their functioning.

5. *Disbursement and allocation of funds*: A proper and accurate record of all the disbursement made by the sports federation throughout the financial year should be maintained and documented. Such records, if required, may be made subjected to the relevant policy for disbursement which should be formulated by the federation.

6. *Risk management*: Sports federations shall ensure formulation of proper and effective arrangements for risk management which shall aid them to identify, control, assess and mitigate risks associated with their activities.

7. *Confidentiality*: Sports federations shall enforce and develop rigorous confidentiality protocols and standards.

Democratic Process

Most sports federations have a system wherein there is an internal compliance and sanctioning system in place but, imperatively, they lack a legislative branch, thereby ensuring that they are run as an authoritarian system containing rule-setting and regulations in the form of diktats. Such a high degree of autonomy has allowed the world of sport administration to function according to its own whims and prioritise its own interests which, as a result, has had repercussions on the internal democratic functioning.

Sports federations should allow democratic participation in their administration and accountability for the athletes and their member associations. However, aristocratic governance in sports is a major source of conflict as persons who are excluded from the decision-making process challenge the regulations and the decisions of the sport federation. Consequently, this leads to development of rival factions within the sport federation which seriously affects the functioning of the sport federation. Such development of rival factions and the resultant splits also lead to negative publicity of the sport federation in the media and affect its commercial revenues.

Democracy and minimum standards of democratic process can be achieved by any sports organisation by complying with the following points:

1. *Clear organisational framework*: Sports federations should ensure formulation of proper and effective organisational framework for allocation of membership and establish appropriate parameters of the decision-making power of the representatives who should be elected after following the due procedure of democratic elections. Furthermore, all decisions of the elected members should be up for a review vis-à-vis objectives, plans and vision (individual and organisation/group) of the sport federation.

2. *Decision-making bodies*: In the organisational set-up of a sport federation, there must be a cooperative relationship among all the decision-making bodies. The Memorandum and Articles of Association of the concerned sport federation should clearly demarcate the responsibilities along with the decision-making authority of each and every decision-making body.

   In order to facilitate proper functioning of the decision-making bodies, the sport federation must clearly identify the rights and liabilities of all the stakeholders whilst participating in consultation or decision-making process.

3. *Role and rights of members and stakeholders*: The notifications issued by the sport federation as well as its website must include details of members who will have a right to vote at meetings, order of business under consideration and the opportunity to make representations. There should be strict compliance with the Constitution and procedural rules adopted by the sports federations. The role and rights of all members, stakeholders and participants must be clearly demarcated.

Checks and Balances

'Checks and Balances' are several steps which are implemented so as to serve as crucial tools for implementing accountability and curbing the concentration of power across every level of the sports federations. Absolute power corrupts absolutely. The separation of powers in sport administration between the board and management is an important example of 'Checks and Balances'. Such checks and balances also act as a catalyst to implement internal control procedures.

Checks and balances should also be implemented over personnel working in the departments of a sport federation. This would ensure that no stakeholder or manager or board member or department has absolute control over decisions.

Solidarity

Sports federations at the international level are conforming to demands for ethically, morally and environmentally responsible conduct. They are using the opportunities granted to them by the traction afforded to some media-highlighted controversies to adopt and embrace good governance principles and mould themselves internally in consonance with such good governance principles. Sports federations are also taking inputs from all the stakeholders while establishing the good governance principles. Public exchequer's money is spent for the construction of new stadiums, public transport, building and maintaining new and old training centres, etc. Sports federations which, due to their public health and welfare role, enjoy the benefit of using these public resources are duty-bound to 'give something back' to the community/society.

India seeks to implement these aforementioned good governance principles through guidelines issued by the Government of India in the form of the National Sports Development Code of India (NSDCI), 2011 (amended code to be issued) and the National Sports Development Bill, 2013. In addition to such codes and guidelines, the judiciary through the Lodha Committee recommendations have issued certain mandates, under the aegis of the Hon'ble Supreme Court, which need to be followed by BCCI and hopefully by other national sport federations (NSFs) as well.

National Sports Development Code of India, 2011

NSDCI was introduced by the government to ensure that the NSFs and the Indian Olympic Association (IOA) adopt good governance practices. In order to achieve the goals of good governance and transparency, the Indian government issued comprehensive guidelines in the years 1975, 1988, 1997 and 2001. Pertinently, major changes took place in the Indian sporting fraternity after 2001. Implementation of age and tenure limits for the senior officials and the office-bearers of various NSFs, prevention of sexual harassment of women in sports, anti-doping guidelines and conducting fair and transparent elections for NSFs were some of the changes which were considered imperative towards cleansing sport administration of the malaise and lackadaisical attitude that had crept in. A number of guidelines and circulars issued by the Ministry of Youth Affairs and Sports post 2001 were amalgamated in the NSDCI, 2011. The salient features of the code of 2011 are as follows:

- Vision and mission: The primary vision of NSDCI, 2011, was to adopt and implement good governance principles in sports in India since the development of sports in India in the twenty-first century is of utmost priority and national importance. Sports in today's scenario cannot be viewed in isolation as these promote lifestyle, child and youth development, social inclusiveness, employment opportunities and, above all, a sense of belongingness towards one's motherland.[8] Therefore, upon taking a holistic view of the same, it has become imperative that the sports federations,

[8] Statement of Purpose, National Sports Development Code of India, 2011.

which are responsible for efficient functioning of all sports activities in India and are performing public functions, adopt a good governance policy and be made accountable in case of any inconsistency towards acting in betterment of sports in India.

- NSDCI seeks to develop a categorisation of sports which determines the financial support the government would give to a sport. Under the code of 2011, the government seeks to endorse financial assistance to the athletes, the coaches of various national and regional teams and support personnel for holding appropriate approved coaching camps. However, the scales of support will be notified by the government to the respective sport organisation after consultation with Sports Authority of India (SAI). The government included travelling expenses, lodging and boarding expenses, training kits, and medical and insurance expenses under 'financial assistance' as per the NSDCI.

- Equal voting rights among members of each NSF are provided under NSDCI in order to facilitate the concept of good governance in the sports federations in India. Equal participation of all in the election process will ensure that no person with personal interests is elected to any post.

- Sports federations are to be granted recognition by the government only after three years of efficient and transparent functioning. In addition to the threshold of three years, the federations are also bound to support their applications for assistance with audited annual reports and financial reports of the last three years. This step has been taken to avoid the misuse of financial grants or emoluments by the federations which could be rendered to some other needy federation instead.

- All NSFs need to publish important information such as details of coaching camps, the venues which are to hold these camps, rundown of participants and chosen athletes to the camp. All NSFs are also duty-bound to have their examined accounts disseminated on the website six months in advance.

- An NSF should be the central governing body and have two-thirds of the state sports associations affiliated to it. NSFs are required to conduct state and national championships to identify the potential of the sports-persons of that particular sport in that particular state.

- NSFs should have 25 per cent of representation of athletes in executive committees of every sport federation. This helps in ensuring improvement in the performances of the athletes and ensuring a sense of duty and commitment from athletes. Furthermore, the same would serve to preserve selection criteria, using their experience to overcome potential limitations, helping in appropriate exposure of the players and establishing a legitimate grievance redressal procedure to ensure that the athletes can convey their grievance in confidence.

National Sports Development Bill, 2013

- Vision and mission: The National Sports Development Bill of 2013 was introduced with an aim to develop sports and undertake welfare measures for development of sportsmen and sportswomen, promote ethical practices in the arena of sports including preventing doping practices as much as possible, prevent fraud by the athletes while disclosing their age, prevent sexual harassment of women athletes and set up effective bodies to deal with disputes related to aforementioned issues.

- Office-bearers of a sport federation shall be elected officials and bodies such as Dispute Resolution, Ethics Commission and Election Commission should be set-up to promote democratic functioning within the sports organisations. The Bill of 2013 also sought to ensure integrity and ethical standards by proposing Ethics Commission and Independent Code of Ethics to adjudicate on such ethical issues.

- Under the Bill of 2013, the sports bodies were to be made subject to the Right to Information (RTI) Act, 2005, which would ensure that all information pertaining to the functioning of the NSF would be in the public domain and would be disclosed publicly to encourage transparency and accountability.

- NSFs would be under an obligation to procure playing fields and equipment for smooth and better functioning of the events to be organised by the organisations and the respective sport in general. Sports bodies would also be duty-bound to conduct national championships, bid for international events and send the Indian team as part of the public function of NSFs.

- Further, the Bill sought to make a 25 per cent mandatory representation of athletes in executive committee of sports federations to ensure that the athletes have a voice within the federation.

- The Bill of 2013 also proposed that 10 per cent from each gender should be reserved in the general body of the sports federations to make sure that no gender should be discriminated against or harassed keeping in view the growing cases of sexual harassment.

Challenges Faced by Sportswomen in India: The Saga of Gender Discrimination

'No matter how toughened a sportswoman may be, her organism is not cut out to sustain certain shocks.'[9] Gender discrimination in sports has been a smouldering topic since times immemorial and has been the detriment of sports across several nations and cultures. From the early 1900s, the world has moved towards modernisation of the games and sports and a concentrated attempt to empower women and ensure equal opportunities. In 1978, UNESCO recognised sports and physical activities as basic human rights for all by stating that[10]

[9] Baron Pierre de Coubertin, Founder of Modern Olympics.
[10] The International Charter of Physical Education, Physical Activity and Sport, 1978.

Sports have been a vital part of the official school program since the mid-1800s, and were originally incorporated into the curriculum to serve as an important line of defense against the potential feminization of American males by a growing female teaching profession. As a part of the curriculum, sport provided opportunities for physical fitness and competition, as well as a medium through which valued socio-cultural life skills could be learned and practiced. Grounded in ideals of masculinity, sport, more than any other part of the educational curriculum has been, and continues to be, a gender issue.[11]

Gender Discrimination in Indian Sports: An Introduction

The twin issues of race and sexual orientation are often discovered in the realm of sport. When it comes to sports, such segregation is underestimated. However, it repeatedly keeps penetrating our societal structures as well as our sporting establishments. Women in India are still seen as the 'weaker sex', and this attitude unavoidably keeps affecting women in a grave manner, especially in sports. Sports in India continue to be primarily male-oriented, and women have, for a considerable period of time, been denied participation in games by immediate and backhanded social inhibitors.

Case Studies of Gender Discrimination in India

India has seen a plethora of cases wherein women have been subjected time and again to discrimination which has resulted in women being prohibited and prevented from competing equally with men and excelling in the field of sports. The following case studies are prime examples of such incidents in India:

1. **Gender verification:** The determination of eligibility for women athletes to participate in the female category has always been a source of controversy. Testing and

[11] Vishwas Manohar Deshpandey, *Gender Discrimination in Sports*, 3(3) INT'L J. PHY. EDUC. SPORTS HEALTH 545–547 (2016).

establishing the sex or gender of athletes date back to the 1960s where competitors were paraded naked in front of a panel of judges in order to verify the presence of female genitals.

The anti-doping case of short-distance runner Dutee Chand,[12] a 19-year-old athlete, is the best example of gender verification controversy. She showed certain traits of hyperandrogenism, which disqualified her from competing as a female athlete in Glasgow Commonwealth Games 2014. However, the athlete continued her fight against this discrimination and on 25 July 2015, in a landmark ruling, the Court of Arbitration for Sport (CAS) overturned the ban on her owing to the hyperandrogenism rule and suspended the rule, giving IAAF two years to produce scientific evidence in support of such a rule.

2. **Financial issues:** In a patriarchal country like India, job and/or employment opportunities for sportswomen are shockingly inadequate and sport is not considered as a source of adequate income for women. Apart from sports such as cricket, lawn tennis and golf, women in India who participate and compete in various other sports cannot possibly become financially independent by adopting sport as a career.

The case of Kaveri Prakash is one such incident, where the athlete could not participate in national and international events, owing to a lack of adequate finances. Ms Prakash financed herself up until the district level with extreme difficulty, but eventually gave up sports in entirety, as she did not possess the requisite funds to progress to state and national levels.[13]

3. **Homophobia:** In India, any athlete who is accused of being masculine is treated with scorn and subjected to

[12] Dutee Chand v. Athletics Federation of India (AFI) and the International Association of Athletics Federation (IAAF), CAS2014/A/3759.

[13] Kirsten Sparre, *India Lacks Structure to Nurture Athletes*, CHILDREN IN SPORTS (2007), *available at* http://www.playthegame.org/upload/magazine2007/pdf/sections/playthegamemagazine07childreninsport.pdf

physiological probing leading to tremendous psychological trauma. Having features resembling what is labelled as 'manly' seems to be sufficient enough reason to be accused of having an extra Y chromosome and being treated as a criminal. The case of Pinki Praminik is an example, where a 4×100 metre relay Indian athlete was accused of being a man cloaked as a woman by her live-in partner and was subsequently arrested by police for the alleged charges of rape under the Indian Penal Code 1860. But, the alleged rape charges were dropped by the Calcutta High Court[14] and the athlete was proven to be a woman after all the medical tests were conducted and verified.

4. **Sexual harassment:** Women's participation in sports in India is hindered by the cruel acts of sexual harassment. There is a constant threat, vulnerability, susceptibility, abuse and hardships pertaining to sexual harassment among women athletes in India from their coaches, fellow male athletes, federation officials and administrators.

Ranjitha Devi's case in the year 2010 is a leading case study of how women athletes are facing inappropriate and shameful behaviour from coaches in India. In this case, the hockey coach Mr M. K. Kaushik was blamed with charges for sexual harassment and subsequently resigned and quit from the post of the Indian national women's team head coach. Later, in the probe conducted by the committee set-up, it was found that the language of the coach Mr M. K. Kaushik was sexually coloured and abusive towards the athlete.

The Indian Parliament has subsequently passed the Sexual Harassment of Women at Workplace (Prevention, Prohibition and Redressal) Act, 2013. Subsequent to the passing of this Act, a woman who has been subjected to sexual harassment at the work place can file a complaint under Section 2(a) of this Act as a complainant. Sexual harassment under Section 2(n) includes:

---

[14] Pinki Pramanik v. State of West Bengal & Anr, CRR 2848 (2013).

1. Physical contact and advances
2. A demand or request for sexual favours
3. Making sexually coloured remarks
4. Showing pornography
5. Any other unwelcome physical, verbal or non-verbal conduct of a sexual nature

Also, the term 'workplace' has been defined under Section 2(o)(i) of the Act as 'any department, organisation, undertaking, establishment, enterprise, institution, office, branch or unit which is established, owned, controlled or wholly or substantially financed or funded provided directly or indirectly by the appropriate Government'.

Sports Contracts

Every textbook on contract law begins with a section on the foundation of contracts. In the sports industry also there is frequently a genuine question mark over whether a given arrangement evinces sufficient formality and intention to create legal relations so as to constitute a formal contract. A classic example would be where the governing body of a sport requires a specific mandate from its member in order to authorize it to enter into agreement, or on shortage of time requires the closure of the deal in the circumstances where the appropriate agreement cannot be drafted.[15]

Thus, contract law forms the bedrock of varied transactions and commercial relations in the domain of sports. It assists the sports organisations and their governing bodies in determining the framework of rules and regulations which are applicable to that particular sport. Law of contracts also empowers the authorities in any sport organisation to impose a prescribed sanction in order to maintain discipline and ensure that no act which brings disrepute to the sport is committed. Further, the governing bodies of these sports are governed primarily by the following

[15] VEROW ET AL., SPORTS LAW (2005).

facts: (a) whether it is a society, cooperative society, independent association, etc. and (b) the members of these bodies derive their power from the contracts.[16]

A contract is a legally binding agreement. It represents the meeting of the minds of the parties. Contracts in sports are subject to the same principles of contract formation as any other form of employment agreement. There are elements which are necessary to make it a binding and enforceable contract:

- An agreement
- Between competent parties
- Based upon the genuine assent of the parties
- Supported by consideration
- Made for a lawful objective or is not deemed illegal by existing laws
- In the form required by law

Categories of Sports Contracts

1. **Professional services contracts:** Professional services contracts, also known as standard player contracts, are the general, multipurpose contracts that are delivered to all athletes regardless of negotiated salaries or bonuses; these could be contracts 'of service' or 'for service'.

2. **Sponsorships and endorsement contracts:** They are used to govern relationships between athletes and independent sponsors. An endorsement contract allows the sponsor to use the name of the athlete, his/her image or his/her likeness in advertising the products of the sponsors. The trend has been witnessed among all the sports where individual players are prohibited from endorsing alcoholic beverages or tobacco products.[17] The players are signed

---

[16] MUKUL MUDGAL & VIDUSHPAT SINGHANIA, LAW AND SPORTS IN INDIA (2nd ed. 2016).

[17] US Legal, Sports Contracts—Basic Principles, *available at* https://sportslaw.uslegal.com/sports-agents-and-contracts/sports-contracts-basic-principles/

by major endorsement agencies with the aim of encashing the popularity of the players/athletes, given their immense popularity and mass appeal. Athletes provide several important benefits to advertising such as:

a. Increasing brand name recognition.
b. Creating positive associations by transposing positive qualities of the athlete to the product like physical appeal or likeability.
c. Aiding in the development of distinct brand personalities.

3. **Appearance and advertising contracts:** Appearance contracts allow for additional compensation for athletes who choose to appear at public functions, brand launches, advertisement campaigns, sports camps, etc. Appearance contracts are personal appearance agreements for athletes, celebrities, artists and sports stars to make an appearance for a specified period of time at any event or function. A personal appearance agreement document is prepared in order to

a. Hire a popular name for making an appearance for an event.
b. Manage an organisation or company that regularly hires celebrities, speakers or other VIPs.

Under the personal appearance agreement, the contracting parties need to agree upon and be perfectly clear regarding the terms and conditions of the agreement such as the specified time the athlete is to arrive by, how long is the athlete to stay for and what are the defined rights and the obligations as per the agreement. The contract shall be in writing and signed by the concerned sports athlete.

The personal appearance contract includes the following provisions:

a. **Parties:** Name of the artist and the venue where the artist or celebrity will appear.
b. **Terms and conditions:** Sets out the place and date(s) of the engagement, number of shows, the time and length

of the appearance and information regarding sound checks.

c. **Agreed-upon price:** Specifies the amount of any deposit, amount due when contract is signed and when the total balance is due.

d. **Expenses:** Expenses which will be paid by venue including airfare, hotel and travel accommodations.

e. **Promotion/advertising:** Both artist and venue will be responsible for the promotion of the personal appearance, and artist or celebrity agrees to allow venue to use his/her name and likeness for promotional purposes.

f. **Signatures:** Both artist and a representative of the venue must sign this contract.

4. **Broadcasting contracts:** The broadcasting of sports events is the live coverage of sports in the form of a television programme, radio programme or in any other form of broadcasting media. It usually involves one or more sports commentators describing the events as they take place. The broadcasting of sports events require contracts to govern the terms between the parties to the contract. Such broadcasting contracts generally involve parties such as event owner and broadcaster and usually pertain to production, marketing and sponsorships, etc.

Sports broadcasting contracts have become incredibly lucrative in recent years, allowing major professional sports leagues to earn humongous revenues just from telecasting the games and/or sporting events around the globe to different countries.

5. **Naming rights contracts:** The popularity of naming rights has been increasing in recent years as firms look for additional ways to increase brand awareness, brand value and market share. Naming rights are among the many modes chosen by firms to enhance awareness and recognition. In their simplest form, naming rights can be broadly defined as the privilege of associating a sponsor's name with a

building, project or event by including the sponsor's name in the title of the item being named.[18]

A naming rights contract is a financial contract under which a corporation or individual purchases the rights to name a stadium, potentially along with other benefits, for a set period of time in exchange for a financial payment. It is not uncommon for these agreements to be used as part of a sponsor's marketing strategy to deliver greater brand recognition and improved sales revenue.

The origin of naming rights agreements is rooted in American sports and particularly within baseball. The first recorded agreement was in 1912 when the Boston Red Sox's stadium was renamed Fenway Park in order to create publicity for the stadium owner's real estate company (Fenway Realty). A second example is the Chicago Cubs who renamed their stadium Wrigley Field to promote the owner's chewing gum company.

Peculiarity in Sports Contracts

Peculiarity has always been associated with sports contracts and to justify the same, the most peculiar issue in sports contract is a contract with a minor. The sporting bodies often organise junior and sub-junior sporting events. There are certain problems which are faced while contracting with minors such as how to decide whether a minor is competent to decide about his/her revenues, participation and training. The settled position in law with respect to contract with minors is that the guardian can enter into a contract on behalf of the minor but the issue of minors being affected from such consent has yet not been answered by Indian courts or legislation. Not only in India but sports contracts with minors have also been haunting the global sporting community

---

[18] GREG C. ASHLEY & MICHAEL J. O'HARA, *Valuing Naming Rights*. Paper presented at the 76th annual meeting of the Academy of Legal Studies in Business (2001), *available at* http://cba2.unomaha.edu/faculty/mohara/web/ALSB01ValuingNamingRights.pdf

since the early twentieth century. Thus, it becomes important to mention that International Olympic Association has set no age bar for the athletes to participate in the sporting events. However, international sports federations of particular sports administer the limit for participation in Olympic events.[19]

At times, sports contracts also contain certain peculiar clauses which prescribe that 'a player shall not be involved in any incident which brings shame to the sport and spoils the "image of the sport".' Considering the meteoric rise in the popularity and usage of social media and the emergence of a trend where players routinely engage with their fans via social media and other means on the Internet, clauses with respect to players' social media presence are put in sports contracts to avoid any controversy with respect to online and social media.

Termination of Sports Contracts

Sports contracts are often considered as lopsided agreements due to the simple fact that sports governing bodies are conferred with more powers in a sports contract than the player; that is, one party in the contract has more powers than the others. Even NSFs often exploit the powers conferred upon them and cancel contracts with teams for non-payment of dues like in the case of *Deccan Chronical Holding Limited (DCHL) v. BCCI*[20] or on other myriad grounds like non-fulfilment of requisites before qualification as witnessed in the case of All India Football Federation (AIFF), wherein AIFF cancelled the licences of football clubs such as Churchill Brothers, United SC, Rangdajied United Football Club and Mohammedan Sporting Club.[21]

[19] MUDGAL & SINGHANIA, *supra* note 16, at 179.

[20] ARBP(L) No. 1238 of 2012.

[21] *Times of India, AIFF Club Licensing Appeals Committee to Meet on Tuesday*, 2 June 2014, *available at* http://timesofindia.indiatimes.com/sports/football/top-stories/AIFF-Club-Licensing-Appeals-Committee-to-meet-on-Tuesday/articleshow/35952978.cms

Importance of Sports Contracts

The law of contract plays an increasingly important role for modern sportsmen and sportswomen in the following ways:

1. Determination of employment status of athlete
2. Determination of salary/compensation and bonuses
3. Specification of grievances redressal mechanisms
4. Fundamental in engaging the services of agents
5. Entering into sponsorship deals

Important Areas in Which Sports Contracts Are Required

The law of contract is the cornerstone on which sports law has been built and which is of primary importance in most areas such as[22]

1. Sale of media rights in respect of a sporting event or competition
2. Sponsorship rights
3. Eligibility of athletes or teams to compete in particular competitions or events
4. Selection of athletes for sporting teams
5. Rights to host a major sporting competition or event
6. Management contracts between athletes and managers
7. Membership rights in sporting clubs or organisations

Anti-doping

[Doping is] the administration of or use by a competing athlete of any substance foreign to the body or any physiological substance taken in abnormal quantities or taken by an abnormal route of entry into the body with the sole purpose of increasing,

[22] Alan Sullivan Q. C., *The Role of Contract in Sports Law*, ANZ SPORTS L. J. (2010), *available at* http://www.austlii.edu.au/au/journals/ANZSportsLawJl/2010/2.pdf

in an artificial and unfair manner, his/her performance in the competition.[23]

WADA is the global body established, in 1999, to monitor and check anti-doping activities. WADA works as an independent agency at an international level and is funded primarily by the sport legislatures of the world. The main tasks of WADA include development and promotion of anti-doping capacities, education of athletes and sports agencies, promotion of scientific research, and monitoring and updating the World Anti-Doping Code (WADC).

WADC was created in 2004, subsequently revised in 2009 and then again in 2015. The primary purposes of WADC are as follows:[24]

1. To protect an athlete's right to be a part of doping-free sport and promoting fairness and equality in the sports activities worldwide.
2. To formulate and ensure synchronised and efficient anti-doping programmes at both national and international levels with respect to prevention, detection and deterrence of doping.

The code contains 25 different articles dealing with all the aspects of anti-doping and has been amended frequently as per the need. However, the most important and widely invoked articles in almost all the doping cases are Articles 2 and 10, defining anti-doping rule violations and sanctions on individuals involved in doping respectively.

Article 2 of the WADC: Anti-Doping Rule Violations

Article 2 of the code is primarily based on the principle of 'strict liability' which implies that if the report of any athlete tests

---

[23] Definition of doping by IOC.
[24] WADC, 2015.

positive for adverse analytical finding of a prohibited substance, then s/he shall be solely held liable for the substance being found in his/her body, irrespective of the fact that the substance was consumed intentionally or not.[25]

Article 10 of the WADC: Automatic Disqualification of Individual Results

Article 10 of the code provides for the sanctions that are to be imposed on the athletes found guilty of doping. The sanctions include enforcing a ban on the athlete and forfeiture of medals, points and prizes.[26]

Major Changes in Article 10 after the WADA Anti-Doping Rules, 2015

Following the amendment of the WADC in 2015, the period of ineligibility under Article 10.2 has been increased from two years to four. This increase in the sanctions has found its jurisprudence upon the principle that 'there must be harsher penalties for cheats'.

Even though the sanctions under the amended code have been doubled, certain provisions have also been simultaneously created for reduction of such sanctions. Article 10 enables athletes to establish that they have not cheated intentionally. The reduction in sanctions can be allowed on following possible grounds:[27]

1. Substantial assistance in establishing anti-doping rule violation
2. Admission of the violation of anti-doping rule in case no other evidence is found
3. Prompt admission of the guilt
4. Application on any other grounds for reduction of sanction

[25] MUDGAL & SINGHANIA, *supra* note 16, at 121.
[26] *Supra* note 17.
[27] MUDGAL & SINGHANIA, *supra* note 16, at 122.

National Anti Doping Agency (NADA) was established as an autonomous society and is the primary prosecuting body that seeks to punish Indian athletes who are found violating the anti-doping rules. NADA adopted the WADC in the year 2008 and since then WADA has been charging Indian athletes as per the rules and regulations formulated by WADA. NADA has been acting as an advisor to the Government of India on key issues such as anti-doping policies in the country. Thus, the role of NADA is not only restricted to act as testing and prosecuting agency, but it also plays an active and key role in dissemination of information regarding the norms of anti-doping. It also helps in spreading information and apprising athletes about their obligations under the anti-doping norms.

Defences in Anti-doping Cases

Articles 10.4 and 10.5 of the WADC 2015 apply only to the question of the imposition of sanctions and are not applicable to the question of determination of whether an anti-doping rule violation has occurred. They will only apply in exceptional circumstances such as where an athlete could prove that, despite all due care and caution, s/he was sabotaged by a competitor. Conversely, 'No Fault or Negligence' would not apply in the following circumstances:

1. A positive test resulting from a mislabelled or contaminated vitamin or nutritional supplement (athletes are responsible for what they ingest [Article 2.1.1] and have been warned against the possibility of supplement contamination).
2. The administration of a prohibited substance by the athlete's personal physician or trainer without disclosure to the athlete (athletes are responsible for their choice of medical personnel and for advising medical personnel that they cannot be given any prohibited substance).
3. Sabotage of the athlete's food or drink by a spouse, coach or other person within the athlete's circle of associates (athletes are responsible for what they ingest and for the

conduct of those persons to whom they entrust access to their food and drink).

However, depending on the unique facts of a particular case, any of the referenced illustrations could result in a reduced sanction under Article 10.4 based on 'No Fault or Negligence' argument and Article 10.5 based on 'No Significant Fault or Negligence' argument.[28]

Article 10.5 of Anti-Doping Rules, 2015

The WADC 2015 defines 'No Significant Fault or Negligence' as follows:

> The Athlete or other Person's establishing that his or her Fault or negligence, when viewed in the totality of the circumstances and taking into account the criteria for No Fault or Negligence, was not significant in relationship to the antidoping rule violation. Except in the case of a Minor, for any violation of Article 2.1, the Athlete must also establish how the Prohibited Substance entered his or her system. [Comment: For Cannabinoids, an athlete may establish No Significant Fault or Negligence by clearly demonstrating that the context of the use was unrelated to sport performance.]

Article 10.5 of the NADA Anti-Doping Regulations, 2015, provides defences which can be used in order to reduce the sanction imposed on the athlete who is liable merely by violating the anti-doping rules; that is, to say, a reduction from four years of punishment to two years can be expected by the athlete if in the case s/he is successfully able to establish 'No Significant Fault or Negligence' argument before the anti-doping tribunal. In order for him/her to bring his/her case within the purview of Article 10.5, the following prerequisites need to be satisfied:

1. How the substance entered the athlete's body
2. Precautions reasonably exercised
3. Degree of fault and appropriate sanction

[28] *Supra* note 24.

UKAD v. *Gareth Warburton and Rhys Williams*[29] *(UKAD—2015)*

In this case, the panel imposed six months and four months as periods of ineligibility, respectively. In the case of Warburton, he investigated about the supplement through Facebook and its website. He also accepted the risks that were involved in taking an unknown supplement. He also checked whether the concerned supplements were certified by appropriate authorities and discussed about the same with his agent and an amateur athlete friend.

Rhys Williams had a sports science degree and significant knowledge of nutrition. He researched about the supplement and also referred to the Global Drug Reference website. He also looked up for the supplement on the Informed-Sport website and did not find it. Upon raising this query with the manufacturer, he was told by the manufacturer that the manufacturing company was an accredited Informed-Sport manufacturer.

The panel held that there was an inadvertent ingestion through contamination and there was also no evidence of performance enhancement. Furthermore, since this was their first offence and they had conducted some preliminary research on the product, they were handed the respective bans.

Article 10.4 of the Anti-Doping Rules, 2015

Article 10.4 of NADA Anti-Doping Rules states the principle of 'No Fault or Negligence' and the ineligibility period of four years is waived off completely if the athlete can establish No Fault or Negligence before the anti-doping tribunal. To avail this defence, the athlete has to establish that s/he has exercised his/her duty of utmost care and caution.

The prime example of this argument is the case of judo athlete Charline Van Snick before the CAS in the year 2014.

[29] SR/0000120227 National Anti-Doping Panel (NADP)—2015.

Charline Van Snick v. *Fédération Internationale de Judo*[30]

Charline Van Snick is a judo athlete from Belgium who underwent an in-competition anti-doping test and tested positive for cocaine, a non-specified substance prohibited in competition only. She maintained and argued that she had never seen, touched, let alone ingested a product containing cocaine and maintained that someone sabotaged her drink by giving her favourite sports supplement 'Energy Boost'.

Para 32 of the judgement states that

32. The arguments of the Appellant in support of his claims can be briefly summarized as follows:

A deliberate ingestion of cocaine by Miss Van Snick has been excluded.

Miss Van Snick, a top athlete underwent several doping tests which, except for the control dated 26 August 2013, were all negative including the controls dated 6 July 2013 and 18 September 2013.

Given her performance and world ranking, Miss Van Snick knew that she would certainly be subjected to doping control during competition. It is unlikely that she would take the risk to test positive for doping.

The doctors of the Federation and the Belgian national judo team during the Competition as well as the sports physiotherapist for the Flemish Judo Federation and the Belgian Olympic Committee, who was also present at the Competition, have attested to have found no signs or symptoms indicating the use of cocaine by Miss Van Snick before or on the day of the competition. No sign of anxiety or nervousness may indicate a concern regarding the results of doping control analysis.

This is clear evidence in the case, particularly the test results for the samples collected on August 26, 2013 which showed a very low concentration of cocaine and the conclusions in Prof. Jan Tytgat's report on the analysis of the capillary sample of Miss Van Snick, that she is not a cocaine consumer. Cocaine

---

[30] TAS 2014/A/3475.

metabolites in her urine were in such small quantity that their presence can be explained by an isolated and accidental contamination, and could not have influenced her performance.

Professor Jan Tytgat's analysis of the contents of the powder box of 'Energy Boost', which had not been opened since 26 August 2013, and an infusion of tea consumed by Miss Van Snick during the Competition revealed the presence of cocaine in the powder 'Energy Boost' but its absence in the infusion. Therefore, he appears almost certain that a malicious third party mixed a tiny amount of the banned substance in the powder 'Energy Boost', customarily used in competitions, without the knowledge of Miss Van Snick.

The most likely explanation for the presence of the prohibited substance in Miss Van Snick's body is an act of sabotage before or during a fight when her bag containing the box of 'Energy Boost' powder was lying unattended in the warm-up room of the Competition, which was accessible to anyone with an accreditation.

After reading Professor Tytgat's conclusions, Miss Van Snick filed a civil action complaint against an unidentified person before an investigating judge at the Court of First Instance in Liège, Belgium, with the chief offenses being those under Articles 402 and 405 of the Belgian Criminal Code that punishes anyone causing another illness or personal incapacity by administering substances that can seriously affect the health, and any other offense that the investigation would reveal. In her complaint, Miss Van Snick said she could not blame anyone for sure but suspected someone in her sports entourage with malice towards her was responsible.

Miss Van Snick could not have reasonably anticipated that a malicious person would open her bag and mix the banned substance in her 'Energy Boost' powder. Therefore, she did not commit any fault or showed negligence within the definitions of RAD FIJ and the CMA.

The CAS panel relied solely upon circumstantial evidence and accepted her explanation and found that the violation was committed with 'No Fault or Negligence', thus completely eliminating the associated period of 'ineligibility'.

In this case, the CAS has accepted sabotage by an unidentified person as a valid manner to prove No Fault or Negligence:

104. Furthermore, the Athlete is clearly convinced that an identifiable third party could intentionally harm her sporting career and would have been able to commit sabotage. The CAS Panel noted all evidence presented by the athlete, including the existence of a criminal complaint against X (currently instruction) and the facts revealed during the hearing and the comments submitted subsequently by the parties (v. para. 30 above). Given the weak evidence provided by the Athlete on the identity of the third party, the Arbitral Panel is not able to determine with certainty that an identifiable third party was linked to this sabotage.

105. However, the CAS Panel considered, in light of all the material presented before it and the improbable (or unlikely) nature of the other scenarios, the scenario of sabotage by a malicious third party is, as the standard of balance of probabilities, the most likely scenario.anti-doping: *Charline Van Snick* v. *Fédération Internationale de Judo*P12

109. In light of the comment, and in any event, the case of sabotage by a malicious third is a situation of no fault of the Athlete.

Match-fixing and Spot-fixing

Every sport is indulged in and permitted its minor insufficiencies for as long as its heart is inherently seen as spotless. However, Hansie Cronje's confession about taking payments from a bookie[31] had shaken the foundations of cricket and changed the way the gentleman's game came to be seen. Like a putrid infection, match-fixing and betting have permeated cricket's circulation system to the point where the principles that served as the embodiment of cricket have been broken. The foundation of sport is its inherent credibility, and it is shaking like a leaf in a sudden tempest.

Allegations of match-fixing were first asserted in 1979–1980 against the visiting Pakistan team in the third test match played

[31] ESP Ncricinfo, *Wisden Obituary*, *available at* http://www.espncricinfo. com/India/content/player/44485.html

between India and Pakistan at Mumbai, and it was alleged that they had lost the test match intentionally.[32] In 1992–1993, Australian player Dean Jones asserted that an Indian offered him $40,000 to leak team information about strategies and tactics.[33] In 1998, the Australian Cricket Board conceded that Mark Waugh and Shane Warne had given data regarding the pitch and the climate to bookies, and further in 2000 Hansie Cronje's affirmation that he passed on information to a bookie in exchange for $10,000 shook the world of sport.[34]

In India, Justice Y. V. Chandrachud's 94-page archive on betting and match-fixing in the game of cricket in India is kept under wraps for reasons unknown. The Chandrachud report[35] stated that 'It will be a sad day, if the common men and women on whose support the game has occupied its pride of place believe that bookies and not the chosen eleven play the game.'

In February 1995, Mark Waugh and Shane Warne confessed that they had acknowledged instalments ranging from $2,500 to $15,000 from bookies for giving information.[36] The Australian Cricket Board fined Waugh $10,000 and Warne $8,080[37] but kept the matter secret and shrouded in mystery, and the fine

---

[32] Rohit Brijnath, *Sarfaraz Nawaz Says Sunil Gavaskar Involved in Fixing Matches, Claim Finds Few Takers*, India Today (1999), *available at* http://indiatoday.intoday.in/story/sarfaraz-nawaz-says-sunil-gavaskar-involved-in-fixing-matches-claim-finds-few-takers/1/253539.html

[33] S. Satyanarayanan & M. S. Unnikrishnan, *CBI Names Nine Foreign Cricketers*, The Tribune, 1 November 2000, *available at* http://www.tribuneindia.com/2000/20001101/main1.html

[34] *Supra* note 24.

[35] Chandrachud Commission Report on Match Fixing (2000), *available at* http://www.rediff.com/sports/2000/apr/20report.html

[36] Mark Ray, Greg Baum & Martin Blake, *Warne, Mark Waugh Took Bookie's Cash*, The Age, 9 December 1998, *available at* http://www.theage.com.au/articles/1998/12/09/1060588497968.html

[37] Peter Roebuck & Rohit Brijnath, *Lifting the Covers*, India Today, 28 December 1998, *available at* http://indiatoday.intoday.in/story/acb-breaks-silence-admits-shane-warne-and-mark-waugh-accepted-money-from-bookie/1/265554.html

forced on the cricketers was an extremely gentle punishment considering the magnitude of the data that they had leaked.

One of the proposals recommended by the International Cricket Council's (ICC) Code of Conduct Commission is that there must be 'a commitment on the part of the players to report to the team manager or captain about any approach made to them by bookmakers or information of such an approach made to some other player' with the result that 'inability to make such a report be made a punishable offense'.[38] It is for the players to help keep their game unblemished, for a polluted sport implies that even the legitimate elements will be under investigation.

Prevention of Sporting Fraud Bill, 2013

The bill was introduced to prevent and combat sporting fraud affecting the integrity of sports and fair play in relation to national and international sporting events and for matters connected therewith or incidental thereto.[39]

Objectives of the Bill

The objectives of the Sporting Fraud Bill, 2013, are as follows:

1. Demonstrating a zero-tolerance policy to corruption in sport.
2. Introducing specific policies on match/spot-fixing in player agreements.
3. Undertaking integrity with due diligence of the support staff and experts hired to work with players.
4. Monitoring financial transactions including those involving players pertaining to issues of sponsorship/publicity or any other arrangements.
5. Conducting education programmes for players explaining the obligations under the relevant statutes and codes set forth by the relevant sport governing authorities.

[38] Article 2.4.1 of the ICC Anti-Corruption Code.
[39] Prevention of Sporting Fraud Bill, 2013.

Key Provisions

Section 3: A person is said to commit the offence of sporting fraud in relation to a sporting event if he/she, directly or indirectly,

1. Manipulates sports results
2. Misapplies rules of sports
3. Wilfully fails to perform to his/her true potential for economic or any other advantage
4. Possesses and discloses inside information likely resulting in financial gain
5. Fails to disclose knowledge of or attempt for sporting fraud

Section 4: Whoever gets any information as to the commission of any of the acts referred to in Section 3 shall, within such time as may be prescribed, give the information regarding the same to the appropriate authority or the team management or the NSF, in writing. The team management or NSF shall inform the appropriate authority within three working days of receiving such information.

Pakistan Cricket Team Spot-fixing Scandal, 2010

The Pakistan cricket spot-fixing scandal in 2010 involved Pakistan's national cricket team players Salman Butt, Mohd Amir and Mohd Asif who were convicted of taking bribes from a bookmaker, Mazhar Majeed, to underperform deliberately at decided intervals in a test match played between England and Pakistan at Lord's, London, in 2010.

Undercover reporters from *News of the World* secretly videotaped Mazhar Majeed accepting money and informing the reporters that fast bowlers Mohd Asif and Mohd Amir would deliberately bowl no-balls at specific points in an over. This information could be used by gamblers to place bets with the help of this inside information.[40] In response, the Scotland Yard arrested Majeed on the charge of match-fixing.

Two days later, after the test match had been completed, three more arrests were made (two unidentified men and one unidentified woman) on suspicion of money laundering in connection with the allegations.[41] Police also seized the cell phones of Mohd Asif, Mohd Amir and Salman Butt as part of their investigations. Scotland Yard announced on 17 September 2010 that the initial file of the investigation had been passed on to the Crown Prosecution Service for them to decide whether to charge the players or not.

On 5 November 2010, Scotland Yard announced that they had passed on the second file of fixing evidence to the Crown Prosecution Service. Criminal charges for conspiracy were brought against the four defendants under the Prevention of Corruption Act, 1906; Criminal Law Act, 1977; and Gambling Act, 2005. Contravention of the first two Acts carried a maximum penalty of seven years' imprisonment and contravention of the Gambling Act carried a maximum sentence of two years' imprisonment.

Evidence produced at the trial in the form of information from secret recordings and text messages from the undercover sting, along with cross-examination of the defendants, gave the jury an insight into the tricks and subterfuge that connected betting syndicates with the sport, and convinced the jury to find the defendants guilty unanimously.

On 1 November 2011, at Southwark Crown Court, Majeed, Asif, Amir and Butt were found guilty of conspiracy to cheat at gambling and conspiracy to accept corrupt payments. Majeed and Amir

[40] Vic Marks, *Pakistan Embroiled in No-ball Betting Scandal against England*, The Guardian, 29 August 2010.

[41] ESP Ncricinfo, *Three More Arrests in Fixing Investigation* (31 August 2010), *available at* http://www.espn.in/cricket/story/_/id/22521393/three-more-arrests-fixing-investigation

were convicted following guilty pleas. The judge, Jeremy Cooke, rejected a plea in mitigation from Amir that he had been involved in spot-fixing on only one occasion, on the grounds that the contents of text messages submitted as evidence suggested otherwise.[42]

Conclusion

Sports industry in India has progressed by leaps and bounds since in the modern era and is considered to be a gold mine. Twenty-first-century India witnessed emergence of corporate and commercial interests in sports. With expanding markets and requirement for clear, concise and far-reaching legal documentation, legal issues in sports are gradually coming into the limelight and the issues related to contracts such as capacity to elucidate each party's desires and commitments, securing the athlete's and brand's image, and due consideration of the inherently inalienable administrative, lawful and different risks prevailing in the industry are subject of much needed focus.

The sport industry of India has reached a phase where it now needs a whole new legislation/enactment which deals with sports. India's disappointing results at international sporting events highlight the poor framework, infrastructure and corruption which have permeated within the structure of sports and sports federations at different levels in India. The Government of India should, therefore, try to aim to improve the prevailing situation and meet the demands of the evolving scenario in sports at national and international levels. Therefore, it is absolutely vital for the Government of India to secure for the country an improved and amended version of the National Sports Code with specific goals kept in mind for athletes, coaches, stakeholders, members of NSFs, etc.

---

[42] Matt Scott, '*Judge Rejects Mohammad Amir's Plea that Spot-fixing Role Was One-off*', *The Guardian*, 2 November 2011, *available at* https://www.theguardian.com/sport/2011/nov/02/judge-rejects-mohammad-amir-plea

Public Interest Litigation and Sports in India

Shivam Singh and Shreeyash Uday Lalit

Introduction

Public interest litigation (hereinafter 'PIL') or social interest litigation is a classic case of the judiciary exercising its expansive powers to offer relief and protection for the greater social good without being bound by the strict requirements of either substantive or procedural law. It permits the courts to exercise its jurisdiction, without having the person who is the victim of the violation of his/her right to approach the court in person.

In the recent past, PILs have become an extremely efficient legal tool to ensure effective justice delivery. At the same time, they have evoked sharp criticism for providing the judiciary with untrammelled powers that run contrary to the separation of powers doctrine.

In this chapter, we shall focus on two broad areas. In the first part of this chapter, we shall analyse the concept of PILs and their application to the branch of sports law. Within this portion, we shall also include issues relating to the criticisms of the

PIL jurisprudence in the Indian set-up. The second section of this chapter shall analyse some leading PIL decisions by the Indian courts in the sphere of Indian sports law.

Concept of PIL and Its Applicability in Sports Law

The Indian Constitution does not employ the phrase 'public interest litigation', and its evolution in the Indian context can be put down to judicial innovation. In India, PIL has been developed as a result of the consciousness of the court of its constitutional commitment.[1]

Prior to the 1980s, only a person with locus standi—Americans call it standing—was a *sine qua non* for the maintainability of any petition. Locus standi is Latin for 'place to stand' or, in law, the right to bring an action.[2] In effect, it stipulates that only a person who has sufficient connection to an action or omission and is harmed from the said action or omission can thereafter challenge that action or omission in a court of law and seek any proper remedy as may be fit. Therefore, the principle bars any person from bringing forth any petition or application who does not have any locus standi in the matter.

However, this scenario gradually changed post emergency when India underwent a tumultuous period, wherein various rights of underprivileged and downtrodden were want only infringed without due process. Soon thereafter, the attitude of the Supreme Court (SC) also drastically changed with regard to PILs.

Justice Krishna Iyer in the case of *Mumbai Kamagar Sabha* v. *Abdul Thai*[3] initiated the first step towards this dynamic shift in perspective. Although first addressed in the aforesaid case, Justice Krishna Iyer delineated the reasons and the analyses behind

---

[1] Sudhir Krishnaswamy & Rajgopal Saikumar, *Restoring Legitimacy to PILs*, The Hindu, 3 May 2014, *available at* http://www.thehindu.com/todays-paper/tp-opinion/restoring-legitimacy-to-pils/article5971744.ece

[2] https://en.oxforddictionaries.com/definition/locus_standi

[3] *Mumbai Kamagar Sabha* v. *Abdul Thai*, AIR 1976 SC 1455.

liberalisation of the locus standi rule in *Fertilizer Corporation Kamgar* v. *Union of India*,[4] which further blossomed in *S. P. Gupta* v. *Union of India*[5] with the help of Justice P. N. Bhagwati.

In the *Fertilizer Corporation* case,[6] the SC observed that 'public interest litigation is part of the process of participative justice and "standing" in civil litigation of that pattern must have liberal reception at the judicial doorsteps'. Furthermore, in *People's Union for Democratic Rights & Others* v. *Union of India & Others*,[7] the SC defined 'PIL' and observed that the 'Public interest litigation is a cooperative or collaborative effort by the petitioner, the State of public authority and the judiciary to secure observance of constitutional or basic human rights, benefits and privileges upon poor, downtrodden and vulnerable sections of the society'.

Even in *Ramsharan Autyanuprasi & Another* v. *Union of India & Others*,[8] it was observed by the Court that the PIL is for making basic human rights meaningful to the deprived and vulnerable sections of the community and to assure them social, economic and political justice.

Thus, the concept of liberalisation of locus standi and thereafter boosting the PILs has provided an impetus to the government and its officers to make intrinsic human rights meaningful to the underprivileged and susceptible sections of the society. PIL is not in the nature of adversarial litigation and ensures social and economic justice, which is the essence of our Constitution.

Among the major criticisms of the PIL jurisprudence has been that it has allowed the judiciary to unilaterally expand its constitutionally guaranteed powers of judicial review. This has been

---

[4] Fertilizer Corporation Kamgar v. Union of India, AIR 1981 SC 344.

[5] S. P. Gupta v. Union of India, AIR 1982 SC 149.

[6] Fertilizer Corporation Kamgar v. Union of India, AIR 1981 SC 344.

[7] People's Union for Democratic Rights & Others v. Union of India & Others, (1982) 3 SCC 235.

[8] Ramsharan Autyanuprasi & Another v. Union of India & Others, AIR 1989 SC 549.

done with scant regard to the doctrine of separation of powers and has resulted in its performing acts of judicial overreach.[9] The counterpoint in support of this ever-expanding PIL jurisprudence has been that this is a situation wherein the courts as a last resort have been called upon to perform constitutional duties since the legislature and the executive have chosen to abdicate their functions especially vis-à-vis the marginalised sections of society.[10] These counter-narratives best represent the most important ongoing debate vis-à-vis sports law jurisprudence in the Indian context, and sports law is no exception to it.

For sports law, PILs have been used to ensure the accountability of various governmental institutions to persons having no proximity to harm or injury caused due to the actions or omissions of the institution.

This brings in the applicability of sports law to the concept of PIL. Sport has now come to be seen as a public function which governs a cultural good intrinsic to the functioning of the society. Thus, it necessitates the State to assume the role of provider of such public functions and makes no distinction between a private body taking charge of such functions and a governmental body working under the auspices of a statute. If both these bodies cater to an essential public function, namely sports, then the same should be amenable to PILs.

An Examination of the PIL Jurisprudence Vis-à-Vis Indian Sports Law

Sarita Devi Case

The arena of sports is not alien to the concept and usage of PIL. Recently, the Indian boxer Sarita Devi's case gained publicity

---

[9] *See*, generally, *Arun Shourie, Courts and Their Judgments—Premises, Perquisites, Consequences* (2001).

[10] Lavanya Rajamani, *Public Interest Litigation in India: Exploring Issues of Access, Participation, Equity, Effectiveness and Sustainability*, 9(3) *J Env. L.* 293 (2007).

when on 1 October 2014, she refused to accept her bronze medal in the 57–60 kg category at the 17th Asian Games Incheon 2014, claiming that the judges were biased against her even though she felt she had dominated the round. Choosing to hang the medal around the neck of her semi-final opponent, Park Ji-Na,[11] Devi invited a huge amount of criticism from the International Boxing Association (AIBA).

Devi believed that the result of the semi-final bout, which she was adjudged to have lost, was biased and incorrect and that she had clearly won the fight. Devi protested the decision immediately after the result was declared;[12] however, she failed in her protest as, pursuant to Rule 5 of the Association Internationale de Boxe Amateur Technical Rules (Protest), a boxer cannot appeal the judges' decision. Article 3.1 of the AIBA Disciplinary Code also states that 'All persons subject to this Disciplinary Code must: (e) at all times behave with respect towards each other, (f) respect the principles of honesty, integrity and sportsmanship, and (g) act in accordance with the principle of fair-play.'

As a counter blast to Devi's actions, the AIBA decided to ban Devi for a year.[13] The case caused huge bustle in India owing to the austerity of AIBA's ban, and the inadequacy of a congruous legal challenge. The responses of various relevant governing bodies were questioned and the criticisms reached such a degree that a PIL was filed to address the issues regarding the general inaccuracy encompassing the dispute resolution processes.

---

[11] The Hindu, *Bitter Sarita Refuses Bronze Medal*, 2014, *available at* http://www.thehindu.com/sport/other-sports/incheon-asian-games-2014-in-consolable-sarita-refuses-bronze-medal-with-organisers/article6464951.ece

[12] J. Linden, *Sarita Devi Given 'Strong Warning' after Medal Protest*, *Reuters* (2014), *available at* http://in.reuters.com/article/2014/10/04/asian-games-sarita-bronze-protest-idINKCN0HT05V20141004

[13] Y. B. Sarangi, *Sarita Devi, Coaches and Chef-de-mission Suspended*, *The Hindu*, 2014, *available at* http://www.thehindu.com/sport/other-sports/aiba-suspends-sarita-devi-coachesand-chefdemission/article6524543.ece

Questions with regard to the appropriate responses of the governing bodies became relevant, with the crux of the matter falling under the following issues:

- Whether there was an effective appeal to the Court of Arbitration for Sport (CAS).
- The general lack of clarity surrounding sports dispute resolution processes.

While it is important to see that an ad hoc division of the CAS was operating at the time of the games, however, the general unawareness of such processes ensured that Devi could not approach the same. An ad hoc division can decide within 24 hours of the dispute, which was unavailable since crucial time was spent in ignorance of any such provision.

Mr Rajiv Dutta, senior advocate in the SC, filed a PIL in the Delhi High Court against the Department of Sports, the Indian Olympic Association (IOA) and Boxing Federation of India.[14] The principal argument was that there was no guidance provided to Sarita Devi about the possibilities of appeal of the AIBA decision coupled with the lack of guidelines for resolution of such disputes with international sports governing bodies. This lacunae in law and policy was disturbing to say the least, and he therefore requested the Court to ensure that national sports federations (NSFs) include a provision for appeal to CAS in their draft bills.

While the Court simply heard the petition, the Ministry of Youth Affairs and Sports (MYAS) issued an advisory direction to all NSFs to establish an 'effective, transparent and fair grievance redressal system and mechanism' which is compliant with international sports dispute resolution processes and also mandated

[14] Rajiv Dutta v. Union of India, WP(C) 8734/2014, Delhi High Court decision of 15 January 2016. Note: The author Shivam Singh was one of the lawyers who appeared in this case before the Delhi High Court along with Mr Rajiv Dutta, Senior Advocate.

them to incorporate guidelines for provisions of appeal to CAS which would be made available to athletes.[15]

Both these changes once implemented would have far-reaching consequences for sports. Thus, the concept of PIL is extremely beneficial in ensuring the transparency, accountability and efficiency of sports organisations. It also helps reveal any present lacunae in the system, so that the same may be rectified through a proper channel. It would have been inconceivable to reflect any change in the functioning of sports bodies if not for the constructive outcome of the PIL on the Sarita Devi case which was only possible due to the relaxation of the rule of locus standi.

Cricket Association of Bihar Case

The game of cricket in India has always managed to be in the spotlight, and not always for the right reasons. The improper and inefficient functioning of the governing body for cricket has not only brought irreverence to the people behind its administration but also portrayed the sport in bad light.[16]

A cursory look at Entry 33 of the State List in the VII Schedule of the Constitution sheds light on how sport is to be governed within the territory of India. While these were intended to be State List subjects, however, the presence of international sporting events made the government reconsider. The Department of Youth Affairs and Sports was subsequently converted into a full ministry and, thereafter, segregated into two independent secretaries. These secretaries find mention in the Government of India (Allocation of Business) Rules, 1961.

---

[15] MINISTRY OF YOUTH AFFAIRS AND SPORTS, GOVERNMENT OF INDIA, SAFEGUARDING THE INTERESTS OF SPORTS PERSONS AND PROVISION OF EFFECTIVE GRIEVANCE REDRESSAL SYSTEM IN THE CONSTITUTION OF NATIONAL SPORTS FEDERATIONS (17 June 2016), *available at* http://pib.nic.in/newsite/PrintRelease.aspx?relid=146295

[16] *Economic and Political Weekly, Big Business: Not Cricket* (2004), *available at* http://www.epw.in/journal/2004/40/editorials/big-business-not-cricket.html

The functions of these secretaries also extend to matters relating to the IOA and NSFs. The latter are established as autonomous bodies which are not under direct control of the government. In effect, they are private associations that exercise essential public functions, which ideally should be exercised by the government. Representing the nation at an international platform is a task which is supposed to be undertaken by the government. Therefore, it would necessarily cover the dimension of a public function.

NSFs such as the 'All India Tennis Association' and 'All India Football Federation' or even state federations such as 'Cricket Association of Bengal' and 'Delhi Basketball Association' are all examples of associations which have their own rules, bye-laws and regulations. Even domestic and international sporting tournaments act as independent organisations over which the NSFs have no control or jurisdiction. Thus, they act as independent and autonomous organisations, having no uniformity in their structure.

It is only for the betterment of the sport if these authorities and organisations are brought under the inclusive definition of 'State' under Article 12 of the Indian Constitution. Since these private bodies are exercising public functions, it also brings into fore a certain element of responsibility and accountability of these organisations to the Indian public. On account of them being private, they cannot be permitted to operate at their whims. Rights such as those of equality and equal opportunity need to be incorporated in these organisations. Thus, proclaiming them as 'State' gathers a vital significance.

An attempt has been made by the SC in the case of *Board of Control for Cricket in India* v. *Cricket Association of Bihar*[17] at curbing the influence of people akin to its functioning and bringing about responsibility in the affairs of the Board in relation to cricket administration in this country.

---

[17] Board of Control for Cricket in India v. Cricket Association of Bihar, (2015) 1 MLJ 711.

This case primarily dealt with the issue of Board of Control for Cricket in India (BCCI) being 'State' under Article 12 or not. If BCCI were to be held a State, then it could be open to writ proceedings under Article 32 or Article 226 of the Constitution. Article 32 allows the SC to take original jurisdiction over actions directly infringing upon fundamental rights (FRs). However, the scope of Article 226 is wider which permits the High Court (HC) to pass a writ for not only FR infringements but also infringements of other legal rights.

The two-judge bench held that BCCI was not 'State' for the purpose of this Article. However, before the *Cricket Association of Bihar (CAB)* case is discussed, it is important that we review another case that came prior to the *CAB* case, namely *Zee Telefilms* v. *Union of India*,[18] which expanded upon the public function test as talked about in the *CAB* case.

In *Zee Telefilms*, the direct issue that arose was whether BCCI could be considered a State as under Article 12 of the Indian Constitution. The backdrop of the case relates to a bid for telecast rights made by Zee Telefilms Ltd for a few tournaments which was promptly cancelled by BCCI. As a counter, Zee Telefilms filed a civil writ petition and argued that BCCI had discriminated against the petitioners. To this effect, they intended on proving that BCCI as recognised by the MYAS falls under 'any other authority' as enumerated in Article 12 of the Constitution and is therefore subject to a writ under Article 32/226 of the Constitution.

Split by 3:2, the SC held that private bodies exercising public functions such as BCCI could be amendable to a writ under Article 226 as the scope of the said Article is far more extensive as compared to Article 32 of the Constitution. The primary reason for not allowing BCCI to be considered a State under this 2005 verdict was the 'floodgate' theory, under which the SC believed that any and every private body exercising a remotely public

---

[18] Zee Telefilms v. Union of India, AIR 2005 SC 2677.

function would become subject to writ proceedings, thereby defeating the intent of Article 32.

The *CAB* case can be analysed in this perspective. When BCCI in 2007 decided to launch the Indian Premier League (IPL), it decided to appoint Mr N. Srinivasan as secretary of BCCI and amended its regulation 6.2.4 in order to exclude the IPL and Champions League T20 from its purview. In April 2013, Delhi Police retrieved information in relation to spot-fixing in IPL and charges were levelled against Raj Kundra, the owner of Rajasthan Royals, and Gurunath Meiyappan, the son-in-law of N. Srinivasan who was also the owner of the IPL team Chennai Super Kings.[19]

BCCI constituted a committee headed by Shri Sanjay Jagdale and two retired judges of Madras High Court. After Mr Jagdale's resignation, the probe committee consisted of the two retired judges. A PIL was filed by CAB before the Bombay High Court, seeking a declaration that the constitution of the committee be declared ultra-vires the Constitution and further sought the appointment of retired SC judges in the panel.

The SC ruled out BCCI as State due to the 'lack of deep and pervasive control and lack of substantial government funding', on the basis of the tests clearly laid out in the cases of *R. D. Shetty* v. *Union of India*[20] and *Ajay Hasia* v. *Khalid Mujib*.[21] Upholding its decision in the case of *Zee Telefilms* v. *Union of India*,[22] the Court held BCCI to be a non-State entity, amenable under the writ jurisdiction of the HC under Article 226 of the Constitution of India, even though the Board performed important public functions that were akin to State functions. All sports federations

[19] *The Economic Times*, BCCI Panel 'Illegal', *Against Its Own Rules: Bombay HC*, 31 July 2013, *available at* https://economictimes.indiatimes. com/news/politics-and-nation/bcci-panel-illegal-against-its-own-rules-bombay-hc/articleshow/21508002.cms

[20] R. D. Shetty v. Union of India, AIR 1979 SC 1628.

[21] Ajay Hasia v. Khalid Mujib, AIR 1981 SC 487.

[22] Zee Telefilms v. Union of India, AIR 2005 SC 2677.

and other institutions having a similar mode of operations have, therefore, been covered by the instant judgement.

While admitting that BCCI performs a few public functions, the Court held that

> It cannot be denied that the Board does discharge some duties like the selection of an Indian cricket team, controlling the activities of the players and others involved in the game of cricket. These activities can be said to be akin to public duties or State functions and if there is any violation of any constitutional or statutory obligation or rights of other citizens, the aggrieved party may not have a relief by way of a petition under Article 32. But that does not mean that the violator of such right would go scot-free merely because it or he is not a State. Under the Indian jurisprudence there is always a just remedy for violation of a right of a citizen. Though the remedy under Article 32 is not available, an aggrieved party can always seek a remedy under the ordinary course of law or by way of a writ petition under Article 226 of the Constitution which is much wider than Article 32.[23]

It did incorporate the 'nature of duties and functions' test while charting a middle path between the 'ratio' of *Zee Telefilms* and the position before by expanding on the 'floodgate' principle to include a focus on the public functions and nature of duties to determine what would amount to be a 'State'. As an extension, they also mentioned that the same public functions would require a determination to consider if the jurisdiction under Article 226 would be available or not.

Furthermore, in relation to the issue of Raj Kundra and Gurunath Meiyappan being 'team officials' for the purpose of disciplinary matters or not, the Court ruled that since they were commissioned locally or centrally by BCCI for matters pertaining to the IPL, they were to be considered 'team officials' subject to the terms and conditions of the IPL operational rules.

[23] Board of Control for Cricket in India v. Cricket Association of Bihar, (2015) 1 MLJ 711.

In relation to the issue of amendment to Rule 6.2.4 of IPL regulations being illegal, the SC observed that

> An amendment which strikes at the very essence of the game as stated in the Anti Corruption Code cannot obviously co-exist with the fundamental imperatives. Conflict of interest situation is a complete anti-thesis to everything recognized by BCCI as constituting fundamental imperatives of the game hence unsustainable and impermissible in law.[24]

What is of importance is that aggrieved persons can move the superior courts under Article 226 of the Constitution even though sports federations have not been termed as 'State' under Article 12. While this may be a compensatory mechanism that may hold the fort for now, the best course of action for effective management of sports organisations would be to bring in greater accountability of these federations, which would necessarily involve their inclusion under Article 12.

A crucial development that took place in this case was that the SC assigned the task of suggesting cricketing reforms to a panel of three retired SC judges, namely Former CJI Lodha, Justice Bhan and Justice Raveendran. The wide-scale reforms suggested by the Lodha panel resulted in the whittling down of powers enjoyed by the BCCI incumbents. Among the multiple reforms put forth by the Lodha panel, the most contentious ones related to age caps, tenure caps and ensuring that BCCI remained immune from political interference. The effect of these proposed recommendations was that a large section of the BCCI officials who had served for long periods of time were no longer capable of discharging their functions as cricket administrators and had to demit office. This set the stage for a bitter tug of war between the SC and the BCCI dispensation.[25]

---

[24] 'Amendment to rule 6.2.4 is "true villain": Supreme Court', http://www.dnaindia.com/sports/report-amendment-to-rule-624-is-true-villain-supreme-court-2054875

[25] Sambit Bal, *No One Is Bigger than the Game*, ESPNCRICINFO (2 January 2017), *available at* http://www.espncricinfo.com/india/content/story/1075205.html

BCCI steadfastly refused to accept the SC's verdict, appointed a retired SC Judge, that is, Justice Katju, to advise it about its future course of action and unsuccessfully sought a review[26] of the SC verdict. The matter came to a head wherein the SC stripped the BCCI President Anurag Thakur and BCCI Secretary Ajay Shrike from their posts. It further issued a show cause notice to the sacked BCCI president and asked him to respond to charges of perjury and contempt of the Court as he had allegedly filed a false affidavit with a view to obstruct the implementation of the SC's orders.[27]

As on date, the ex-BCCI President Anurag Thakur has appeared before the SC and tendered an unconditional apology for his conduct. The hearing on his application to tender an apology was heard on 17 April 2017.[28]

IPL Drought Case

In the 2013 edition of the IPL, about 66 lakh litres of water was spent on maintaining pitches at the Wankhede Stadium in Mumbai, D. Y. Patil Stadium in Navi Mumbai and Sahara Stadium in Pune.[29]

---

[26] Curative Petition (Civil) No. 440/2016 disposed on 15 December 2016 and Review Petition (Civil) No. 3433-3437/2016 disposed on 10 November 2016.

[27] Utkarsh Anand, *Supreme Court Sacks BCCI Chief, Secretary; Anurag Thakur Says 'All the Best'*, The Indian Express, 2017, *available at* http://indianexpress.com/article/sports/cricket/supreme-court-sacks-bcci-chief-secretary-anurag-thakur-says-all-the-best-4456134/

[28] Samanwaya Rautray, *Anurag Thakur Tenders Unconditional Apology to Supreme Court*, The Economic Times, 7 March 2017, *available at* http://economictimes.indiatimes.com/news/sports/anurag-thakur-tenders-unconditional-apology-to-supreme-court/articleshow/57496728.cms

[29] *The Times of India, Scribe Files PIL, Demands IPL to Pay Penalty to Drought-hit M'rashtra*, 2016, *available at* http://timesofindia.indiatimes.com/sports/ipl/news/Scribe-files-PIL-demands-IPL-to-pay-penalty-to-drought-hit-Mrashtra/articleshow/51710928.cms

In the 2016 edition of the series, matches were scheduled to be held in Maharashtra when the state was going through one of the worst droughts. It was in the backdrop of this scenario that a PIL[30] was filed challenging the use of water for maintaining IPL pitches, in the Bombay High Court. In a bid to receive a penalty from the organisers to meet the expenses of delivering water to the drought-affected areas, the PIL sought a direction to the IPL commissioner to pay tax on water, as about 60,000 litres per day would be required to maintain the pitches.

According to the PIL, the pitch maintenance in these stadiums would consume 60,000 litres of water every day. The Bombay High Court sought an explanation from BCCI and the three state associations in Maharashtra on why water should be 'wasted' on hosting IPL 2016 matches when the state was facing one of its worst-ever droughts.[31]

The HC had ordered shifting of all IPL matches scheduled in Maharashtra after 30 April to another state. The direction had come even as BCCI had given an assurance that IPL franchises of Mumbai and Pune had agreed to contribute ₹5 crore to chief minister's drought relief fund.[32]

The division bench comprising Justices V. M. Kanade and M. S. Karnik while hearing the PIL filed by the NGO Loksatta Movement noted: 'We agree that merely shifting of IPL matches out of the state will not be a solution, but diverting water to villages which otherwise would have been used for maintaining pitches will help resolve the problem to a large extent.'

According to the petitioner, the real reason behind filing the PIL was not shifting the IPL venue but penalising the Maharashtra

[30] PIL No. 33/2016 (Bombay High Court).

[31] ESPNcricinfo, *Bombay High Court Questions Hosting IPL Matches in Drought-hit State*, 2016, *available at* http://www.espncricinfo.com/indian-premier-league-2016/content/story/995409.html

[32] *The Indian Express, Supreme Setback for MI, Pune as Top Court Quashes Appeal for IPL in May*, 2016, *available at*, http://indianexpress.com/article/sports/cricket/no-ipl-2016-matches-in-maharashtra-in-may-supreme-court-cancels-mca-plea-2772661/

government to arrange for an infrastructure to deliver water to these drought-affected districts which should be equivalent to ₹1,000 per litre. The petition demanded that at least 1,000 litres of water should be delivered to each family in the drought-stricken districts if the matches were to be arranged.

BCCI and Maharashtra Cricket Association[33] and Mumbai Cricket Association[34] approached the SC by way of a special leave petition seeking a stay on the Bombay High Court order. Counsels appearing for the state cricket bodies maintained that potable water would not be used for any cricketing activity in stadiums in Mumbai and Pune and treated sewage water would be used.

The SC of India on 27 April 2016 via CJI T. S. Thakur and Justices R. Bhanumati and U. U. Lalit dismissed the plea that Maharashtra Cricket Association and Mumbai Cricket Association had filed against the Bombay High Court order and directed shifting of IPL matches outside the drought-hit state.[35] The IPL drought case is a classic scenario of holding larger public interest on a higher footing than the interest of a cash-rich few.

Sachin Tendulkar Bharat Ratna Case

A lot of controversy followed the announcement of presenting Sachin Tendulkar with the Bharat Ratna, the highest civilian award in the country. Tendulkar, who retired from all forms of cricket in November 2013, is one of the most accomplished cricketers in the world. He has 15,921 runs from a record 200 test matches at an average of 53.58 and 51 centuries and 18,426

[33] Maharashtra Cricket Association v. Loksatta Movement & Ors, Special Leave Petition (Civil) No. 11202/2016

[34] Mumbai Cricket Association (Through its Joint Secretary) v. Loksatta Movement & Ors., Special Leave Petition (Civil) No. 11566/2016.

[35] Ashok K. M., *SC Refuses to Allow IPL Matches in Drought Hit Maharashtra in May*, LIVE LAW (2016), *available at* http://www.livelaw.in/sc-refuses-allow-ipl-matches-drought-hit-maharashtra-may/

runs from 463 ODIs with an average of 44.83 including 49 centuries. He was also the first to score a double-century in the 50-over format.

Many eyebrows were raised when after getting the award, Tendulkar was seen doing commercial advertisements. Alleging misuse of the prestigious award for commercial purpose, a PIL[36] was filed by V. K. Naswa in the Madhya Pradesh High Court demanding Tendulkar to return this award on moral grounds. In the alternative, it demanded that the government should take it back since the use of this honour for commercial purpose was 'illegitimate'.[37]

The petitioner charged Prime Minister Manmohan Singh, Union Home Minister Sushil Kumar Shinde, Union Sports Minister Bhanwar Jitendra Singh and Secretary to the Union Sports Ministry with hurting the people's sentiments by deleting Dhyanchand's name to accommodate Tendulkar's wish for the highest national honours.

Madhya Pradesh High Court through Justices A. M. Khanwilkar and K. K. Trivedi admitted the PIL and issued a directive to the additional solicitor general to find out if there are any SC guidelines on use of award for promotion of commercial products by awardees of country's highest honour.

However, the SC of India while taking cognisance of the special leave petition[38] filed against the order passed by the division bench of Madhya Pradesh High Court dismissed the PIL on 18 July 2016. The bench of Justices Dipak Misra and D. Y. Chandrachud noted the absence of any statutory provisions, rules

---

[36] V. K. Naswa v. Union of India & Ors, Writ Petition Civil No. 7513/2015, Madhya Pradesh High Court at Jabalpur.

[37] Firstpost, *PIL Filed Seeking Sachin Tendulkar to Surrender Bharat Ratna for Appearing in Commercials*, 2015, *available at* http://www.firstpost.com/sports/pil-filed-seeking-sachin-tendulkar-to-surrender-bharat-ratna-for-appearing-in-commercials-2303544.html#

[38] V. K. Naswa v. Union of India & Ors, Special Leave Petition (Civil) No. 20140/2016.

or regulations which would deal with the allegations meted out against Sachin Tendulkar.[39]

While adverting to the two grievances raised by the petitioner, namely that various books have been published on Tendulkar citing him as a Bharat Ratna and secondly that he is profiting from his Bharat Ratna by participating in commercial activities, the bench held:

> In our considered opinion, what the petitioner intends to contend is that in the realm of regulation of conduct of an awardee which, we are disposed to think, cannot be gone into by this Court in the absence of any statutory provision. Had the Respondent No. 2 written a book by using the words 'Bharat Ratna' as a 'prefix' or 'suffix', the matter would have been different. When a third party writes a book, we have no hesitation in our mind that the Respondent No. 2 cannot be held responsible.[40]

Therefore, raison d'être for the order was that the book, which was disputed to be a form of profit-making exercise from a national award, was written and published by a third party, and therefore Tendulkar's liability in the same would be absolutely precluded. However, that brings forth the question of the possibility of liability of a sportsperson if s/he had written the book himself/herself. What would the position of the sportsperson be in that scenario? Whether the award of a national honour such as Bharat Ratna prohibits the person from using that title to describe himself? Whether using it as 'suffix' or 'prefix' in a book title, even by a person duly awarded the national honour, acts as an effort to commercially exploit the said honour? These are all questions which have been left unanswered and deserve a deep understanding of various disciplines of law to arrive at a proper conclusion.

<hr>

[39] Live Law, *SC Dismisses Petition Against Sachin Tendulkar's Bharat Ratna* (2016), *available at* http://www.livelaw.in/sc-dismisses-petition-sachin-tendulkars-bharat-ratna/

[40] 'SC dismisses plea against Tendulkar for "misusing" Bharat Ratna', https://timesofindia.indiatimes.com/india/SC-dismisses-plea-against-Tendulkar-for-misusing-Bharat-Ratna/articleshow/53267930.cms

Privacy Issues and Sports in India

Agnidipto Tarafder and Carmel Sharma

Introduction

The intersection between privacy rights and anti-doping rules within the realm of sports law throws up some peculiar concerns. The functioning of anti-doping organisations (hereinafter ADOs), in their quest to maintain the integrity and competitiveness of sports, sometimes require adherence to exacting standards for athletes, often at the cost of their individual privacy. Disclosure requirements put fetters on an athlete's rights and liberties in a number of ways, crucial among which are issues relating to bodily integrity, informational privacy and decisional autonomy. The cost of playing sport entails the possibility of substantially sacrificing these inherent rights in the name of compliance requirements. While the integrity of sport is paramount, whether the pursuit of any vocation should involve a waiver of an individual's basic rights as a necessary precondition needs to be explored thoroughly from a legal, social and perhaps even a moral perspective.

The operation of the World Anti-Doping Code (WADC) as well as International Standards has stirred controversies in the past and has raised several concerns about the rights of an athlete being compromised. It has been argued that these are 'voluntary' trade-offs that athletes make in order to participate in a system that is striving to keep sports free from doping, and therefore place all athletes at an equal pedestal and retain competitiveness that is associated with sports.[1] This chapter analyses certain significant legal questions pertaining to the right to privacy of an athlete that might be violated by virtue of his/her participation in sporting activities, with a special focus on the issues that might arise in the context of anti-doping measures. The second section provides a broad overview of the WADC. The third focuses on the issues of bodily integrity and personal autonomy which stand compromised due to the application of the whereabouts rule. The fourth section discusses the implications of the anti-doping practices on data protection. The fifth section attempts to highlight the need for greater restraint in journalistic expression and the issue of defamation, in light of an athlete's right to privacy.

A Basic Overview of the WADC

The World Anti-Doping Agency (hereinafter WADA) is the leading international organisation that was established in 1999 in Toronto, Canada, by the International Olympic Committee to promote, coordinate and monitor the combat doping in sport. WADA aims to do this through means of education, research and development of anti-doping capacities and through the monitoring of compliance with the WADC.[2] The WADC is the document that harmonises anti-doping policies for all sports in all countries to protect athletes' right to participate in doping-free sport which would ultimately help in promoting fairness and equality between them.[3] The WADC was first implemented in 2004 and

[1] McChrystal M. K., *Privacy in Sports: Recent Developments in the Federal Courts*, 12(1) MARQ. SPORTS L. REV. 397, 398, 399 (2001).

[2] WADA, *The Code* (2017), *available at* https://www.wada-ama.org/en/what-we-do/the-code

[3] *Id.*

has subsequently been revised twice since then, first in 2009 and subsequently in 2015, which is currently in force.

The code lays down the conditions that have to be met by athletes as well as their support personnel for participation in sporting events, the manner of collecting samples for doping tests and the prescribed procedure for conducting proceedings in cases of violation of the code. The World Anti-Doping Programme envisages a three-tier mechanism to ensure uniformity and inclusion of best practices at the international as well as national level programmes being run by ADOs.[4] The first level is that of the WADC. The second includes various 'International Standards' that have been prescribed by WADA for different technical and operational areas such as testing and sample collection, Therapeutic Use Exemptions (hereinafter TUEs), Prohibited Substances and Methods and for the protection of privacy and personal information of athletes. The WADC requires mandatory adherence to such International Standards to ensure harmonisation among ADOs. The third level comprises of Models of Best Practice and Guidelines which are recommended by WADA but compliance with them has not been made mandatory for the signatories to the code.[5]

With the aim of ensuring effectiveness of the application of the code, in 2005 the UNESCO adopted the International Convention against Doping in Sport, wherein several governments across the world came to agree to apply the force of international law to fight doping in sports.[6] The convention, which came into force in 2007 and has been accepted by over 186 state parties, creates a legal framework under which governments can address certain areas of anti-doping that remain outside the control of the sports

[4] WADA, *World Anti-Doping Code* (W2017), *available at* https://www.wada-ama.org/en/resources/the-code/world-anti-doping-code

[5] *Id.*

[6] UNESCO, *Background to the International Convention against Doping in Sport, available at,* http://www.unesco.org/new/en/social-and-human-sciences/themes/anti-doping/international-convention-against-doping-in-sport/background/

movement that consists of sports governing bodies and federations and helps in formalising international anti-doping rules, policies and guidelines.[7] States that are parties to the convention have agreed to commit themselves to the principles that have been enshrined in the WADC and its fundamental role in keeping sports free from doping.[8]

India is a signatory to the International Convention against Doping in Sport and ratified the treaty in 2007. In pursuance of this obligation, the Ministry of Youth Affairs and Sports (MYAS) established the National Anti-Doping Agency (hereinafter NADA) in 2009.[9] NADA is a government-controlled body that works with the primary objectives of implementing anti-doping rules as per WADC and the relevant standards prescribed therein, regulating dope control programme, promoting education and research, and creating awareness about doping and its harmful consequences.[10]

Implications on Personal Liberty and Bodily Integrity

WADA has prescribed a procedure that needs to be followed for effective testing under the International Standard for Testing and Investigations (hereinafter ISTI). ISTI covers how ADOs should effectively plan testing, notify athletes, take samples while maintaining their integrity and identity and even transport such samples for carrying out analysis.[11] ISTI, read with the WADC, prescribes procedure for both in-competition and

---

[7] *Id.*

[8] Article 4, International Convention against Doping in Sport.

[9] Lovely Dasgupta, *Catch Me If You Can! Anti-Doping Policy In India*, LawInSport (2013), *available at*, https://www.lawinsport.com/features/item/catch-me-if-you-can-anti-doping-policy-in-india

[10] NADA, *Primary Function* (2017), *available at* http://nada.nic.in/View/PRIMARYFUNCTION.aspx

[11] WADA, *International Standard for Testing and Investigations (ISTI)* (2016), *available at* https://www.wada-ama.org/en/resources/

out-of-competition testing for their Anti-Doping Programme. WADA emphasises on the importance of out-of-competition testing because the use of number of prohibited methods and substances remains traceable only for a short period of time in the athlete's body while delivering the performance enhancing effect.[12] To reduce the chances of such use going undetected, ADOs are required to run programmes that focus on conducting unexpected tests on athletes which WADA views as one of the most effective means of ensuring deterrence.[13] Several athletes have raised objections relating to invasion of their privacy and bodily integrity due to the procedures for random testing. However, it appears that the most contentious provision in this regard has been the 'whereabouts rule' violation under Article 2.4 of the WADC.[14]

WADA introduced the whereabouts rule for the first time in 2004 as specified obligations for a limited pool of elite athletes only. Under the rule, athletes were required to report where they would be located at specified points of time to their respective National Anti-Doping Organization (NADO). Initially, there was considerable ambiguity over the specificities of how this rule would be applied because a considerable amount of discretion was accorded to NADOs. This resulted in there being several dissimilar versions of the rule being applied. Not only was the definition of the term 'missed test' varying across ADOs but there was also a difference in the number of maximum permissible tests that an athlete could miss and the penalties that would be imposed in case of such violations.[15] There existed a lack

world-anti-doping-program/international-standard-for-testing-and-investigations-isti-0

[12] Oskar MacGregor et al., *Anti-Doping, Purported Rights to Privacy and WADA'S Whereabouts Requirements: A Legal Analysis*, 1 FAIR PLAY REVISTA DE FILOSOFÍA, ÉTICA Y DERECHO DEL DEPORTE 13, 15–17 (2013), *available at* http://www.raco.cat/index.php/FairPlay/article/view/269796/357382

[13] WADA, *Athlete Reference Guide to the 2015 World Anti-Doping Code* (2015), *available at* https://www.wada-ama.org/sites/default/files/resources/files/wada-reference-guide-to-2015-code.pdf

[14] Article 2.6 of the 2015 version of WADC and Annexure I of the ISTI.

[15] *See supra* note 12.

of standardisation, and athletes pursuing different sports were being treated differently.[16] As a response to these issues, WADA implemented a second version of the whereabouts rule in 2009 under Article 11 of ISTI with the aim of bringing in uniformity in application to athletes across the board.[17] This version of the rule not only clearly defined what essentials needed to be satisfied for a violation of this rule to amount an Anti-Doping Rule Violation but also specified which athletes would qualify and form a part of the 'Registered Pool' for testing under the rule and would be required to submit their whereabouts filings prior to the commencement of each annual quarter.[18] Compliance with this rule also included specifying a 60 minutes' time slot between 6 AM and 11 PM for each day of the quarter with details of a location the athlete could be found for testing.[19] The rule also specified that the maximum permissible number of tests for an athlete would be 3, in a period of 18 months.[20]

Several concerns regarding violation of individual privacy were raised in addition to the obvious concerns of impracticality of imposing such reporting by athletes months in advance. Prominent sports governing bodies such as the Federation Internationale de Football Association (FIFA) and Union of European Football Associations (UEFA) had strongly opposed the imposition of this rule and even went as far as labelling it a sign of disrespect to the private lives of individual athletes, a 'fundamental element of individual liberty'.[21] The Board of Control for Cricket in India (hereinafter BCCI) had also strongly opposed the implementation of this rule citing privacy and security concerns for cricketers, who already attract a considerable amount of

---

[16] Id.

[17] Id.

[18] See supra note 12.

[19] Section 11, WADA's ISTI (2009).

[20] Id.

[21] FIFA, FIFA and UEFA Reject WADA 'Whereabouts' Rule (2009), available at http://www.fifa.com/development/news/y=2009/m=3/news=fifa-and-uefa-reject-wada-whereabouts-rule-1040455.html

public attention in India.[22] It must be noted that BCCI is not a signatory to NADA; however, the International Cricket Council (ICC) became a signatory to the WADC in 2006 and accepted the application of the rule in 2010, which is still not being applied by BCCI in entirety.[23]

WADA in 2015 came up with the latest version of the rule under Article 2.4 of the code and Annexure I of ISTI.[24] Through this amendment, WADA sought to make the rule more flexible. The window period within which 3 tests could be missed was shortened from 18 months to 12 months, to be more accommodative for athletes who might be careless with such administrative compliances.[25] If an athlete commits three whereabouts failures within this period, s/he would be deemed to have committed an Anti-Doping Rule Violation.[26] The amended version of the rule also goes as far as prescribing what should constitute a Registered Testing Pool of athletes while still leaving discretionary power with ADOs to prepare these lists. However, it fails to address any of the privacy concerns that have been raised since 2009.[27] In fact, additional concerns relating to proportionality of retention period are raised as the data collected under this rule is retained

---

[22] *See* Sabi Hussain, *NADA Plans to Test Cricketers for Doping in Domestic Circuit*, The Tribune, 2017, *available at* http://www.tribuneindia.com/news/sport/nada-plans-to-test-cricketers-for-doping-in-domestic-circuit/409496.html

[23] *See Hindustan Times, Whereabouts Clause Issue Resolved, Says Lorgat*, 2010, *available at* http://www.hindustantimes.com/cricket/whereabouts-clause-issue-resolved-says-lorgat/story-M7yJxVdD7YUECtTQXX6a0I.html

[24] Article 2.4 of WADC states that whereabouts failures are 'Any combination of three missed tests and/or filing failures, as defined in the International Standard for Testing and Investigations, within a twelve-month period by an Athlete in a Registered Testing Pool', *see* Annexure I of the ISTI.

[25] *Id.*

[26] *Id.*

[27] WADA, *Significant Changes Between the 2009 Code and the 2015 Code, Version 4.0* (2017), *available at* https://www.wada-ama.org/sites/default/files/wadc-2015-draft-version-4.0-significant-changes-to-2009-en.pdf

for a period of 18 months, even though the violation window has been reduced to 12 months.[28]

Stakeholders and commentators have consistently argued that the imposition of the rule amounts to a transgression on the right to privacy of individuals. A majority of these challenges have been under European Union (hereinafter EU) privacy laws[29] on grounds ranging from data protection concerns to being in violation of their right to work as athletes, by way of contract, consent to constant surveillance by ADOs by furnishing their whereabouts.[30] This results in athletes practically having no 'off-days' as they can potentially be tested at any time—even while they are out on a personal holiday. It has been argued that the rule is in contravention to EU law and likely to be struck down if an athlete challenges its validity before a suitable court of law. This is because it disregards any respect for the privacy and personal life which is expressly protected under EU laws.[31] The rule has been said to be in conflict with the European Working Time Directive that gives individuals an entitlement to at least four weeks of holiday time each year and other such rights to ensure the protection of privacy of workers and their personal lives.[32]

The position on whether a challenge to the Whereabouts Rule would be successful before courts in India remains unclear

[28] Antonio Rigozzi, Marjolaine Viret & Emily Wisnosky, *Does the World Anti-Doping Code Revision Live Up to Its Promises? A Preliminary Survey of the Main Changes in the Final Draft of the 2015 WADA Code*, JUSLETTER (2013), *available at* http://lk-k.com/wp-content/uploads/RIGOZZI-VIRET-WISNOSKY-WADC-Revision-11-November-2013.pdf

[29] Article 8 of the European Convention on Human Rights guarantees the right to privacy to individuals.

[30] *See supra* note 12. *See also* James Halt, *Where is the Privacy in WADA's 'Whereabouts' Rule?* 20 MARQ. SPORTS L. REV. (2009), *available at* http://scholarship.law.marquette.edu/cgi/viewcontent.cgi?article=1017 &context=sportslaw

[31] *Id.*

[32] Council Directive (EC) 93/104 concerning certain aspects of the organisation of working time (1993) OJ L307/18 (Working Time Directive); Halt, *supra* note 30.

as there is an absence of express provisions relating to athlete's privacy like in the EU. It must be borne in mind that the whereabouts rule is designed in a way that compels an athlete to disclose accurate information regarding not only his/her residence, training locations, office addresses, address of school, university and places where the athlete might be competing but also any party or personal outings. The athlete would then be under an obligation to undertake a 'no-notice' drug test or risk it being marked a 'missed test'.[33] This essentially means that the athlete is under perpetual surveillance by his/her respective NADO or the international sport federation. NADO is a government-controlled authority that was established by the MYAS in 2005 under the Societies Registration Act, 1890. It had adopted the WADC in 2009 and subsequently the latest version from 2015. It is, therefore, responsible for the implementation of the rule. A possible challenge to the whereabouts rule could lie before the Indian courts on the basis of it amounting to disproportionate surveillance by the state, being in contravention to the right to privacy guaranteed under Article 21 of the Constitution of India.

Another area of challenge lies in the requirement of furnishing details for the 60 minutes' time slot during which an athlete would have to be present at the location specified by them in the whereabouts filing. This places a heavy burden on an athlete to be present at the specified location for the entirety of one hour on each day of the year. This essentially restricts the ability of an individual to move freely from one place to another of their choice, a right that has been guaranteed under Article 19(1)(d) of the Constitution. The only justification for the imposition of such a restriction on their right to free movement is 'public interest', as contemplated within Article 19(5). However, restrictions allowed under Article 19(5) ought to be 'reasonable'. The principle of reasonability would demand that the restriction be proportionate to the amount of threat that is posed in the absence of such restriction. This would require the courts to delve into what would be the least restrictive way in which NADO could run a

---

[33] Halt, *id.*

successful anti-doping programme, something which ought to be the expertise of only ADOs. The courts would be forced to recognise that surprise testing for which whereabouts details is an essential requirement for maintaining the integrity of sports and might have to come up with a middle path to balance this with the competing rights of the individual athlete.

In the Indian context, it is interesting to note that the operationalisation of the whereabouts rule has been consistently resisted in case of the nation's favourite sport, Cricket. Compared by the apex court to be equivalent to religion in this country, BCCI, the nodal authority for the sport, have always had reservations against extending the mandate to cricketers—national or provincial.[34] Recently, however, BCCI has made statements indicating that the rule may be applied as a test case in the regional tournaments, the Ranji and Irani Trophy formats.[35] This development may be of significance. If the rule is implemented, BCCI which is a private entity shall certainly be called to question for authorising invasive testing which are clear violations of the individual's right to privacy. In India, where fundamental rights (FRs) cannot be waived by an individual, unless an express exception to the right to privacy covers this case, it seems unlikely that the courts will be convinced that the right be ignored for active sports-persons. Whether sports-persons constitute a separate class to whom differential standards can be applied is another dilemma the courts may have to resolve, incidental to the core question of infringement.

The argument that testing is done upon the express consent of the player seems to lack merit, since consent requires to be

---

[34] K. P. Mohan, *No, BCCI, Cricket in Olympics Won't Mean Indian Players Will Have to Compromise on Privacy, Scroll.in* (2017), *available at* https://thefield.scroll.in/847393/no-bcci-the-wadas-whereabouts-clause-does-not-infringe-upon-the-privacy-of-your-star-cricketers

[35] Sabi Hussain, *NADA Plans to Test Cricketers for Doping in Domestic Circuit, The Tribune*, 2017, *available at* http://www.tribuneindia.com/news/sport/nada-plans-to-test-cricketers-for-doping-in-domestic-circuit/409496.html

voluntary and not obtained through coercion. If the regulations are made mandatory for participation in a sport, the athlete has no choice but to consent to them in order to participate. The idea of mandatory regulations does not leave any room for consent. This is particularly problematic since participation in sport is connected to the issue of livelihood, in case of professional sports-persons. If one is required to waive fundamental human rights in lieu of the license to ply one's trade, such a stipulation raises questions that travel far beyond the realm of sports and competition, attracting issues of human dignity and individual autonomy.

Anti-doping Programmes: Implications on Privacy and Data Protection

It is essential for ADOs, that are signatories to the WADC, to collect and process several types of information about athletes to be able to run effective anti-doping programmes. This includes results of blood and urine samples of athletes which are collected both in and out of competition, any existing medical conditions that an athlete might be suffering from and medication that has been prescribed for such conditions and might be relevant for the grant of TUEs.[36] Information can also be in the form of the training and competition schedules of an athlete which might be relevant for arranging dope tests and in the form of the controversial whereabouts rule as mentioned under Article 2.4 of the WADC or any other personal information that athletes might have to furnish to comply with the provisions of the WADC 2015.

As data protection and privacy legislations lack uniformity across jurisdictions, WADA drafted a policy to ensure the safety

---

[36] Abby Brindley & Ed Carder, *Do WADA'S International Standards Sufficiently Protect Athletes' Personal Data?* LawInSport (2016), *available at* https://www.lawinsport.com/articles/item/do-wada-s-international-standards-sufficiently-protect-athletes-personal-data?highlight=WyJwcml2YWN5IiwiJ3ByaXZhY3kiLCJwcml2YWN5JywiLCJwcml2YWN5JyJd#references

of such information through imposition of mandatory compliance with the minimum standards of protection. This has been done through the mandatory International Standard for the Protection of Privacy and Personal Information (hereinafter ISPPPI)[37] that applies to signatory to the WADC.[38] The ISPPPI comes into play when data that has been collected and 'processed' as a result of anti-doping activities that might be carried out by ADOs to identify possible violations of anti-doping rules.[39] This standard specifies that ADOs can collect and process data only when certain conditions are met. These include obtaining express written consent of the individual athlete or fulfilment of valid legal reasons for processing the data.[40] However, exceptions to obtaining the consent of the athlete or cases where consent is withdrawn by the athlete are also covered under the standard. These include situations where processing data is necessary for commencing or pursuing anti-doping investigations involving the athlete; or for conducting proceedings relating to Anti-Doping Rule Violations involving the said athlete; or for establishing a case or defence in legal proceedings.[41]

In addition to this, the ISPPPI expressly prohibits ADOs from obtaining unnecessary or irrelevant information from not only athletes but also third parties.[42] It also places an express restriction on ADOs processing data for any reasons apart from anti-doping activities or in contravention of any existing (national or international) privacy or data protection laws that might

[37] The latest version of the ISPPPI came into effect in January 2015.

[38] As per Para 3.1 of the ISPPPI, a signatory has been defined as any ADO that is 'responsible for adopting rules for initiating, implementing or enforcing any part of the Doping Control process'.

[39] See supra note 36. The term 'process' is a broad term that includes collection, computation, filing, analysis, storage, etc. of such data.

[40] Para 6.1 of the ISPPPI.

[41] Para 6.2 of the ISPPPI. Commentary provided within the ISPPPI states that these exceptions have been created to avoid 'withdrawal of consent' being used as a means to avoid or circumvent anti-doping exercises or for including detection of violations.

[42] Para 5.2 of the ISPPPI.

be applicable to the ADO.[43] The standard, therefore, not only recognises and addresses concerns that an individual might have in relation to not sharing unnecessary personal information but also attempts to respect the extent of their consent accorded to processing such information and balancing it with the main objective of implementing effective anti-doping measures.

The ISPPPI creates two distinct categories of information that is collected, that is, personal information and sensitive personal information, and mandates a higher degree of protection for the latter.[44] This distinction has also been made in India under the Information Technology Act, 2000,[45] as amended in 2008 (hereinafter IT Act) read with Information Technology (Reasonable Security Practices and Procedures and Sensitive Personal Data or Information) Rules, 2011 (hereinafter SPDI Rules). The legislation read with the rules framed therein[46] provides for mandating certain minimum standards for protection of such data that might be collected and processed or dealt with in electronic form. An obligation is placed on every 'body corporate' that processes, deals or handles any sensitive personal data or information (hereinafter SPDI). The term 'body corporate' has been defined as 'any company and includes a firm, sole proprietorship or other association of individuals engaged in commercial or professional activities'.[47] However, it remains unclear if this definition may be extended to ADOs including NADA by classifying them as associations engaged in professional activities and by extension,

---

[43] *Id.*

[44] According to the commentary provided within the ISPPPI, the term personal information includes the name of the athlete, date of birth, contact details, sporting affiliations, test results, details about their doctors or physiotherapists etc. and is an umbrella term that includes Sensitive Personal Information such as ethnic or racial background of an athlete, any previous convictions, data about an athlete's health and genetic make-up based on samples collected for testing etc.

[45] Act No. 21 of 2000.

[46] Information Technology (Reasonable Security Practices and Procedures and Sensitive Personal Data or Information) Rules, 2011.

[47] Section 43A of the Information Technology (Amendment) Act, 2008.

whether an aggrieved athlete can ask for recourse or compensation under Section 43A of IT Act in case of breaches on part of the respective ADO.[48] Beyond this, however, no separate recourse exists. Even an application made before the Court of Arbitration for Sport (CAS) would entail expenditure which is practically impossible for most sports-persons to bear, especially in India, where apart from in a handful of sports, the lack of financial incentives ensures that professional athletes have to struggle to ensure basic nutrition and access to quality equipment. The availability of remedies under the IT Act is of importance, considering the fact that the ISPPPI does not contain direct provisions for payment of compensation or other similar reliefs to an individual who might have suffered an injury due to the fault or negligence on the part of an ADO.

Under the ISPPPI, ADOs have been mandated to put into place a fair complaints procedure to address any concerns that an individual might have with regard to the organisation's practices, procedures or decisions within the organisation.[49] In cases where the ADO is unwilling or not able to resolve a complaint in a satisfactory fashion, the complaint can then be made to WADA or be taken up at CAS.[50] While taking up the complaint with WADA could be effective, pursuing the complaint at CAS might not be. This is primarily because of the extremely high costs associated with pursuing arbitration proceedings at the international forum, which might not be affordable by a large majority, barring a few elite athletes in India. This makes it all the more important for athletes to have recourse under the existing national legal mechanism and is implicitly recognised by the standard.[51]

---

[48] Section 43A provides for compensation to be payable in case of wrongful loss or wrongful gain to any person due to the negligence of the body corporate. This compensation can be an amount of up to ₹5 crore being payable to the person affected.

[49] Para 11.5 of the ISPPPI; Brindley & Carder, *supra* note 36. The term 'process' is a broad term that includes collection, computation, filing, analysis, storage, etc. of such data.

[50] *Id.*

[51] *Id.*

The IT Act sets out the obligations on the 'body corporate' to maintain the security of sensitive personal data by maintaining 'reasonable security practices and procedures' to protect from unauthorised access, damage, use, modification, disclosure or impairment.[52] Reasonable security practices and procedures that are to be observed may vary from case to case, depending upon the relationship between the provider of SPDI and the body corporate. In case there exists an agreement that specifies protection from unauthorised access, the minimum standards to be followed in safeguarding such information would be governed by the agreement.[53] In the absence of such an agreement, the standards applicable would have to be in conformity with any laws in force in the time being.[54] In absence of both of the mentioned conditions, such standards as may be prescribed by the Central government in consultation with such professional bodies or associations would be applicable.[55]

In case of ADOs such as NADA, the standards of data security that should be applicable should be the ones prescribed under the ISPPPI. This is because of the contractual nature of relationship that exists between ADOs and athletes, who submit to ADOs with their written consent before being subjected to scrutiny under anti-doping regimes. Under the ISPPPI, ADOs are required to take 'all necessary security safeguards, including physical, organizational, technical, environmental and other measures, to prevent the loss, theft, or unauthorized access, destruction, use, modification or disclosure (including disclosures made via electronic networks) of Personal Information'.[56] ADOs are required to adhere to an even higher standard of care to ensure the protection of sensitive personal data considering the greater amount of risk that an individual would be exposed to, if this information were to be disclosed unlawfully.[57] The standard also casts a duty

---

[52] Section 43A of the Information Technology (Amendment) Act, 2008.
[53] Id.
[54] Id.
[55] Id.
[56] Para 9.2 of the ISPPPI.
[57] Para 9.3 of the ISPPPI.

on the ADO to immediately inform the affected athlete in the event of a breach as soon as possible, along with the nature and other details of the measures taken by the ADO to minimise such damage such as engaging specialists and approaching courts for injunction orders as may be needed to secure the breach.[58]

Despite the safeguards contained in the latest standard, there have been various instances of unauthorised and illegal data leaks and publication of confidential data relating to athletes in the past that was stored on the WADA's Anti-Doping Administration and Management System (hereinafter ADAMS).[59] ADAMS is a web-based database management system that assists in simplifying the documentation of data involving all stakeholders and athletes that form a part of the anti-doping mechanism across the globe and it contains multi-level access systems to protect the confidentiality and safety of data contained.[60] It stores information such as laboratory test results of samples collected from athletes, regarding TUEs, past records of Anti-Doping Rule Violations and whereabouts information of athletes and facilitates the transfer of information between relevant organisations. The system has been put in place to promote effectiveness and to prevent inconvenience arising out of multiplicity of forums where athletes have to enter their information for the purposes of compliance.[61]

In September 2016, several concerns regarding the sufficiency of security of the ADAMS were raised after a series of leaks by a cyber-espionage group that called itself 'Fancy Bear' were reported. Confidential medical data of athletes, such as the

---

[58] *See supra* note 36. *See also* Abby Brindley & Ed Carder, *The IAAF Blood Test Data Leak: Was Publishing the Data Lawful?* LawInSport (2017), *available at* https://www.lawinsport.com/articles/item/the-iaaf-blood-test-data-leak-was-publishing-the-data-lawful

[59] ISSF, *Privacy Issues in the World of Anti-Doping* (2016), *available at* http://www.issf-sports.org/getfile.aspx?mod=docf&pane=1&inst=257&file=IPOD-ISSFNEWS_2016-06.pdf

[60] WADA, *ADAMS* (2017), *available at* https://www.wada-ama.org/en/adams

[61] *Id.*

grant of TUEs, was acquired from the International Olympic Committee's account that was created for the purpose of the Rio 2016 Olympic Games.[62] As an immediate response, WADA formed a multidisciplinary response team for investigating the security breach and to chalk out the future course of action to take down the leaked information from websites and to inform the relevant stakeholders about the incident.[63] This merely highlights that the security of personal information is a constant challenge and even with the existence of the highest levels of security, there may be no incontrovertible solution to such threats. However, what the standard does is provide individual stakeholders with some assurance that WADA does take the safety of their data seriously.

Implications of Disclosers: Defamation and Journalistic Responsibility

The threat of unauthorised invasion has loomed large over the lives of celebrities across the world. In the age of social media and citizen journalism, the effects of such invasion on the life of a public personality have often given rise to intense debate regarding the role and responsibilities of the press. While celebrities from every walk of life are accustomed to certain exacting standards of public scrutiny, the impact of adverse and often irresponsible reporting holds a greater potential for harm in case of sports personalities. Athletes, unlike film personalities, have a relatively shorter shelf life, and the damage to their reputation resulting from such invasions of their private space may jeopardise whole careers.

The most infamous instance of this was seen during the media trial of O. J. Simpson, the National Football League player of international repute. Charged with murdering his wife and another, his much-publicised trial became a public spectacle on

---

[62] ISSF, *supra* note 59.
[63] *Id.*

national television with prime-time news anchors conducting a trial within their studios, most often pronouncing him guilty, based on their 'investigations'. The public perception created against Simpson, owing largely due to the press coverage of this incident, severely affected his private life even after the court acquitted him of the charge of murder. O. J. Simpson's trial was dubbed the 'trial of the century' and has become a case study on the adverse effects of a media-frenzy surrounding law enforcement and sensationalistic journalism, the likes of which are prevalent until this day.[64]

Unauthorised publication of personal information of athletes, especially confidential medical data and test results, can not only lead to serious repercussions on their privacy but also result in defamation. The interpretation of blood-sample results, for instance, is a highly specialised task which requires not only expert medical professionals but also an understanding of the pre-existing medical condition of an athlete. An incomplete understanding of background circumstances may lead to incorrect inferences of doping allegations against an innocent athlete which could result in defamation.[65] Allegations of doping could potentially destroy an innocent athlete's career and have long-term effects such as backlash from both the general public and existing and potential sponsors.

On the occurrence of such disclosures, athletes are often forced to divulge more personal information to the general public to control the damage to their public image. An example of such forceful disclosures was due to the leak of confidential data held by the International Association of Athletics Federations (hereinafter IAAF) in 2015. Several media houses such as *The Sunday Times* in the UK and ARD/WDR in Germany credited the leak to a 'whistle-blower' who intended to bring to light instances of cheating by athletes at leading events, a claim which was later

---

[64] Andrew McStay, PRIVACY AND THE MEDIA (1st ed. 2017).
[65] *See* Brindley & Carder, *supra* note 58.

rebutted strongly by IAAF.[66] While these media agencies had reached out to individual athletes to obtain their consent for the publication of such information, such consent was not necessarily 'free'. A threat of inferences of doping violations being drawn is always present in case an athlete decides to not share information or give consent for publication of personal information in such situations.[67] Such concerns also arise when there are reports that state that an athlete 'potentially' could be guilty of Anti-Doping Rule Violations based on such personal information and test results.[68]

An adverse impact on the reputation and privacy of athletes as a result of public disclosures is not limited to only data that has been obtained illegally or in an unauthorised manner. It can also extend to data that has been obtained legitimately and disclosed by sports governing bodies, ADOs or other authorities in the course of them discharging their duties. There have been various instances in the past where commissions have been set up to look into allegations of systematic doping prevalent in certain countries or sports due to corruption or mismanagement.[69] Commissions gather the information they need from ADOs and other sports governing authorities while being limited in their scope and power by the ISPPPI, in addition to other national

---

[66] *Id. See also WADA Confirms that Leaked Athletics Database Does Not Originate from Its Anti-Doping Administration & Management System (ADAMS)*, LawInSport (2016), *available at* https://www.lawinsport.com/sports-law-news/item/wada-confirms-that-leaked-athletics-database-does-not-originate-from-its-anti-doping-administration-management-system-adams

[67] *See* Ben Bloom, *Paula Radcliffe Insists She Is Not Guilty of Doping*, *The Telegraph*, 2017, *available at* http://www.telegraph.co.uk/sport/othersports/athletics/11851409/Paula-Radcliffe-insists-she-is-not-guilty-of-doping.html

[68] *See supra* note 36.

[69] In 2015–2016, WADA published two reports by two independent commissions that were set up to look into allegations of systematic doping practices being prevalent in Russia. Cycliste Internationale also published a report by an expert commission to look into such practices in the sport.

laws that might be applicable.[70] Legal issues such as defamation may arise on the publication of reports that are prepared by such commissions. This is because, in the event that the report indicates the prevalence of systematic and widespread doping, clean athletes might also suffer repercussions such as loss of reputation, among other consequences. While civil remedies like defamation can be used as an effective tool to address these concerns, the consequential damage due to irresponsible disclosure is often far greater than financially quantifiable. ADOs and sports governing bodies should, therefore, take into account such ramifications before publication. However, this legal risk has to be balanced with their own interests of rebuilding the integrity of sport through transparency in the publication, which could prove to be a difficult exercise.[71]

Conclusion

The issue of privacy rights of public personalities has always been a contentious one. The surrender of privacy rights is considered an occupational hazard for celebrities, big or small. Such invasions, often excessive and unjustified, continue under the pretext of 'newsworthiness' where the commercial interest of the media, fed by the curiosity of its audience, sets the parameters for public acceptability. Athletes are especially vulnerable to misreporting and media excesses, since their reputation as sports-persons is contingent on the public's faith in their integrity. While instances of doping and failure to comply must certainly be brought to light, the opportunity cost in case of misreporting even a single such case demands adherence to the highest standards of journalistic responsibility and restraint.

[70] Kendrah Potts, *Investigating Systemic Doping in Sports: How Independent Commissions Are Established and Run*, LAWINSPORT (2016), *available at* https://www.lawinsport.com/features/item/investigating-systemic-doping-in-sports-how-independent-commissions-are-established-and-run?highlight=WyJwcml2YWN5IiwiJ3ByaXZhY3kiLCJwcml2YWN5JywiLCJwcml2YWN5JyJd

[71] *Id.*

The importance of ensuring transparency and fair play in the competitive world of professional sports has led to many innovations over the years, and the introduction of the WADA rules is but a step in the same direction. The controversies surrounding these rules, particularly the claims relating to violation of privacy, however, seriously undermine the legitimacy of the regulations. Questions continue to remain regarding the twin issues of necessity and proportionality of these measures. Whether the implementation of the WADA rules is found to be necessary or excessive depends heavily on the standards of privacy protection in each separate jurisdiction. The judiciary is, therefore, faced with the momentous task of balancing the conflicting interests of the individual's right to privacy and the need for greater accountability in sports. While the sporting fraternity braces itself for a tough fight, there remains hope that if the sports-persons exert enough influence collectively, the possibility for the removal of these provisions may be effected even without a gruelling courtroom battle. Instead of assiduously advocating for greater acceptability of the regulations, one would imagine that a more profitable outcome may emerge if greater stress was laid on finding an alternate system, wherein the already limited private space of the athlete does not suffer more shrinkage at the gunpoint of compliance.

Doping and Sports in India

Richa R. Mulchandani

Introduction

In the world of sports, doping is one of the most serious issues which has a very negative effect on those who are part of it. The use of banned drugs to enhance performance during the game is considered unethical, and it also adversely affects the mental and physical health of players. Whether it is at the national or international level, in sports or in general, using, administering, possessing and trafficking of prohibited drugs are subject to punitive action. Doping or use of prohibited substances in sports is always seen as a pest that hampers the 'spirit of Olympism' as it goes against the 'spirit of fair play'.

The historical evolution of doping regulations suggests that protection of athletes from effects of cheating, health hazard and degradation in moral strength is the key reason to adopt and implement an anti-doping code. In addition to maintaining sports as a 'clean game', it gives the innocent participants equal and just opportunities to compete on the basis of their natural abilities.

It has been observed that since 1960, many efforts have been made to restrict, minimise and prohibit the use of performance enhancement drugs in sports. However, more organised efforts have been made since the beginning of the twenty-first century with the establishment of World Anti-Doping Agency (WADA). The World Anti-Doping Code (WADC) was first adopted in 2003 and came into effect in 2004. To maintain the sanctity of sports and to meet the challenges, it is updated and amended on a regular basis. It was first amended in 2009 and then the whole code was revised in 2013 and 2015. The revised and updated version has been implemented since then effectively.

WADA ensures that the athletes are benefited from the anti-doping protocols and they are protected regardless of their nationality, the sport or the country where it is played. The ultimate goal is to have a safe and fair competition worldwide, for which WADA facilitates the coordination of Regional Anti-Doping Organizations (RADOs) which perform various functions like testing, result management and adjudication. One of WADA's most vital responsibilities is to provide anti-doping education and spread awareness regarding its effects. The working of these organisations is largely affected by the government's efforts and funding. Hereby a comparative study has been made of six countries, the USA, UK, China, France, Australia and India, in terms of identifying activities undertaken in the field of anti-doping education to have more clarity on what countries need to learn more on this subject.

Article 18 of WADC describes principles and education programme to be adopted and followed by RADOs.

It reads as follows:

18.1 Basic Principle and Primary Goal

The basic principle for information and education programs for doping-free sport is to preserve the spirit of sport, as described in the Introduction to the Code, from being undermined by doping. The primary goal of such programs is prevention. The objective shall be to prevent the intentional or unintentional Use by Athletes of Prohibited Substances and Prohibited Methods.

Information programs should focus on providing basic information to Athletes as described in Article 18.2. Education programs should focus on prevention. Prevention programs should be values based and directed towards Athletes and Athlete Support Personnel with a particular focus on young people through implementation in school curricula.

All Signatories shall within their means and scope of responsibility and in cooperation with each other, plan, implement, evaluate and monitor information, education, and prevention programs for doping-free sport.

18.2 Programs and Activities

These programs shall provide Athletes and other Persons with updated and accurate information on at least the following issues:

- Substances and methods of the Prohibited List.
- Anti-doping Rule Violations (ADRVs).
- Consequences of doping, including sanctions, health, and social consequences.
- Doping Control procedures.
- Athletes' and Athlete Support Personnel's rights and responsibilities.
- Therapeutic Use Exemptions (TUEs).
- Managing the risks of nutritional supplements.
- Harm of doping to the spirit of sport.

The programmes should promote the spirit of sport in order to establish an environment that is strongly conducive to the doping-free sport and will have a positive and long-term influence on the choices made by Athletes and other Persons.

Prevention programs shall be primarily directed at young people, appropriate to their stage of development, in school and sports clubs, parents, adult athletes, sport officials, coaches, medical personnel and the media.

Athlete Support Personnel shall educate and counsel Athletes regarding anti-doping policies and rules adopted pursuant to the Code.

All Signatories shall promote and support active participation by Athletes and Athlete Support Personnel in education programs for doping-free sport.

18.3 Professional Codes of Conduct

All Signatories shall cooperate with each other and governments to encourage relevant, competent professional associations and institutions to develop and implement appropriate Codes of Conduct, good practice and ethics related to sport practice regarding anti-doping, as well as sanctions, which are consistent with the Code.

18.4 Coordination and Cooperation

WADA shall act as a central clearinghouse for informational and educational resources and/or programs developed by WADA or Anti-Doping Organizations.

All Signatories and Athletes and other Persons shall cooperate with each other and governments to coordinate their efforts in anti-doping information and education in order to share experience and ensure the effectiveness of these programs in preventing doping in sport.

The targeted audience for these programmes are the youth. It is appropriate since at this stage of development, schools, sports clubs, parents, adult athletes, sports officials, coaches, medical personnel and media play a huge role in a youngster's life. (The media should also support and create awareness regarding substance abuse.) Athlete support personnel should educate and counsel athletes regarding anti-doping policies and rules adopted pursuant to the code. All signatories should promote and support active participation by athletes and athlete support personnel in programmes for a doping-free sport.

It has been found that not only Article 18 but also

- Article 20.1.9 describes roles and responsibilities of the International Olympic Committee (IOC) in promoting anti-doping education.
- Article 20.2.8 describes roles and responsibilities of the International Paralympic Committee to promote anti-doping education.
- Article 20.3.12 describes roles and responsibilities of international federations to promote anti-doping education, including requiring national federations to conduct anti-doping education in coordination with the applicable National Anti-Doping Organization (NADO).
- Article 20.4.11 describes roles and responsibilities of National Olympic Committees and National Paralympic Committees to promote anti-doping education, including requiring national federations to conduct anti-doping education in coordination with the applicable NADO.
- Article 20.5.8 describes roles and responsibilities of NADOs to promote anti-doping education.
- Article 20.6.7 describes roles and responsibilities of major event organisations to promote anti-doping education.
- Article 20.7.6 describes roles and responsibilities of WADA to promote, conduct, commission, fund and coordinate anti-doping research and to promote anti-doping education.
- Article 21.3.6 describes roles and responsibilities of RADOs to promote anti-doping education.

WADA makes it the responsibility of various stakeholders to promote education programmes regarding anti-doping. However, it does not mean that any announcement or half an hour session on awareness is an 'education programme'.

The education programme is important as it is essential to minimise the cases of doping in sports. It has been found that

RADOs play an important role in educating the sports-persons, and failure in discharging their duty to provide education leads to more cases of doping. It has been found that in majority of the cases, the accused sportsperson stated that s/he used prohibited drugs unintentionally or was unaware of the fact that those drugs were prohibited. So here the question arises as to why they are unaware. Education is the only tool to counter this unawareness.

Anti-doping Education Programmes: The Global Experiences

It is time to delve into the anti-doping education programmes of other countries in order to observe how they are conducted and what India could learn in order to design its own framework.

The USA

Earlier, the education department of the US Anti-Doping Agency (USADA) had focused on educating athletes at the Olympic and Paralympic levels about the anti-doping programme. At the same time, USADA had also taught athletes at a young age and at grass-roots levels about clean competition.[1]

Recently, they have created two high-performance teams with different target groups. This includes:

- Olympic education which focuses primarily on elite-level athletes. It includes those who are in the Registered Testing Pool (RTP) of USADA.
- TrueSport is a relatively new initiative which focuses on teaching the spirit of sports to young athletes, their parents and youth sports stakeholders.

---

[1] USADA, *Then and Now: Education* (2016), *available at* http://www.usada.org/then-now-education/

USADA reports that they have undertaken the anti-doping education programmes in a way that it benefits the athletes. Apart from informing about the rules and regulations, they help athletes to connect and engage in interactive games and activities as part of their education programme.

They have a separate section on their website called 'athletes' where athletes can get educated about their responsibilities, duties and the regulations.[2]

USADA has made it compulsory for RTP athletes to take the Athlete's Advantage Tutorial which provides invaluable information and serves as an overview of their anti-doping rights and responsibilities. It has evolved with passage of time and is updated every year.

USADA has a list of all athletes who have ever been found positive of anti-doping tests and has published it on their official website.[3] It also publishes an annual report of the work that it has done.[4] The USA is also faced with the problem of doping in sports such as baseball and football, although the numbers are decreasing. Importantly, it does not fall among the top 10 countries who violated Anti-doping Rule in 2014.

Dr Larry Bowers, member, USADA, and internationally acclaimed anti-doping scientist, rightly observed:

> I'm saying that to highlight the point that anti-doping science can be both complicated and formidable, but the reality is that we have very talented, bright people on our side who get up every morning and continue to fight the good fight. Doing our best to protect clean athletes and helping to preserve the integrity of sport makes going to work every day a pleasure.[5]

[2] USADA, *Athletes* (2016), *available at* http://www.usada.org/athletes/
[3] USADA, *Results Management and Adjudication* (2016), *available at* http://www.usada.org/testing/results
[4] ASADA, *Annual Reports* (2016), *available at* https://www.asada.gov.au/about-asada/corporate-information/annual-reports
[5] https://www.usada.org/anti-doping-from-science-perspective/

He went on to opine:

> These are defining days in the fight for clean sport, and ultimately, we want clean athletes around the world to know that there is a committed group of people at the U.S. Anti-Doping Agency who wake up every day and work as hard as they can to preserve a level playing field. That's what this is all about.[6]

Furthermore, it must also be noted that the US lobbyists are pushing for doping regulation to be imposed on horse racing. To quote Joe Pitts, the republican representative of Pennsylvania:

> Last year, I chaired a hearing that took a deep look into the problems of both legal and illegal drugs in horse racing. We heard testimony about how abuse of drugs is killing horses and imperiling riders. Before more people and animals are hurt, we need to put a responsible national authority in charge of cleaning up racing. This is a sensible, bipartisan measure to restore trust in racing and protect lives.[7]

The UK

The UK Anti-Doping (UKAD) provides online education for all persons related to sports in one way or the other. It has the athlete zone, the parents' zone, the coaches' zone and the support personnel zone in the education section.[8]

UKAD had prepared a strategic plan for the years 2014–2017, in which it had included its vision, mission and objectives. The document for the strategic plan 2014–2017 is there on the website.[9]

---

[6] *Id.*

[7] http://www.nytimes.com/2013/05/01/sports/prroposed-bill-would-give-usada-authority-over-horse-racing.html?rref=collection%2Ftimestopic%2F United%20States%20Anti-Doping%20Agency

[8] UKAD, *Education* (2016), *available at* http://www.ukad.org.uk/education/

[9] UKAD, *Strategic Objectives* (2016), *available at* http://www.ukad.org.uk/our-organisation/strategic-objectives/

UKAD also hosts a series of additional forums as part of its commitment to engage with key stakeholders and their members that include university forum, research forum and educator forum for accredited educators along with athlete support personnel forum for active practitioners currently involved in the sport.

They are currently working on a revised prevention through education strategy in line with the 2015 code. Their aim is to develop a framework for doping prevention, one in which all their partners can contribute to, and actively support, the clean sports agenda in the UK. UKAD also provides a list of all anti-doping cases that have occurred there since 1997.[10] This ensures transparency in the working of the agency. It also uploads all the minutes of the board meetings on its website.

One of the interesting education programmes conducted by them is called 'What is 100% me?'

100% me is about being a true athlete. It is about being able to say that my performance is 100% me. There is no secret to one's success—just hard work, determination and talent. It encourages sports-persons to get involved and be a part of 100% me and keep up-to-date with all by registering on its website. It promotes its education through Twitter, Facebook and its blog.

One has to remember that not only lack of information and lack of penal measures bolster drug abuse, but curiosity about the banned drugs also acts as an important element in anti-doping violations.

As Dan Stevens, amateur cyclist in UK, mentioned:

I think it is just a way of modern day life—we are living in a phar-macised world. I took thyroxine and testosterone on prescription, and EPO out of 'curiosity'. I'd always been a clean athlete and this situation happened to me when I was 39 years old. But the real

---

[10] UKAD, *Providing a List of All Anti-Doping Rule Violations* (2016), *available at* http://ukad.org.uk/anti-doping-rule-violations/current-violations

thing for me wasn't really about racing—I didn't do a lot of racing on these substances. The main thing was curiosity. I don't think in the amateur ranks it is about winning. You've got a situation where someone is overweight, a little bit fat, need to lean down, get in shape. And they get in shape. They then get railroaded into doing a marathon or a long bike ride or some kind of competitive event and they improve their fitness levels again and they become a healthier individual and become more body conscious and more health-orientated.[11]

Furthermore, inability of the dispute resolution bodies to effectively combat drug issues also has a negative impact on mental health of the athletes. For example, Britain's troubled former heavyweight world champion Tyson Fury has not fought since his shock defeat to Wladimir Klitschko. He is waiting to appear before UKAD hearing after being charged with a doping offence over a year ago.[12]

To quote Tyson Fury,

It's been 15 months since I've been under investigation, you're keeping an innocent man from fulfilling his destiny and from providing for his family. How long must I be held up and kept out of action? Surely there must be a human rights law preventing this from happening to people! Either ban me or set me free as I've been in limbo for a long time! I want to move on with my life![13]

However, it needs to be observed that UK does not fall among the top 10 nations' list of ADRV.

Australia

The Australian Sports Anti-Doping Authority (ASADA) offers a wide range of anti-doping education opportunities. These programmes are there for everyone, ranging from individuals to

---

[11] http://www.bbc.com/sport/38884801
[12] http://sports.inquirer.net/265405/tyson-fury-urges-uk-anti-doping-resolution
[13] *Id.*

national sporting organisations. Most programmes and resources are available free of charge.

It has developed an e-learning programme, where anyone who wants to learn about the anti-doping laws can join.[14]

The course is divided into two parts:

- **Level 1—Anti-doping course:** It is a 70-minute online course which covers the 6 key areas of anti-doping and gives a certificate on completing the course. This enables and allows the individual to participate in Level 2.
- **Level 2—Anti-doping test:** This covers a greater deal of topic and goes into the advanced areas of anti-doping. It is updated every year.[15]

It also has other education programmes like face-to-face anti-doping presentations, where an expert in anti-doping will attend the training session and deliver a presentation to a group of athletes or support personnel. This is advantageous as the athletes can interact as well as ask questions. Sessions are generally offered free of charge to national teams and squads of recognised national sporting organisations, while sessions for other groups may be on a user pays basis.

At the school level, lesson plans and resources for teachers are also provided by ASADA online. It is for the students from years 9 to 10 on issues explored in the National Curriculum for Health and Physical Education. The plans are adaptable for use in a senior secondary environment.

The two new e-courses which were added by them are: Level 1 Anti-doping course and Level 2 Anti-doping test. Out of the two courses, one is meant for anyone who wants to learn, and the other is meant exclusively for medical practitioners and for athlete medical support personnel.

[14] ASADA, *ASADA ELearning* (2016), *available at* https://elearning.asada.gov.au/
[15] *Id.*

ASADA also publishes a report every year since 2005 regarding the work it has done in the past one year. These annual reports include everything. These have information regarding its annual performance, operations, management and accountability, financial information and statistics.[16] These give a detailed report on the violations of anti-doping laws, the educational programmes that were undertaken and their results. Forty-nine cases of ADRV were reported in 2014 and twenty-one cases of ADRV assertion were reported in the same year.

ASADA has also appointed an ex-policeman to bust the abuse of drugs. It has adopted a more aggressive approach towards cutting the supply of drugs and minimise it along with it.

According to Greg Hunt, the Australian sports minister,

> As we get closer to the Gold Coast 2018 Commonwealth Games, we all want to see athletes do well and achieve their potential but we also want to continue to be confident that all competition is clean and fair.[17]

The effort of Australian government about anti-doping definitely deserves appreciation.

France

The national doping agency of France (Agence française de Lutte Contre le dopage; AFLD) has a website which is in their national language, French. There also exists an English version of the website.[18] The English version is very basic and contains just the main page. Therefore, non-French speakers may have limited access to it.

AFLD publishes a report annually. The data collected in these reports indicate a decrease in the use of doping substances

---

[16] ASADA, *supra* note 4.

[17] https://www.insidethegames.biz/articles/1054579/australian-sports-anti-doping-authority-appoint-policeman-as-new-chief-executive

[18] https://www.afld.fr/

by athletes in France from 2013 to 2014. The educational programmes have been successful in bringing down the doping rate.

AFLD partners with many organisations and individuals for its education programmes. These include:

- Doping organisation or sports institution: NADO, sports federations, CREPS (Centres de Ressources, d'Expertise et de Performance Sportive), clubs, etc. are privileged partners of the agency. The exchanges may include services, information, intelligence exchanges, providing advice, setting up of awareness and training programme, etc.
- A public or private laboratory: Research and scientific knowledge base is clearly a priority for the agency, which assigns every year an ever larger share of its resources to advance scientific knowledge. Participation by other actors and contributors also greatly improves and develop its detection methods.
- A higher education institution: The higher education institutions specialising not only in law, political science, sports, medicine, chemistry or biology but also in areas such as media communication, graphic design, management, etc. are engaged in a partnership with the agency.

China

The China Anti-Doping Agency (CHINADA) has taken quite a few steps for its education programme. It too has a dedicated tab on its website for 'Education'. It has a few sections under it. They are:

- **Access Control Programme:** The Access Control Programme is with regard to the effort that the athletes must make to gain anti-doping education and must take part in the anti-doping knowledge exam when they join a sports team at every level or are promoted to a higher sports rank, and they can only obtain the corresponding qualification after passing the exam.

At the moment, the Access Control Programme is mainly applied in the access of qualification for large-scale sports events. Since 2009, the Access Control Programme has been successfully implemented on athletes and their assistant personnel participating in such large-scale domestic and international sports events such as the 11th National Games, the 16th Asian Games, the 7th City Games, the 12th National Winter Games, the 30th Summer Olympic Games and the 22nd Winter Olympic Games.

- **Outreach Program:** Carrying out anti-doping education outreach activities (outreach targeting for athletes under 18 is Play True Generation) during important events (e.g., Olympic games) is an effective educational approach created and promoted by WADA. A place for the anti-doping education outreach activities is usually set up in the athletes' village, where the athletes stay; hence, it is easy to attract their attentions. Interesting activities are designed to engage the athletes and their assistant personnel to participate in the anti-doping knowledge question–answer sessions. The anti-doping knowledge will be spread by teaching through interesting activities via face-to-face communication with the athletes.

- **Training Courses:** The lecture on the anti-doping knowledge refers to a way of education in which training lecturers identified by the anti-doping agency spread the anti-doping knowledge to the athletes, their assistant personnel and the public through face-to-face communication, within the specified time, so as to improve their anti-doping awareness.

- **Tools:** The agency has specific training programmes for trainers, coaches and athletes. It has quizzes on its website, which makes the learning experience more interactive. To strengthen the anti-doping publicity, the anti-doping agency publishes a monthly journal named the *Anti-Doping*

Developments, which was revised in 2011 and 2015 respectively to realise excellence in the picture and its accompanying essay and expand the issuing scope. The anti-doping developments are sent to offices in charge of various sports bureaus in each province, anti-doping agency at the provincial level, sports science research institute at the provincial level, national high-level talents base and the doping checking sites, etc. each month, and the electronic copy of the anti-doping developments is uploaded on the website of the agency for download.

China does have anti-doping cases reported regularly and also falls in the category of top 10 countries under ADRV with 49 cases reported in ADRV. Therefore, putting more efforts to curb the practice, China has launched a more extensive anti-doping education programme that covers university students and senior high school students that are about to take sports tests to enter higher education. The programme includes adding anti-doping lessons to university curriculum and giving lectures to university applicants with sports specialty.

According to Du Lijun, director, CHINADA,

> From every level of our government, we have a very clear goal for our Chinese athletes, and that is for no positive doping cases to occur during the Olympics. This agency doesn't care about how many gold medals we have. We've been working very hard to cleanse China's name after some really bad situations ruined China's image.[19]

India

National Anti-Doping Agency (NADA), India, has taken quite a few steps towards education and outreach. Like other countries discussed previously, it is paying attention to follow Article 18.

---

[19] http://www.nytimes.com/2008/08/04/sports/olympics/04drugs.html

NADA has developed an extensive education programme, namely Programme for Education and Awareness on Anti Doping in Sports (PEADS). To know the exact requirement for this purpose, an Information and Education Committee (IEC) expert group has been constituted under the chairmanship of director general, NADA, to assist and advice NADA. PEADS is a comprehensive programme that has been planned with an objective to deal with different stakeholders in the country. Each stakeholder is clearly defined in this programme. The main stakeholders are NADA, Sports Authority of India (SAI) and National Dope Testing Laboratory (NDTL).

However, according to this research finding, it can be inferred that NADA's plan for education has all the right intentions but enforcement has been not as per the expectation.

A Pilot Study on the Awareness on Anti-Doping among Indian Sports-persons

To ascertain grass-roots reality more clearly on anti-doping education, a pilot sample of 75 national and international sportsperson residing in Gujarat was collected. The sample collection of 75 opinions was primarily made on the basis of general awareness about anti-doping regulation, understanding on ADRV and TUE, revised code of WADA 2015, and their opinion on need to go through a proper training. The research analysed the opinions of sports-persons, sports authorities, coaches and professors of a sports university who participated as sample. Their identity which forms the valuable sample of the research has been kept confidential. The researcher admits the limitation of research as it is a very comprehensive sample collected with limited number of questions. The scope of the research provides a reality check to understand optimum requirement to educate sports-persons. The same is also reflected from the responses of the athletes.

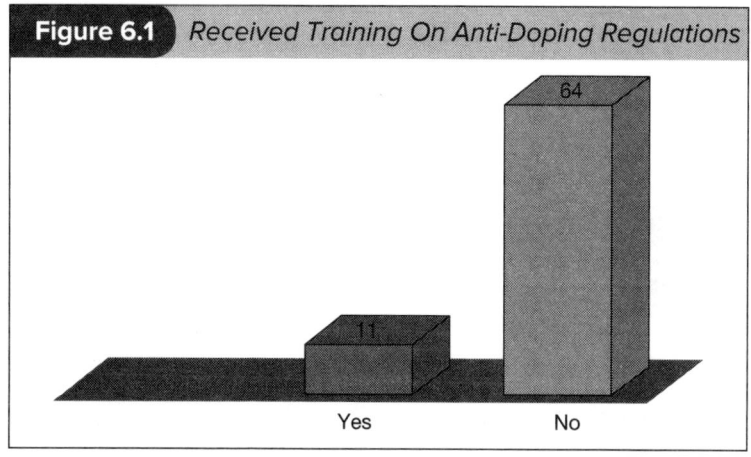

Figure 6.1 *Received Training On Anti-Doping Regulations*

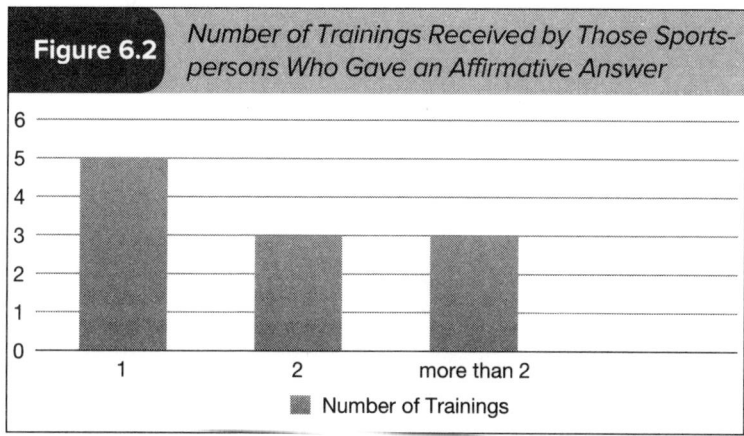

Figure 6.2 *Number of Trainings Received by Those Sportspersons Who Gave an Affirmative Answer*

Research Findings

Out of the total number of respondents, 85 per cent have informed that they have not received training on anti-doping regulations. Although a majority of them are aware of the test conducted by WADA, they were unaware of what actually involves in the regulation.

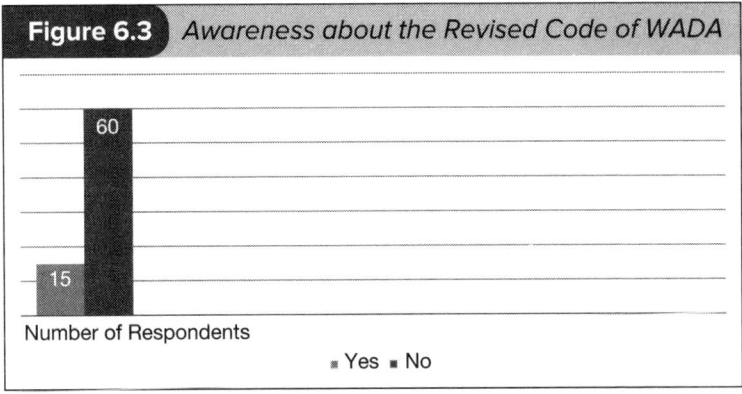

Figure 6.3 Awareness about the Revised Code of WADA

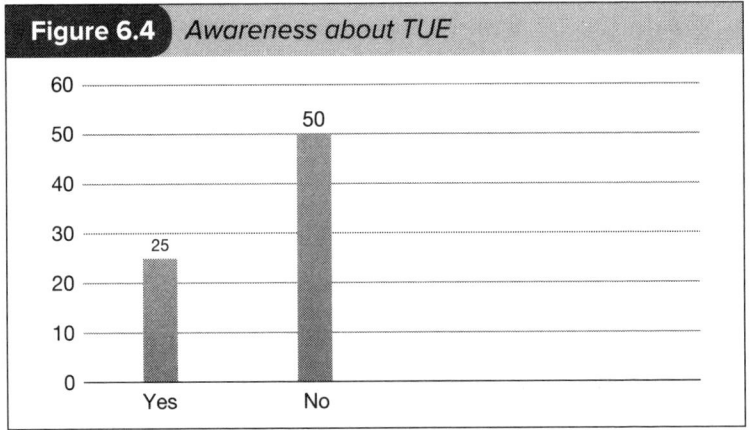

Figure 6.4 Awareness about TUE

Out of the total number of respondents, 44 per cent have received 1 training, 33 per cent have received 2 trainings and only 33 per cent have received more than 2 trainings.

Out of the total number of respondents, only 20 per cent were aware of the revised code of WADA 2015, while 80 per cent sports-persons were unaware of it.

Out of total number of respondents, 33 per cent respondents were aware of the TUE, while 67 per cent sports-persons were unaware of it.

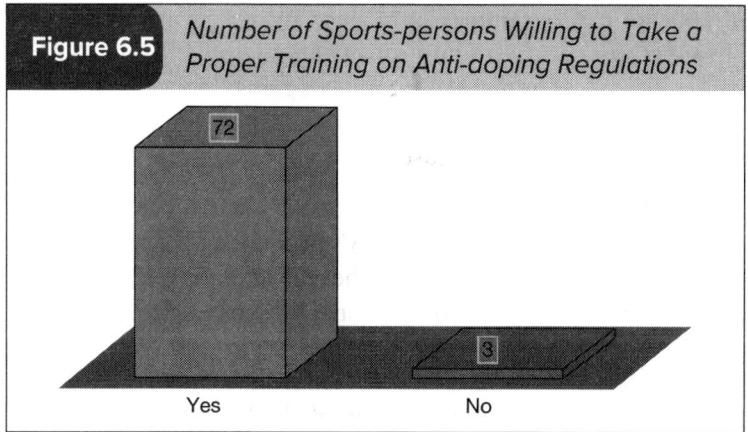

Figure 6.5 Number of Sports-persons Willing to Take a Proper Training on Anti-doping Regulations

Out of the total number of respondents, 96 per cent were willing to take to take a proper training on anti-doping regulations.

It was found that except some, most sports-persons were aware of NADA's responsibility of education, but they knew nothing of the details. When asked further questions on the basic understanding of ADRV, they knew very little or were more or less unaware of it. While having discussion with sports–persons, it was generally found that peculiarities related to whereabouts, ADDP (Anti Doping Disciplinary Panel) and ADAP (Anti Doping Appeal Panel) sports associates were unknown to the athletes or the knowledge was limited. Due to this, their separate findings are not shown in graph.[20]

The findings of the empirical study are further substantiated by the questions that were asked by Shri Chandu Lal Sahu and Shri Raghav Lakhanpal in Lok Sabha. The same was answered by Shri Vijay Goel, then minister of state (independent charge) for youth affairs and sports, making a proclamation that the number

---

[20] The researcher would like to set a disclaimer as this is to assist the government to determine its future policy and it does not intend to demean the efforts of the government.

of education programmes have been increased in 2014–2015. However, as per the requisition mentioned in PEADS, NADA conducted 55 training programmes against the requisition of 60.[21] This is even less than their own set target. At the same time, numbers of doping cases have increased from 95 in 2014 to 120 in 2015.[22]

Another problem is with NADA's pedagogy. The programmes undertaken by NADA, involving the education of sports-persons, consist of a very general conventional style of teaching. The language used is English, which may not be understood by everyone. Hence, stress should be given on vernacular and the script used in the presentation should also be of the local language of the sports-persons for better understanding by the sports-persons. The presentation should be more attractive, entertaining, engaging, interactive and at the same time simple so that the athletes can easily get acquainted with technicalities of doping, and mission of education regarding anti-doping (Article 18) can be accomplished.

Conclusion

To conclude, it can be definitely asserted that India is continuously making efforts to comply with the standard set by WADA to obtain its goal of 'dope-free sport'. However, India has a long way to go before it can be at par with the efforts and measures taken by other nations in these regards. There is a need to create a mass-level programme reaching up to amateur sports culture. It is high time to take proper measures because just increasing the number of training programmes by NADA as compared to the preceding year does not seem to be effective for reducing the doping cases of Indian athletes. On the contrary, the number

[21] PEADS, NADA.
[22] Starred Question No. 159, Lok Sabha Government of India, Ministry of Youth Affairs and Sports (Department of Sports).

of cases had increased drastically in the year 2015. As a result, like various other nations, organisational endeavour needs to be studied and appropriate measures should to be taken to curb the menace of doping in India.

There are many areas where education programmes need improvement in India.

Certainly, NADA needs to play a more active role in imparting education, being the leading RADO of India. Certain extra-mile efforts programme is expected from NADA in the era of Digital India; also, it must be more athlete-friendly rather than being authoritative. It should be on social media like other RADOs or can come up with a 'Mobile Application' on anti-doping education as well as can start an online course.

Looking at the other side, NADA cannot be blamed totally for the poor quality of education. Reason being its very limited staff and a very limited infrastructure facility. It has only nine members from a director general to a peon, and expecting success from a team of just nine members would be unjust. It would be more appropriate that state-based education bodies are set up under the vigilance of NADA. In 2010, China had a team of 60, and I am pretty sure that the number must have increased by now.

As per Article 18.2 of WADC, government as well as NADA must take the support of media in diffusing the information. The way Indian media is promoting Swachh Bharat Abhiyan for the spirit of clean India, it can be an inspiration to start a campaign for *clean sports and fairness in the game.*

Incorporating anti-doping information in physical education curriculum in State Board and NCERT books can further help students to have a better understanding of doping-free sports.

Last and most importantly, there has to be a more collective and conducive effort towards enforcement of education programme to bring down the issue of doping.

Religious Dictates and Sports in India

Saurabh Mishra and Shreya Mishra

Introduction and Scope

Given the universal reach and pervasive nature of sport, it is hardly surprising that factors effecting as well as affecting globalisation today are manifest in various examples within sport. While such manifestation is usually positive, given the inherently inclusive nature of sports which are globally prevalent, every once in a while we find ourselves standing at a crossroads between the rules of a game and various sociocultural norms. This chapter examines such an instance which occurred within the realm of professional basketball.

During the fifth edition of the Asia Cup in China, hosted in 2015, two Sikh members of the Indian contingent, namely Amritpal Singh and Amjyot Singh, were required to remove their turbans in order for them to be allowed to compete.[1] However,

---

[1] M. Kulkarni, *Sikh Basketball Players Required to Remove Turbans in Controversial Decision*, LawInSport (1 August 2014), *available at* http://www.lawinsport.com/blog/indian-sports-law/item/

the same came as a surprise to the athletes on account of having been allowed to play the sport with their turbans in the past. A positive fallout from the incident was the Government of India, through the Ministry of Youth Affairs and Sports, writing to the International Olympic Committee (IOC) in a bid for the IOC to introduce a regulation with regard to certain permitted headgear,[2] as an exception to the rule in concern. It is possible that an increased commercial presence of the sport in India today is something that encouraged the government to make a contentious representation.

A nation like India becomes a crucial party in any such instance, due to the same being home to various cultures. Consequently, a large number of athletes practising a plethora of religions would be affected by any regulation which would curtail their right to do so. Additionally, Asia's rise as a viable market for global sports aids the nation's influence when it comes to advocating for a change. A good example of this would indeed be the case being discussed herein, which portrays the benefit of sport becoming a global phenomenon, to the extent that it now needs to accommodate culture.

Prior to examining the intricacies of the predicament which forms the subject matter of this particular chapter, it is imperative that the authors lay down certain basic facts in order to provide a first-time reader with a comprehensive yet simple background to the issue at hand. In order to go about the same in a systematic manner, this chapter has primarily been divided into four key portions, after Introduction.

In the second part, the authors introduce Article 4.4.2 of the Federation of International Basketball Association (FIBA) regulations as it stood prior to its recent amendment, and examine the implications of the same from an athlete's perspective.

---

sikh-basketball-players-required-to-remove-turbans-in-controversial-decision?highlight=WyJ0dXJiYW4iXQ==
  [2] *Id.*

The third part analyses the human rights aspect of sport in general and goes on to ascertain whether FIBA has indeed made an effort to ensure that inclusiveness and secularism form the backbone of the regulating legislation.

The fourth part looks at the remedial steps taken by FIBA to rectify a discriminatory application of the impugned provision.

In the fifth part, prior to concluding, the authors elucidate upon FIBA's final decision and compare the same to a similar amendment effected previously by Federation Internationale de Football Association (FIFA).

Article 4.4.2 of the FIBA Regulations (Erstwhile): An Athlete's Perspective

The premise of this chapter revolves, albeit indirectly, around the global nature of sport, especially the athletic competitions which are a part of the Olympic Movement, since the same has as its objective the uniform development of the world through sport at a global level through cooperation as well as inclusiveness.[3] Essentially, each and every sport is regulated more or less in a uniform manner, with a pyramidal structure in place, with the IOC at the top of the same, overseeing the entities operating at the lower rungs, namely the international federations as well as the national bodies supervising the respective sport within the territorial boundaries of the member states.

Effective propagation of every sport would ideally require a streamlined set-up, incorporating all such entities, where the same cooperate with each other in their functioning. However, due to an ever-changing geopolitical scenario, which carries with it an undeniable element of cultural dynamism, it is becoming rather

---

[3] International Olympic Committee, *Factsheet: The Olympic Movement* (April 2015), *available at* http://www.olympic.org/Documents/Reference_documents_Factsheets/The_Olympic_Movement.pdf

challenging to reconcile the uniformity of the regulations, with the cultural diversity actively becoming a part of sport.

A prime example of such a conflict, therefore, is FIBA's erstwhile rule regarding headgear in basketball, as per Article 4.4.2 of the statute:[4]

> Players shall not wear equipment (objects) that may cause injury to other players.
>
> - The following are not permitted:
>   - Finger, hand, wrist, elbow or forearm guards, casts or braces made of leather, plastic, pliable (soft) plastic, metal or any other hard substance, even if covered with soft padding.
>   - Objects that could cut or cause abrasions (fingernails must be closely cut).
>   - Headgear, hair accessories and jewellery.
> - The following are permitted:
>   - Shoulder, upper arm, thigh or lower leg protective equipment if the material is sufficiently padded.
>   - Compression sleeves of the same dominant colour as the shirts.
>   - Compression stockings of the same dominant colour as the shorts. If for the upper leg it must end above the knee; if for the lower leg it must end below the knee.
>   - Knee braces if they are properly covered.
>   - Protector for an injured nose, even if made of a hard material.
>   - Non-coloured transparent mouth guard.
>   - Spectacles, if they do not pose a danger to other players.
>   - Headbands, maximum 5 cm in width, made of non-abrasive, unicolour cloth, pliable plastic or rubber.
>   - Non-coloured transparent taping of arms, shoulders, legs, etc.

The statute banned an athlete from using any sort of headgear, except a headband consistent with the specifications stated

---

[4] Article 4.4.2, Official Basketball Rules 2014, Approved by the FIBA Central Board on 2 February 2014, *available at* https://www.fiba.com/downloads/Rules/2014/Official_Basketball_Rules_2014_Y.pdf

within the provision itself. This was stated by the federation to be a safety measure necessary in order to prevent injuries while a game is in progress.

However, a negative fallout of the same was felt, in recent times, by athletes who chose to wear headgear for reasons unconnected to sport, with the same being linked mostly to cultural identity. Multiple incidents regarding a clash between this particular rule of the game and religious diktats of varying nature led to a major rethink. This is largely owing to the fact that even though the rule itself was purported to be a safety measure,[5] the inadvertent, yet adverse, impact it had on the effort to increase inclusiveness and secularism in sport is rather undeniable. A direct result was palpable tension with regard to the implementation of such a rule, without reasonable exceptions being put in place to provide against extraneous factors.

The aim herein is to explore such a conflict and the process of resolving the same from varying perspectives. The primary aim of such a process is to establish the federation's rationale behind persisting with the provision in concern even in the face of constant, and rather severe criticism emanating from the other key stakeholder, the athlete. Furthermore, a significant fallout of such a stance is the effect such a rule could have on the long-term cooperation between the different rungs of the aforementioned pyramid within the sport of basketball.

As the game has expanded to new territories, aside from the commercial as well as athletic challenges to such expansion, it now has to deal with a rather sensitive element in the form of racial and cultural segregation. As such, the rule was challenged keeping in mind the very ethos of the Olympic Movement, which aims at secular expansion of sport. Therefore, the debate herein was also regarding whether the rule itself can be reconciled with the universally guaranteed freedom of an athlete to propagate his/her religion.

[5] Wordbulletin, *FIBA Defends Decision on Qatar Hijab Row* (26 September 2014), *available at* http://www.worldbulletin.net/news/145228/fiba-defends-decision-on-qatar-hijab-row

Sports and Human Rights: How Inclusive Are the Statutes?

In this regard, Article 1.3 of the FIBA General Statutes assumes relevance, owing to the same setting the premise, at the very outset, to be that of a sport which values inclusiveness and secularism above all else.

> FIBA maintains absolute political and religious neutrality and does not tolerate any form of discrimination.[6]

However, while a combined reading of Article 4.4.2 of the FIBA statute and the aforementioned provision does not necessarily give rise to a conflict, the effect of the former certainly put FIBA in a spot of bother, owing to there being an apparent inconsistency in the way the rules of the game have been designed. While FIBA's fundamental stance regarding secularism and neutrality on all contentious fronts being the basic elements is rather admirable, perhaps the federation's lack of long-term vision becomes evident upon reading the specific provision in concern, in as much as a uniform application of a rule as strictly worded as Article 4.4.2 is rather impossible, practically speaking.

The aim of the federation, in their defence, was to ensure that the rules as per the statute are interpreted as well as implemented in a purely sporting context, with no other factor influencing the same. However, given the rapidly expanding reach of the sport, aided further by commercial considerations, such factors intertwining with the fundamental rules of the game was but an inevitability. As such, assuming a non-contentious operation of any such rule would be a rather naïve notion.

A rather popular example in this regard is that of Bilqis Abdul-Qaadir, who after plying her trade in the NCAA Division I in

---

[6] Article 1.3, FIBA General Statutes, Approved at the FIBA Congress of 28–29 August 2014, *available at* https://www.fiba.com/downloads/Regulations/2014/ FIBAGeneralStatutes_ApprovedbyExtraordinaryCongress16March2014_ English.pdf

the USA decided to pursue a career in professional basketball, albeit in Europe.[7] However, she found her way blocked by the FIBA regulation in concern, since European basketball operates under the aegis of FIBA, which meant that unlike in the USA, she would have to compete without religious headgear owing to the same being banned under Article 4.4.2. Interestingly enough, the NCAA Rulebook states that 'Head decorations, head wear and jewellery are illegal'.[8] However, players are allowed to compete regardless of religious headgear, which clearly implies a much more accommodative stance towards the same, as compared to that of the international federation, at the time.

Another incident along the same lines saw Indira Kaljo,[9] a Bosnian athlete based in California, who was having to choose between a career in basketball and her faith, since she belatedly chose to wear a hijab while pursuing a career as a professional athlete. However, her path too was hindered by the provision in concern. While launching a petition[10] to do away with the rule itself, Kaljo raised a valid point about a tightly worded provision indirectly disallowing a large number of people from pursuing the sport while representing their ideologies at the same time, and that in itself is a rather serious prospect, in as much as it creates an entry barrier into basketball, which is largely unrelated to sport, despite the federation's stance regarding neutrality with regard to the operation of the regulations.

[7] Z. V. Kanno-Youngs, *For Bilqis Abdul-Qaadir, a Wish that FIBA Would Catch Up to FIFA*, USA TODAY (6 July 2015), *available at* http://www.usatoday.com/story/sports/olympics/2015/07/05/fiba-fifa-headscarves-scarf-muslim-rules-bilqis-abdul-qaadir/29605587/

[8] Rule 3, Section 9, Article 7, NCAA Basketball Men's and Women's Rules, *available at* http://www.naia.org/fls/27900/1NAIA/resources/sid/Rule%20Books/BASKETR.pdf?DB_OEM_ID=27900

[9] Al Jazeera, *Basketball OKs Use of Religious Headwear* (16 September 2014), *available at* http://america.aljazeera.com/articles/2014/9/16/basketball-oks-playerheadgear.html

[10] I. Kaljo, *Remove Ban on Wearing Head Scarf during Competition*, CHANGE.ORG, *available at* https://www.change.org/p/fiba-f%C3%A9d%C3%A9ration-internationale-de-basketball-remove-ban-on-wearing-head-scarf-during-competition

Looking at the issue from an athlete's perspective such as in this case, it becomes clear why the controversy also has a human rights angle attached to it. There is a clear choice to be made between pursuing one's right to livelihood and the freedom to practise a religion. The Universal Declaration of Human Rights (UDHR) guarantees a person's freedom to choose and manifest any religion, under Article 18[11] of the instrument.

Everyone has the right to freedom of thought, conscience and religion; this right includes freedom to change his religion or belief, and freedom, either alone or in community with others and in public or private, to manifest his religion or belief in teaching, practice, worship and observance.

In light of this, application of the impugned provision seemed to go against a universally accepted principle of human rights, in as much as it hindered the right and freedom mentioned previously and, therefore, assumed the character of being discriminatory in nature. In this regard, Human Rights Watch, in the aftermath of the Asian Games, launched a scathing attack on the federation by stating that 'it is difficult to see how a ban on the headscarf is anything other than an unnecessary restriction on the players' rights to religious freedom and personal autonomy'.[12]

The situation became all the more perplexing due to inconsistencies within the game itself, which allows for the headgear to be used in competitions not being regulated by FIBA. Thus, the athletes were right in questioning the rationale behind such a selective application of a safety measure, especially since uniformity within the sport is a major argument being presented by the federation in defence of this provision.

A lack of clarity in this regard has in the past led to confusion regarding the application of the rule itself at the top level, which

[11] Article 18, Universal Declaration of Human Rights.
[12] N. Kim, *Archers Take Aim at Basketball's Hijab Ban Reuters* (26 September 2014), *available at* http://in.reuters.com/article/2014/09/26/games-asian-archery-hijab-idINKCN0HL0J720140926

was perhaps slightly embarrassing from FIBA's point of view. Differing statements from officials with respect to the permissibility of headgear have, in the past, led to confusion among the athletes, who have consequently suffered in their attempt to represent their nation as well as their faith. A key incident to be cited in this instance perhaps would be the women's basketball team from Qatar withdrawing from the 2014 Asian Games, held in Incheon.[13]

Remedial Steps Taken by FIBA

Debate surrounding the effect of Article 4.4.2 was yet another example of how significant a role is played by sport in general, and bodies in charge of regulating the sport specifically, to ensure that sociocultural inclusiveness is more than just a utopian concept. As a corollary, the negative implementation of such an instrument inadvertently leads to marginalisation at a large scale, which defeats the entire purpose of an Olympic sport, such as basketball. Therefore, where there exists a mischief in the rules of the game, it is imperative that the same be remedied in a manner which is consistent with the rights of those most affected by the mischief in the first place. In this regard, it is the authors' opinion that FIBA's handling of the issue was rather pragmatic, and fair.

In the first meeting of the newly elected Central Board under the leadership of Horacio Muratore, the members discussed the rules regarding uniforms in light of several requests received with regard to the same and suggested the implementation of a testing phase in the consequent press release, for a period of two years.[14] This relaxation, however, was limited in its scope and

[13] M. Kulkarni, *Qatar Women's Basketball Team Withdraw from Asian Games as Hijab Ban Continues*, LAWINSPORT (25 September 2014), *available at* http://www.lawinsport.com/blog/indian-sports-law/item/qatar-women-s-basketball-team-withdraw-from-asian-games-as-hijab-ban-continues

[14] PR No. 56, *Key Appointments Headline First Meeting of Newly-elected Central Board*, FIBA (16 September 2014), *available at* http://www.fiba.com/news/pr-n56–key-appointments-headline-first-meeting-of-newly-elected-central-board

effect, as it was to be implemented at the national level, upon the respective national federation applying for the same. At the international level, the rule was to be relaxed for the 3×3 format of the sport, with the athlete desirous of using headgear in competition required to duly apply for a permission for the same. FIBA also required the national federations to submit follow-up reports twice a year. Such reports were then monitored by FIBA, with focus on any instances threatening player safety.

– Relaxing the current rules regarding headgear in order to enable national federations to request, as of now, exceptions to be applied at the national level within their territory without incurring any sanctions for violation of FIBA's Official Basketball Rules. National Federations wishing to apply for such an exception to the uniform regulations shall submit a detailed request to FIBA. Once approved, they shall submit follow-up reports twice a year to monitor the use of such exceptions.

– The players will be allowed to play in FIBA endorsed 3×3 competitions—both nationally and internationally—wearing headgear without restrictions, unless the latter presents a direct threat to their safety or that of other players on the court. Players wishing to take part in such competitions with headgear must ensure that a detailed request for approval is addressed to FIBA.[15]

The move was celebrated as a victory by organisations such as the Sikh American Legal Defense and Education Fund (SALDEF), which advocated, through various online petitions, a rethink of the policy in concern, citing the often quoted belief regarding sports being a means of uniting people from diverse cultures, religions and races.[16]

With regard to the monitoring of exemptions, a number of parameters were to be looked by FIBA, such as the

[15] *Id.*

[16] F. K. Wang, *Basketball Federation Refuses to Rule on Turban Ban,* NBC News (28 August 2014), *available at* http://www.nbcnews.com/news/asian-america/basketball-federation-refuses-rule-turban-ban-n191316

specifications regarding the headgear itself,[17] in as much as it would have to be manufactured in a manner which is most suitable with regard to safety of the athletes as well as the uniformity of equipment.[18] This was an attempt to ensure that the essence of the provision itself is not derogated, which is fair enough. Furthermore, an important criteria to be considered is the effect such a measure would have on participation in basketball within the territories vying for the rule to be amended.[19] This is especially encouraging since the same pointed to a tacit recognition, from the Board, of the fact that a secular expansion of sport is perhaps not possible without leaving scope for a certain amount of flexibility in order to accommodate the various cultural beliefs that come with the propagation of any movement at a global level.

A primary report was to be provided to the Central Board in 2015, following which a full review of the developments in the relaxation period was to be done. This full review was to be conducted after the Summer Olympics in Rio, held last year.[20] Only after this segmented analysis was FIBA to rule upon the need for a relaxation of the impugned provision. Subsequently, the FIBA Central Board, during its first conference of the calendar year 2017, analysed a report centred on the impact of such exceptional application of the rule, and recommended that the rule be accordingly modified.[21]

> After initiating a revision process of the headgear rule (Article 4.4.2) of the Official Basketball Rules in September 2014, the Board received a report on the impact of the exceptions applied on a domestic level during a two-year period. It favoured a modification of the rule and issued a mandate for the Technical

[17] *Id.*
[18] *Id.*
[19] *Id.*
[20] *Id.*
[21] FIBA, *FIBA Central Board Makes Key Decisions during First Meeting of 2017* (30 January 2017), *available at* http://www.fiba.com/news/ fiba-central-board-makes-key-decisions-during-first-meeting-of-2017

Commission to come forward with a proposal that would allow headgear to be worn safely by athletes.

The FIBA and the FIFA: A Comparative Study of the Headgear Rules

Such recommendation of the Board, arrived at after analysing all the data available in this regard, was warmly welcomed by all those who had been rallying against the erstwhile application of Article 4.4.2.[22] Crucially, the recommendation was ratified unanimously at FIBA's first ever mid-term Congress held in Hong Kong in May 2017.[23] The result of this process was an amendment to the impugned regulation, to the effect that athletes of faith no longer have to strike a compromise between sport and religion. The new rule, effective from 1 October 2017, allows headgear to be worn by the athletes, provided the same adhere to the guidelines as issued by FIBA previously.[24] To clarify, these guidelines are reasonable as well as broad enough so as to not bar any form of religious headgear, and in fact have been directly imported to form the new rule:[25]

The following are permitted:

Headgear of the same dominant colour as the shirts, or black, or white, but all players on the team must wear the same colour. The

[22] CAIR, *CAIR Welcomes FIBA's Move to Allow Religious Headgear* (5 February 2017), *available at* https://www.cair.com/press-center/press-releases/14087-cair-welcomes-fiba-s-move-to-allow-religious-headgear.html; House Democrats, *Crowley and Bera Announce Major Step Forward in Fight Against International Basketball Federation's Discriminatory Policy on Sikh Players* (2 February 2017), *available at* http://www.dems.gov/crowley-bera-announce-major-step-forward-fight-international-basketball-federations-discriminatory-policy-sikh-players/
[23] FIBA, *FIBA's Mid-Term Congress Unanimously Ratifies New Headgear Rule* (4 May 2017), *available at* http://www.fiba.com/news/fibas-mid-term-congress-ratifies-new-headgear-rule
[24] *Id.*
[25] Article 4.4.2, Official Basketball Rules 2017, *available at* http://www.fiba.basketball/OBR2017/v11/15Aug2017.pdf

headgear shall not cover any part of the face entirely or partially (eyes, nose, lips etc.) and shall not be dangerous to the player wearing it and/or to other players. The headgear shall not have opening/closing elements around the face and/or neck and shall not have any parts extruding from its surface.

Of course, this is not the first time that such a rule has been successfully challenged, with FIFA having witnessed a similar conundrum in the past. Having originally banned the use of headgear while playing football, once again on the grounds of safety,[26] FIFA undertook a similar process whereby it monitored the use of the same during a two-year long trial period.[27] Subsequently, the ban was lifted, and the rule in concern was accordingly amended:[28]

> Where head covers are worn, they must
>
> - be black or of the same main colour as the jersey (provided that the players of the same team wear the same colour)
>
> - be in keeping with the professional appearance of the player's equipment
>
> - not be attached to the shirt
>
> - not be dangerous to the player wearing it or any other player (e.g. opening/closing mechanism around neck)
>
> - not have any part(s) extending out from the surface (protruding elements)

The language of this provision, issued by the International Football Association Board (IFAB), is evidently similar to the headgear rule as amended by FIBA. The timing of the changes by

[26] Reuters/AFP, *FIFA Lifts Ban on Hijab for Women Footballers The Tribune*, 6 July 2012, *available at* http://tribune.com.pk/story/404321/fifa-lifts-ban-on-headscarves-for-women-footballers/

[27] Al Jazeera, *FIFA Lifts Ban on Head Covers* (1 March 2014), *available at* http://www.aljazeera.com/sport/football/2014/03/fifa-allows-hijab-turban-players-20143113053667394.html

[28] Law 4 (4), Laws of the Game 2017/18, IFAB, *available at* http://www.the-afc.com/uploads/afc/files/IFAB-laws-of-the-game-2017-2018.pdf

FIBA was perhaps strategic, given that the same was to take effect just prior to the Africa Champions Cup, as well as the FIBA U-16 Asian Championship, in 2017. Indeed, a somewhat persuasive factor for such a change at the time was Jordan's successful bid to host the U-17 Women's World Cup in 2016,[29] which once again underlines the interplay between sport and society.

Conclusion

At this point in time, basketball is at a crossroads, in as much as expansion into newer territories, in order to truly be regarded as a global phenomenon, is very much the next step for the sport. An amendment to aid inclusiveness, therefore, should help FIBA in achieving any such objective. However, regardless of motive, there is little doubt that FIBA handled the situation as best it could, and the outcome has been immensely positive. The procedural commonalities shared with FIFA could mean that such gradual progression can be viewed as a blueprint to be followed by other sporting organisations, if the need shall so arise. Given the dynamic nature of both, sport and society, such a conflict of rules is perhaps inevitable. As such, the reach of basketball as well as the rapid expansion of the sport that is underway, a somewhat radical change in position by an important sporting federation sets a positive precedent.

[29] *Id.*

Arbitration and Sports Disputes in India

Daniel Mathew

As in all matters, disputes remain a silent yet potent possibility in sports. Given the high stakes in terms of athletes' career, and technicalities including pressures of time that is involved, over the years enormous investment has gone into structuring efficient dispute resolution mechanisms to resolve sports disputes. These mechanisms are highly customised and continuously fine-tuned to render a timely award that remains relevant given the short duration over which a sporting event takes place. This piece aims to delve deeper into issues surrounding utilisation on one specific method of alternate dispute resolution, namely arbitration in resolving sports disputes. Over the years, arbitration has emerged as the method of choice for resolving sports-related disputes with Court of Arbitration for Sports (CAS) being a widely acclaimed success story. However, for arbitration to operationalise, presence of certain core requirements such as existence of valid arbitration agreement and jurisdictional competence of the arbitral tribunal must first materialise. The attempt here is to explore some of these core issues in the context of arbitration laws of India, namely the Arbitration and Conciliation Act, 1996 (1996 Act), as amended in 2015. The first part of the chapter would briefly discuss the intersection of arbitration and resolution of sports disputes. The second part would explore issues of consent that constitutes an imperative requirement of any arbitration. The third part would explore the legality of multi-tier arbitration clause routinely provided for in sporting regulations such as constitution of Indian Olympic Association (IOA) in light of recent decisions of the Supreme Court of India. The fourth part would evaluate the establishment of arbitral tribunals under applicable rules for its conformity to the standards of independence and impartiality as expanded upon by the Indian judiciary.

Introduction

The need for alternate methods of dispute resolution arose out of the disillusionment from state-based methods of dispute resolution, namely the courts. Lengthy, costly and highly technical and complex procedures ensured that the outcome was often of little consequence if at all any to the litigants.[1] Faced with a judicial system that was fast losing its ability to deliver on promises of speedy and effective justice, efforts were intensified to find meaningful alternates that would assist and in some instances replace the courts as the primary mechanisms for resolving disputes.

India has a well-documented history of extensive utilisation of non-state-based methods of dispute resolution. Be it panchayats,

[1] M/s Guru Nanak Foundations v. M/s Rattan Singh & Sons, AIR 1981 SC 2075.

Interminable, time consuming, complex and expensive Court procedures impelled jurists to search for an alternative forum, less formal, more effective and speedy for resolution of disputes avoiding procedural claptrap and this led them to the Arbitration Act 1940. However the way in which the proceedings under the Act are conducted and without an exception challenged in Courts, has made lawyers laugh and legal philosophers weep.

Similar comments were reiterated by the Supreme Court in Food Corporation of India v. Joginderpal Mohinderpal, AIR 1989 SC 1263.

Puga, Sreni and *Kula*[2] early texts are replete with references to board of persons entrusted with the duty of amicably resolving disputes in a society, community, village or among traders and artisans.[3] Early colonial efforts such as regulations of 1772, 1781, 1813 and 1822 aimed at consolidating and systematising previous ad hoc methods and bringing them within a state-sanctioned and recognised system of resolving disputes through arbitration. Legal developments, both pre and post independence, ensured that law relating to ADR (Alternate Dispute Resolution) methods was continuously updated, keeping pace with the ever-growing and complex demands of an increasingly aware polity.

In 1996, the Indian arbitration law was updated to bring it in line with prevailing international standards. In sharp contrast to earlier regulations, the 1996 Act was expanded to allow for arbitration of a wide range of disputes. Arbitration is a private and consensual method of resolving disputes, with the following key elements:[4] (a) agreement to arbitrate (consent and intention); (b) a legal dispute; (c) submission of dispute to a neutral independent party for its determination; and (d) binding end result.

However, not all types of disputes are arbitrable. Even though the 1996 Act does not explicitly list types of disputes that cannot be arbitrated, both legislative and judicial limitations on the nature of disputes that are considered inarbitrable have been readily established.[5] In other words, every civil or commercial disputer, either contractual or otherwise, which could be decided by a court was in principle capable of being adjudicated and resolved by arbitration unless excluded either expressly or by

[2] These are Sanskrit/Hindi terms considered forerunners to a formal arbitral tribunal.

[3] Law Commission of India, *Arbitration Act, 1940* (Law Com No. 76, 1978), paras 1.11–1.12. V. A. MOHTA & ANOOP V. MOHTA, ARBITRATION, CONCILIATION AND MEDIATION 2 (2nd ed. 2008).

[4] NIGEL BLACKABY ET AL., REDFERN AND HUNTER ON INTERNATIONAL ARBITRATION 2 (6th ed. September 2015).

[5] Section 2(4): 'A dispute concerning a matter which by virtue of a law is made inarbitrable, cannot be referred to arbitration under the 1996 Act'.

necessary implication. In a similar vein, certain set of disputes have been held to be of such nature that renders it unsuitable to be arbitrated. In *Booz Allen* v. *SBI Home Finance*[6] (Booz Allen), the Supreme Court of India had crystallised the principle of inarbitrability, noting that the disputes of certain nature could not be referred to arbitration. Consequently, the 1996 Act applies to all arbitration that take place in India, and portions of it apply to arbitral awards from arbitration that happen outside India and which are sought to be enforced within the territory of India.[7]

Sports disputes do not fall within the exclusion list drawn up by the 1996 Act and the Booz Allen formula, and therefore are amenable to arbitration within the Indian jurisdiction. Even globally, arbitration is the most preferred method of resolving sports dispute, with CAS being the most prominent example of the alliance.[8] Adjudication of sports disputes through arbitration in India would be regulated by the Memorandum and Rules and Regulations of Indian Olympic Association,[9] rules arbitration

---

[6] Booz Allen v. SBI Home Finance, (2011) 5 SCC 532.

The well recognized examples of non-arbitrable disputes are: (i) disputes relating to rights and liabilities which give rise to or arise out of criminal offences; (ii) matrimonial disputes relating to divorce, judicial separation, restitution of conjugal rights, child custody; (iii) guardianship matters; (iv) insolvency and winding up matters; (v) testamentary matters (grant of probate, letters of administration and succession certificate); and (vi) eviction or tenancy matters governed by special statutes where the tenant enjoys statutory protection against eviction and only the specified courts are conferred jurisdiction to grant eviction or decide the disputes. (para 22)

[7] Part I applies to all arbitration that happen in India and Part II applies to foreign awards sought to be enforced in India. See also Balco Aluminium v. Kaiser Aluminium, (2012) 9 SCC 552.

[8] Hilary A. Findlay, *Symposium: Alternate Dispute Resolution in Sports: Rules of a Sport Specific Arbitration Process as an Instrument of Policy Making*, 16 MARQ. SPORTS L. REV. 73, 73–77 (2005).

[9] IOA Rules, Rule XXII r/w Rule XXIV.

commission (RAC),[10] rules of the sporting federation and the 1996 Act.[11] Although sports disputes render themselves to arbitration, given their nature is not in contention, the structuring of dispute resolution mechanisms within various sporting regulations generates certain crucial issues requiring a deeper look.

Consent: Arbitration Agreement

Arbitration is a method of private dispute resolution and is contingent on the consent of all parties involved therein. Consent, therefore, is the edifice on which the entire arbitration is premised, that is, a pre-requisite of arbitration.[12] In other words, unless a party gives its consent to arbitration, it cannot be compelled to arbitrate its dispute. Consent of the parties is contained within the arbitration agreement, by entering into which the parties voluntarily relinquish their right to have disputes adjudicated through a court-based system. An arbitration agreement indicates the intention of the parties to resolve their matter through arbitration.

Consent for arbitrating sports disputes in India can be found in the Memorandum and Rules and Regulations of the Indian

---

[10] RAC Section 8: Application of the Rules:

These Procedural Rules apply whenever the parties have agreed to refer a sports related dispute to the CAS. Such disputes may arise as a result of various reasons which necessitated the creation of CAS by Indian Olympic Association in accordance with its constitution. All the members of IOA are bound by the Constitution of IOA which mandates the Sports related disputes to be adjudicated by CAS. Such disputes may involve matters of principle relating to sport or matters of pecuniary or other interests brought into play in the practice or the development of sport and, generally speaking, any activity related or connected to sport.

[11] Section 2(2): 'This Part shall apply where the place of arbitration is in India'.

[12] Andrea M. Steingruber, CONSENT IN INTERNATIONAL ARBITRATION (2012), paras 5.43–5.44.

Olympic Association (IOA rules) which requires all NDFs, state Olympic associations, union territory Olympic associations, services sports control board and national federation of Indian sport kho-kho affiliated to IOA to include within their constitution a provision to have their unresolved disputes including sports-related ones arbitrated. This would also include all disputes arising within these federations and associations. The arbitration would be conducted by an arbitration commission (AC) established by IOA, with its members appointed by the latter.[13]

The rules are equally categorical in their requirement that the members of the federation and association voluntarily surrender the right to seek redress in a court of law. Such stipulation is necessary to prevent a party from readily avoiding arbitration by instituting an action before the state courts. Under the 1996 Act, any judicial authority faced with a valid arbitration agreement[14] is mandatorily required to refer that matter to arbitration. Equally clear is that such mandatory reference,[15] which does act as a restraint against legal proceedings, is not illegal. Under the Indian contract law, any agreement attempting to restrain a party from enforcing its rights by way of legal proceedings before an ordinary tribunal is considered void.[16] However, this rule is subject to three exceptions, one of which permits parties to legitimately impose a restriction by way of an arbitration agreement.[17]

At this juncture, it is important to query whether the IOA rules indeed form a valid arbitration agreement. The requirements of a valid arbitration agreement are drawn from both the 1996 Act and the Indian Contract Act, 1872.[18] Thus, in addition to the

---

[13] IOA Rules, Rule XXII(i) and (ii) r/w Rule XXVIII(e).

[14] The recent amendment to the 1996 Act clarified the requirement noting that the reviewing authority is only required to ensure that the arbitration agreement is valid prima facie.

[15] P. Anand Gajapathi Raju v. P. V. G. Raju, AIR 2000 SC 1886.

[16] Indian Contract Act 1872, Section 28.

[17] Indian Contract Act 1872, Exception 1 to Section 28.

[18] A conjoint reading of Arbitration and Conciliation Act, 1996, Section 7, and Indian Contract Act, 1872, Sections 10 and 11. In addition thereto, a series of decisions by the Indian courts has elaborated upon this aspect.

requirement of free consent as noted previously, other requirements, namely of writing, competency to contract and a clear and unequivocal intention to arbitrate, become crucial.[19] Viewed in that light, these rules clearly require a sporting federation or association, affiliated or recognised or desirous of being so by IOA, to provide consent to arbitrating its disputes.

From arbitration standpoint, an important question would be whether these provisions[20] fulfil the requirement of clear and unambiguous consent. The rule clearly notes that any federation affiliated with IOA has to submit to mandatory arbitration. It backs it up with a requirement of a waiver of right to seek remedy in court. All affiliated federations are bound to abide by the rule. On their affiliation, they accept to abide by the rules of IOA, including ones pertaining to dispute resolution. The rules require acceptance in their entirety. A federation cannot pick and choose the rules that it would obey. Thus, the single composite acceptance of all rules would effectively meet the unequivocal consent standard. These rules are similar to the ones found in trade associations which require its members to arbitrate their disputes.[21] In such instances, consent and intent to arbitrate are

[19] Jagdish Chander v. Ramesh Chander, (2007) 5 SCC 719. Mere acquiescence does not confer jurisdiction. See also UP Rajkiya Nirman Nigam Ltd v. Indure Private Ltd, AIR 1996 SC 1373.

[20] For instance, IOA Rules, XXII(i):

All National Sports Federations (subject to regulations and directives of their respective International Federations)/State Olympic Associations/Union Territory Olympic Associations/Services Sports Control Board/National Federation of Indian Sport Kho Kho affiliated to I.O.A. shall include in their Constitution a provision that the Federations/Associations would have all unresolved disputes settled by the Arbitration Commission of the IOA and their Members shall voluntarily surrender their right of seeking redress in any Court of Law.

[21] Groupe Chimique Tunisien SA v. Southern Petrochemicals Industries Corpn Ltd, 2006 (2) ArbLR 435 (SC). The respondent had placed a purchase order with the petitioner for supply of phosphoric acid. The purchase order stipulated that the terms and conditions were as per the Fertiliser Association

presumed on the basis of knowledge and awareness on the part of members; in other words, since the members utilise and work in accordance with the rules, their familiarity with the provisions of the rules including the presence of arbitration agreement within it is presumed. Being aware of the existence, and yet agreeing to operate and abide by the rules, indicates consent on the part of the members to the requirement of arbitration. Consequently, an affiliation or a request thereto translates into an acceptance of the offer to arbitrate. It implies an effective consent on behalf of the sporting federation and association to abide by the requirement and refer all their disputes to arbitration.[22]

There are, however, scholars who argue that consent for arbitration obtained through barring an athlete from participating in an event unless they consent would at least under the Indian law in view of Section 10 of the Indian Contract Act, 1872, vitiate arbitration agreement so entered.[23]

Tiered Arbitration Clauses

A crucial difference in arbitration when compared to the state-based court system is the nature of remedy available against a judgement of the tribunal. For matters wherein decision is rendered by a court, varying remedies, such as review, revision

---

of India (FAI) terms and conditions for sale and purchase of phosphoric acid. Clause 15 of FAI provided for settlement of dispute by arbitration. The question was whether there was arbitration agreement between the parties. The court held that there exists a valid arbitration agreement between the parties. A justification forwarded was that of knowledge or presumed knowledge of the arbitral clause. It was presumed that the members of the association who frequently utilised the rules would be aware of the contents of the rules, including the presence of an agreement to arbitrate disputes.

[22] RAC Section 8 rules provide that all the members of IOA are bound by the Constitution of IOA which mandates the sports-related disputes to be adjudicated by CAS.

[23] Mukul Mudgal, LAW & SPORTS IN INDIA: DEVELOPMENTS, ISSUES AND CHALLENGES 321 (2011).

and appeal, are available. In sharp contradistinction, the only substantial remedy available against an arbitral award would be setting aside of the arbitral award on very limited and specific grounds.[24] Numerous decisions of the apex court have clarified the distinction between an appeal and setting aside of an arbitral award.[25]

As a consequence, an arbitral award cannot be appealed against; it can only be reviewed on specific standards prescribed in the 1996 Act. An interesting issue is presented by the rules for dispute resolution adopted by IOA. The rules designate AC as the highest internal authority for the resolution of sports-related disputes in India.[26] A decision by the AC can be appealed before CAS within 21 days of receiving the decision by the AC.[27] This presents an interesting scenario—once an award is rendered by an arbitral award, unless challenged within the given timeline, it conclusively determines the dispute between the parties and is considered to be final and binding on the parties and persons claiming under them.[28] Further, such an award can be enforced in the same manner as if it were a decree of the court.[29] This is crucial; in other words, once the possibility of limited review passes, the winning party obtains a right based on the finality

---

[24] 1996 Act, Section 34 notes seven grounds for setting aside an arbitral award.

[25] P. R. Shah, Shares & Stock Brokers (P) Ltd v. BHH Securities (P) Ltd, (2012) 1 SCC 594.

A court does not sit in appeal over the award of an arbitral tribunal by reassessing or reappreciating the evidence. An award can be challenged only under the grounds mentioned in Section 34(2) of the Act. [...] Therefore the absence of any ground under Section 34(2) of the Act, it is not possible to re-examine the facts to find out whether a different decision can be arrived at.

[26] IOA Rules, Rule XXIV(b).
[27] IOA Rules, Rule XXIV(c).
[28] 1996 Act, Section 35.
[29] 1996 Act, Section 36.

and bindingness of the award. The state agrees to back such an award through an expedited enforcement mechanism.

In this context, it could well be argued that once the AC has rendered an award, such an award covered under the 1996 Act would be final and binding. It could be challenged before the reviewing court on limited grounds, and if such challenge is not made or made but fails, the award could be enforced against the losing party. Here, the possibility of appeal before CAS from decisions rendered by AC becomes relevant. Given this, is such tiered set-up permissible under Indian arbitration law? This question is relevant, considering that the winning party may enforce the award, while the losing party may proceed to CAS. If the latter wins, then the award rendered in Switzerland could be brought into India for enforcement as a foreign award. It would indeed be a paradoxical situation, wherein the same dispute would have rendered both a domestic and a foreign award.

A very similar situation arose before the apex court and took almost 11 years to be resolved involving the following question: Whether tiered arbitration clauses were permitted under the Indian arbitration law? In *M/s Centrotrade Minerals* v. *Hindustan Copper Ltd*[30] (Centrotrade I), the parties had entered

---

[30] M/s Centrotrade Minerals v. Hindustan Copper Ltd, (2006) 11 SCC 245. Clause 14 of the contract contained an arbitration agreement which reads as follows:

All disputes or differences whatsoever arising between the parties out of, or relating to, the construction, meaning and operation or effect of the contract or the breach thereof shall be settled by arbitration in India through the arbitration panel of the Indian Council of Arbitration in accordance with the Rules of Arbitration of the Indian Council of Arbitration. If either party is in disagreement with the arbitration result in India, either party will have the right to appeal to a second arbitration in London, UK in accordance with the rules of conciliation and arbitration of the International Chamber of Commerce in effect on the date hereof and the results of this second arbitration will be binding on both the parties. Judgment upon the award may be entered in any court in jurisdiction.

into an agreement for procurement of copper for Khetri Plant of HCL. A dispute between the parties arose as to the dry weight of the concentrate copper. Centrotrade invoked the arbitration clause, and the arbitrator appointed by Indian Council of Arbitration made a nil award.[31] Centrotrade initiated the proceedings under the second part of the arbitration agreement before the International Chamber of Commerce. In the second proceedings, the award was rendered in favour of Centrotrade and against HCL. Attempts to enforce the second arbitral award by Centrotrade before the Calcutta High Court was resisted in equal measure by HCL. A division bench of the court observed that though successive arbitrations were permitted, successive awards are mutually destructive. Further, the second award was not a foreign award, and therefore setting aside proceedings could be initiated against it.[32]

Before the Supreme Court, the question was whether Clause 14 of the agreement providing for a two-tier arbitration was valid under the 1996 Act. Could such an arrangement provide for an appeal against a domestic award? And whether the outcome would amount to a foreign award?[33] The matter was heard by a division bench, which could not make up its mind on this question. The two judges gave differing opinions, ranging from such arrangements being void[34] to 1996 Act permitting

[31] Para 3.2.

[32] Para 9.

[33] Before the apex court, Centrotrade argued that being a London-seated arbitration, the award would be a foreign award and therefore Indian courts would lack the jurisdiction to set aside such an award. At best, its enforcement could be prevented that too on the basis of limited grounds noted in Section 48 of the 1996 Act. HCL on the other hand argued that the second part of the arbitration agreement pertaining to appeal against the first arbitral award was void being opposed to public policy. This was so because the 1996 Act envisaged only one award.

[34] Justice Shah observed,

A domestic award, in view of the statutory scheme, is subject to the supervision of a court of law. A challenge to the domestic award can, thus, be made only before a national court designated by the Act itself

such arrangements.[35] Thus, in one view of the matter the appeal mechanism set up by IOA rules would have been void. The logic would be that by entering into such an arrangement, the parties would have negated and contracted out of mandatory requirements (namely setting aside and legal of decree) of a statue. This is not permissible under law, and such an action would be contrary to the public policy.

---

and on the grounds specified in Section 34 of the Act. A fortiori, the validity of a domestic award cannot be questioned before any other forum including the forum chosen by the parties, if any. (para 14.9) It is inconceivable that one part of the arbitration agreement shall be enforceable as a domestic award but the other part would be enforceable as a foreign award. An award made in terms of one arbitration agreement can either be a domestic award or a foreign award (paras 15.1, 15.3) The fundamental legislative policy brought out by the 1996 Act, thus, being not in consonance with having two tier arbitration which had two different statutes governed by two different provisions and would be subject to different procedures, in our opinion, is not valid.[...] A two tier arbitration is invalid in law in the context of the 1996 Act having regard to Section 23 of the Contract Act as statutory jurisdiction cannot be waived by contract. It is, thus, amply clear that the very scheme of the 1996 Act does not contemplate a two tier arbitration agreement of this nature (para 18).

Of relevance here is the agreement between the parties that the 'Clause 16. The contract is to be constructed and to take effect as a contract made in accordance with the laws of India'.

[35] Justice Chatterjee observed that the 1996 Act did not prohibit or ban the parties from entering into a two-tier arbitration arrangement. This was important because admittedly under earlier legislations, it was a permissible possibility. He further noted that the 1996 Act does not intend to curtail powers of the parties to contract and structure their agreement in the manner they approve (para 29).

In my view this section only comes into operation once the arbitration proceedings as a whole which must include appellate arbitrations, if any, have ended.[...] Further, an appeal is an intrinsic part of the original proceeding and it is the final award that comes out after on appeal is preferred from the first award, that is relevant for the purpose of 1996 Act.[...] Such an agreement does not violate the provisions of Sections 34 and 36 of the 1996 Act and it cannot be said to be invalid as being opposed to public policy of India (paras 31–35).

Given the difference of opinion, the matter was referred to a larger bench for consideration.[36] The larger bench considered the following issues: (a) whether two-tier arbitration are permissible under laws of India and (b) assuming it is, whether the award rendered in the appellate arbitration being a foreign award could be enforced under Section 48 of the 1996 Act.[37] The Court addressed only the first issue. It engaged in a plain reading and observed that the contract was unambiguous in as much as the parties had agreed to contractually provide two opportunities for resolving their disputes, namely the first through arbitration in India and the second by way of appeal in arbitration in London.[38] Also clearly understood was that the outcome of the first arbitration was an award, regardless of the nomenclature utilised by parties.[39] The bench observed that neither the 1996 Act nor the Model Law on which the 1996 is based prohibited two-tier arbitration. It referred to reports of various expert committees on this matter to acknowledge that permissibility of two-tier clauses was indeed common.[40] Thus, the apex court settled the issue in favour of permissibility of two-tier arbitration under the 1996 Act.

---

[36] Centrotrade Minerals and Metal Inc v. Hindustan Copper Ltd, AIR 2017 SC 185.

[37] Para 5.

[38] Para 6.

[39] The contract refers to the outcome of the first arbitration as 'arbitration result'. For the Court, this was necessary in a situation where neither party activated the appeal clause; in other words, if it were not considered as an award it could not be enforced in case neither chose to appeal against it.

[40] Report of the Working Group on International Contract Practices on the Work of Its Third Session (A/CN.9/216, point 106), wherein the specific question of whether Model Law should recognise agreement between parties providing for appeal before an arbitral tribunal against an arbitral award was discussed. The bench noted with affirmation the response of the working group, namely that parties were free to agree that the award could be appealed before another arbitral tribunal and that the Model Law could not exclude such practice. *See also* Analytical Commentary on Draft Text of a Model Law on International Commercial Arbitration: Report of the Secretary General (A/CN.9/264, page 71), and explanatory note by the UNCITRAL Secretariat on the 1985 Model Law on International Commercial Arbitration as amended in 2006, *available*

The set-up provided under the IOA rules is similar to the aforementioned situation. In the first instance, the arbitration is conducted before the AC, and after exhausting an internal appeal before the AC, a second appeal against the decision is made before CAS. Drawing an analogy from the Centrotrade II decision, the three arbitrations are essentially part of one single process. Such structuring could be held to be well within the party autonomy, a point that the Centrotrade II bench was at pains to point out. This, however, still does not resolve the question of whether that award would be enforced as a foreign award in India.[41]

Arbitral Tribunal: Appointment of Arbitrators

A crucial principle of decision-making, which is now readily accepted in jurisdictions across the globe, is that no person can be a judge in his/her own cause,[42] since such a set-up would cast serious aspersions on the very ability of the arbitral tribunal to render impartial justice. The 1996 Act, as amended in 2015, imposes strict restrictions on who can act as an arbitrator in a given matter. A threshold requirement concerns absence of pecuniary, personal or professional connection between the arbitrators and the parties, so as to ensure transparent and unblemished

---

at http://www.uncitral.org/pdf/english/texts/arbitration/ml-arb/MLARB-explanatoryNote20-9-07.pdf. 'The fact that recourse to a court is available to a party for challenging an award does not ipso facto prohibit the parties from mutually agreeing to a second look at an award with the intention of an early settlement of disputes and differences' (para 28).

[41] This is important because in such situation there is a change in seat of arbitration and consequently the supervisory courts. Under the Bhatia regime (Bhatia International v. Bulk Trading, AIR 2002 SC 1432), even foreign awards could be set aside (*see* Venture Global Engineering v. Satyam Computer Services Ltd, AIR 2008 SC 1061). However, post September 2012, owing to the decision of apex court in Bharat Aluminium Company v. Kaiser Aluminium Technical Services, (2012) 9 SCC 552, only enforcement of foreign award can be resisted in India. The Court affirmed that the power to set aside an award lay with the courts of seat.

[42] *Nemo judex in sua causa*, the principle was established early by the apex court in Builders Supply Corporation v. UOI, AIR 1965 SC 1061.

decision-making. Presence of justifiable doubts regarding arbitrators' independence and impartiality gives rise to adequate cause for challenging an arbitrator. The 1996 Act further identifies certain connections, presence of which automatically disqualifies a person from being an arbitrator, leaving no room for party autonomy, unless such autonomy is exercised after the dispute has arisen.[43]

The AC which is designated as the highest internal authority for the resolution of sports-related disputes in India[44] also acts the appellate authority against any decision taken by IOA. What is of interest is that all members of the AC are appointed by IOA.[45] Such a set-up raises concerns about the probity of the members of the arbitral tribunal so constituted, especially in instances where IOA is a direct party to dispute pending before them.

The First Civil Division of the Swiss Federal Tribunal (SFT) had in the presence of a similar connection between International Olympic Committee (IOC) and CAS, in *Gundel* v. *International Equestrian Federation (FEI)* (Gundel), observed that even though CAS satisfied essential requirements of an independent arbitral tribunal, given its association with IOC, greater efforts were required to sever the 'organic and economic' ties it had with the latter.[46] To the credit of IOC, severance was initiated through the agreement related to the constitution of the International Council of Arbitration for Sports (ICAS), whereby ICAS was formed to act as CAS's independent executive council. Furthermore, activities of CAS were no longer solely financed by IOC. Changes were also made to ensure that members of ICAS and CAS panel of arbitrators were selected with the aim of protecting athletes' rights.[47] In

---

[43] 1996 Act, Section 12(5) r/w the Fifth Schedule.

[44] IOA Rules, Rule XXIV(b).

[45] IOA Rules, Rule XVI(a)(iv) r/w XVIII(3).

[46] Jack Anderson, Modern Sports Law: A Textbook 80–81 (2010).

[47] TAS/CAS, *Code: Statutes of ICAS and CAS*, Sections 4 and 14, *available at* http://www.tas-cas.org/en/icas/code-statutes-of-icas-and-cas.html

sum, reforms ensured that CAS administratively, legally and for practical purposes became a body independent of IOC.[48]

These reforms were further tested in *Danilova and Lazuntina v. IOC and FIS*[49] before the SFT. Unlike the *Gundel* matter, this case had IOC as a direct party. It was alleged before SFT that existence of financial links between IOC and CAS compromised independence of CAS. The SFT, drawing an analogy between state courts and their financing from the state, noted that even though state courts were financed by the state, in countries governed by rule of law it could not be said that the courts lacked independence or were partial to the state in matters involving the state. The court further noted that even though a close relationship might exist between the lawyers and arbitrator, given the small professional circles they traverse, proof of prejudice had to go beyond *purely subjective reactions*. The CAS code was further amended to partially address this situation, whereby ICAS members can neither appear on list of CAS arbitrators nor appear as counsel for parties in CAS proceedings. Furthermore, CAS arbitrators and mediators could not act as counsel for party before CAS.[50]

In comparison, the IOA rules concerning the AC seem rather primeval. The AC is established by IOA and deemed to be the highest internal authority for the resolution of sports-related disputes in India. Arbitrators to AC are nominated solely by IOA.[51] Furthermore, the IOA rules make it mandatory for federations and associations to have all their disputes resolved through the

---

[48] ANDERSON, *supra* note 45, at 83.

[49] Judgement of 27 May 2003, (2003) 3 Digest of CAS Awards 649. The SFT went on to conclude that CAS was no longer a 'vassal' of IOC.

[50] TAS/CAS, *supra* note 46, Section 18, *available at* http://www.tas-cas.org/en/icas/code-statutes-of-icas-and-cas.html

[51] In sharp contrast, the ICAS appoints personalities to the list of CAS arbitrators after receiving inputs from IOC, international federations (IFs), National Olympic Committees (NOCs) and the athletes' commission of the IOC. Section 14 of the Code of Sports-related Arbitration in force as from 1 January 2017.

aegis of the AC and under no circumstances resort to litigation in court of law. Disregard of the stricture would likely attract sanction and disciplinary action.[52] In addition to the AC, IOA also establishes what is referred to as the Affiliation and Dispute Commission. No information relating to this commission is available, except a reference in the RAC whereby the chairman of the Affiliation and Dispute Commission, IOA, may constitute a panel from the list of arbitrators notified by IOA.[53]

Section 1 of the RAC creates the Indian Court of Arbitration for Sports (I-CAS) tasked with facilitating settlement of sports-related disputes through arbitration and mediation. I-CAS is seated at New Delhi, India, and consists of two divisions: the Ordinary Arbitration Division (OAD) and the Appeals Arbitration Division (AAD).[54] Consequently, the current system

---

[52] IOA Rules, Rule XXVIII(e).

[53] Section 5, *available at* http://www.olympic.ind.in/images/IOA-Committees-23-01-2012.pdf

[54] http://www.olympic.ind.in/images/IOA-Committees-23-01-2012.pdf. The RAC seems to have been drafted in a callous and haphazard manner. For instance, a major concern lies in the nomenclature that is utilised. The IOA and AC rules keep alternating between CAS and AC, without ever clarifying whether they are one and same body. Similar issues arise with authorities. The rules mention Chairman of Affiliation and Dispute Commission, without appropriately clarifying the exact duties and relationship with other dispute settlement bodies created under the rules. It merely notes that CAS would include a court office composed of Chairman of Affiliation and Dispute Resolution and one or more counsel appointed to decide the function of Secretary General (Section 7). Similarly, the rules keep referring to CAS, without clarifying whether the referred to institution is the Indian CAS or the ICAS. This is relevant given certain statements made in the press by IOA officials. For instance, *see* J. Venkatesan, *Justice Lakshmanan to Head Indian Court of Sports Arbitration*, The Hindu, 5 August 2011, *available at* http://www.thehindu.com/sport/justice-lakshmanan-to-head-indian-court-of-sports- arbitration/article2322855.ece, which reported that the Indian CAS was constituted as per directions of IOC, and the disputes before it would be resolved in accordance with the rules and regulations of ICAS. Apart from the ambiguity it generates, it also creates potentials for conflict, considering an arbitration before Indian CAS would be seated in New Delhi, with the Indian arbitration law as the curial law.

puts in place a three-tier mechanism: internal remedy for federation, first instance before I-CAS (OAD), appeal before I-CAS (AAD) and final appeal before ICAS, Switzerland. At this juncture, it is important to note that IOA rules or RAC are silent about the association between AC and CAS. Indeed, very little information is available on the IOA website. In fact, the IOA press release dated 21 July 2011, noting the composition of I-CAS, carries the heading 'Arbitration Commission'. Therefore, one assumes that AC and CAS are one and same body with the over responsibility for resolution of disputes (commercial or disciplinary) falling within the purview of IOA rules.

Given that the seat of arbitration conducted by CAS is New Delhi, the 1996 Act would be the curial law. Concordantly, grounds for challenges to an arbitrator could arise from both the rules of AC and the 1996 Act. In the event of a conflict, the mandatory provisions of the 1996 Act would prevail.[55] Provisions relating to the right of the party to challenge the arbitrator on grounds of lack of independence and impartiality form mandatory part of the 1996 Act.

Although the RAC clearly provides for challenge against the arbitrator, provided legitimate doubts exist with regard to their independence,[56] all challenges to an arbitrator remain in the exclusive power of CAS, which may decide at its discretion.[57] It further suggests that parties have the liberty to decide the method of appointment of arbitrator. In the absence of any agreement, parties have to make a specific request for nominating an arbitrator and that such a request should be made to the chairman of Affiliation and Dispute Commission.[58] Of more interest is the

[55] A seat means the legal jurisdiction to which arbitration is attached. An arbitration is conducted according to the arbitration law at the seat of arbitration (curial law or seat of arbitration), even if hearing or other meetings are held elsewhere. SIMON GREENBERG ET AL., INTERNATIONAL COMMERCIAL ARBITRATION: AN ASIA PACIFIC PERSPECTIVE 55 (2011).

[56] RAC, Section 7 r/w Section 12.

[57] RAC, Section 13.

[58] RAC, Section 17.2.

stipulation that none of the parties will have any objection to the nomination so made.[59] In other words, the parties have no say as to who the arbitrator would be. The only choice they have is from the panel of CAS.[60]

At this juncture, it is important to understand that the 1996 Act lays heavy emphasis on neutrality for both arbitrators and the procedures from the initiation of arbitration all the way to its conclusion, that is, rendering of an award. The 1996 Act, thus, lays down precise rules prohibiting arbitrators from having direct or indirect, previous or existing relationship with or interest in parties or the subject matter of the dispute which may present justifiable doubts as to his/her independence and impartiality.[61] The relationship could be of the nature of financial, business, professional or other kind. Party autonomy, however, is held to be paramount, considering the parties can waive any objection and even in the presence of a relationship proceed to appoint such a person as arbitrator. However, the Act stipulates point of time when party autonomy could be exercised. For instances, it clearly identifies certain relations, presence of which requires the parties to waive the objection by way of a written agreement after the dispute has arisen.[62] This is to ensure that disproportionate bargaining power is not brought to bear during contract negotiations to coerce a party to waive their rights against a suspect arbitrator.

[59] RAC, Sections 16 and 17.

[60] Even though a similar arrangement exist with CAS (Procedural Rules: Code of Sports-related Arbitration in force as from 1 January 2017, Rule 33 requires that every arbitrator shall appear on the list drawn up by the ICAS in accordance with the statutes), the list comprises of 370 arbitrators, and, while appointing, the ICAS shall consider continental representation and different judicial culture. The arbitrators are also required to have recognised competence with regard to sports law and a good knowledge of sports in general (Section 14, Code of Sports-related Arbitration).

[61] 1996 Act, Section 12.

[62] 1996 Act, Section 12(5) r/w Seventh Schedule. Such relations concern relationship (direct or indirect interest) with parties, counsel or disputes. It would include being an employee, advisor, consultant, any past or present business relationship with a party, close family relationship with one of the parties, significant financial interest in one of the parties, etc.

The relationship between IOA and AC seems clear. IOA appoints the commission, selects its arbitrators and funds their payments. Even though individuals of high eminence are nominated to the panel, that alone would be inadequate to secure neutrality of an institution. In a similar instance, the SFT though affirming neutrality of CAS had called for greater distancing of IOC and CAS.[63] Such a delinking is yet to occur in the functioning of IOA. On the other hand, the links between IOA and AC seem explicit and secure both financially and administratively. For instance, another IOA functionary (namely the chairman of Affiliation and Dispute Commission) nominates a panel of arbitrators from I-CAS;[64] as a result, only IOA (even when it is a party) has any say in who would be the arbitrators in the matter, with other parties reduced to the status of mere bystanders. Further, given that the federations and athletes have no choice[65] but to arbitrate their disputes before a panel nominated from ICAS, the independence and impartiality of I-CAS does become suspect.

Conclusion

Under the arbitration law of India, all disputes unless expressly or impliedly prohibited lend themselves to arbitration. Limitation tends to be centred on the nature of the disputes and type of remedy sought.

---

[63] Danilova and Lazuntina v. IOC and FIS, judgement of 27 May 2003, (2003) 3 Digest of CAS Awards 649. The SFT went on to conclude that CAS was no longer a 'vassal' of IOC.

[64] RAC, Section 5: 'The personalities who appear on the list of Arbitrators may be called upon to serve on the panel constituted by Chairman of Affiliation and Dispute Commission—IOA'.

[65] It is interesting to note that RAC Section 8 notes that the rules would apply 'whenever the parties have agreed to refer' a sports-related dispute to CAS. This is in sharp contrast to IOA Rules, Rule XXII and XXIV which require submission of disputes including sports-related disputes for settlement through the process of arbitration with the AC.

Globally, arbitration is the preferred means of sports-related dispute resolution.[66] In India, disputes pertaining to sports, whether contractual or otherwise, are deemed arbitrable with sports arbitration fulfilling the basic requirements of arbitration, namely intention to refer matter to neutral third party, noting of the intention in a written document and agreement to be bound by the final award so rendered. Governing bodies such as IOA establish procedures and mechanisms to allow for arbitration of sports-related disputes. These arbitrations are governed by a combination of provisions found in the 1996 Act and rules of IOA and various federations and associations.

However, there remain certain areas of concern, be it the manner in which consent is obtained, the multi-layered agreement to arbitrate or the manner in which arbitrators are appointed to arbitral tribunal organised to adjudicate sports dispute. On all three parameters, the current legal framework provided by an intersection of the applicable rules, particularly the IOA constitution and RAC, have been found to be wanting. Although such limitation in itself does not vitiate the entire set-up, combined they do put a substantial dent in its overall efficiency.

That said, these issues are neither new nor novel. They have been witnessed and have been adequately addressed on the international level by extensive reforms to IOC, ICAS and CAS. Indian sports bodies led by IOA need to invest more effort and imagination in refining the existing mechanism to provide a genuine alternative in resolving sports disputes.

---

[66] James A. R. Nafziger, Arbitration of Rights and Obligations in the International Sports Arena 358–359 (2001).

Image Rights and Sports in India

David McArdle

Introduction

Colleagues in India will be far more familiar than I am with the nuances of domestic intellectual property law and what appears to be a gap in the legal framework in the protection of celebrities' image rights. They will also doubtless be aware that trying to fill that gap involves recourse to Constitutional provisions and a patchwork of protections which mirrors those found in English law—the common law remedy of passing off and the legislative provisions on trademark and copyright infringement—and that there are arguments for a statutory image right which would provide a more adequate framework. This chapter briefly outlines those existing domestic protections and their limitations, and goes on to discuss an image rights dispute in Caribbean cricket and the remedies available under the domestic laws of the European Union (EU) member states to illustrate that India's situation is far from unique—and that there may indeed be arguments for effective statutory protections.

An Overview of the Indian Law on Image Rights

Given the scale of interest in, for instance, the Bollywood film industry and cricket, it is perhaps a little surprising that image rights in India are not more developed than they are. One might have expected to see a far more extensive body of case law as celebrities seek to control the commercial use of their name, image and likeness or other distinctive features. This is especially so when one considers that, for sports celebrities especially, 'popularity ... is inevitably fleeting (and) any misappropriation of intellectual property should result in strong and immediate action'.[1] Sachin Tendulkar's Test career lasted an incredible 25 years but most mere mortals would be fortunate to play their sport at the very highest level for perhaps a third of that time. Celebrity is transient, and today's heroes are tomorrow's memories as the hamster wheel of fortune passes from one generation to the next.

In *R. Rajagopal* v. *State of Tamil Nadu*,[2] the Supreme Court confirmed that the right to privacy which is derived from Articles 19 and 21 of the Constitution extends to image rights and is violated where a person's name, image or likeness is used without their consent. Beyond that, passing off is a potential remedy—but only if one possesses the 'significant reputation or goodwill' that Justice Laddie outlined in the English case of *Irvine* v. *Talksport* as necessary for a successful action.[3] This was the case in *Titan Industries Ltd* v. *Ramkumar Jewellers*,[4] a successful injunction

[1] R. Narula & N. Kumar, When Your Face Is Your Fortune, October/November TRADEMARK L. R. 106, 106 (2012).

[2] R. Rajagopal v. State of Tamil Nadu, JT 1994 (6) SC 514.

[3] Irvine v. Talksport, (2002) 1 WLR 2355, 2369:

To succeed, the burden on the claimant includes a need to prove at least two, interrelated, facts. First, that at the time of the acts complained of he had a significant reputation or goodwill. Second, that the actions of the defendant gave rise to a false message which would be understood by a not insignificant section of his market that his goods have been endorsed, recommended or approved of by the claimant.

[4] Titan Industries Ltd v. Ramkumar Jewellers, CS (OS) 2662 of 2011.

application, and there have been several cases concerning domain name registration—but as Narula and Kumar noted, the 'few judicial decisions which have accorded protection ... through IP laws have proved to be insufficient. There remains a need for a separate regime and statutory protection for image rights'.[5]

The West Indies Cricket Dispute

India is by no means unique in its reliance on IP remedies that are ill-suited to the particular problem of image rights violation. Perhaps a salutary lesson can be learned from a long-running, high-profile and deeply damaging image rights dispute that beset West Indies cricket over the course of two years from November 2004. In the run-up to a three-team tournament in Australia in early 2005, the West Indies Players' Association (WIPA) asked players who were selected for the touring squad not to accept the letters of invitation to a pre-tour training event sent to them by the West Indies Cricket Board (WICB), the governing body. WIPA, although not a trade union, had taken exception to the fact that despite being the recognised body for negotiating the contract terms and conditions of players selected to represent the West Indies,[6] they had not been involved in negotiations on this occasion. WIPA was of the view that 'some of the conditions stipulated ... represent an attempt to exploit the players for commercial purposes'[7] and 16 of the West Indies' best players acceded to its request and refused to sign the contracts. A last-minute and decidedly short-term compromise allowed all parties to skirt around the issue while the Australia tour took place; but the West Indies won only one of their six games in the tournament, and the dispute undermined relations between the players and the governing body for several years.

---

[5] NARULA & KUMAR, *supra* note 1, at 107.

[6] www.wiplayers.com

[7] ESPNcricinfo, *Battle Brews Between West Indies Board and Players* (10 November 2004), *available at* http://www.espncricinfo.com/westindies/content/story/141561.html

The dispute arose because the proposed players' contract, as drafted by the Board prior to the Australia tour, would oblige the players to inform the WICB of any personal contracts they intended to sign—especially those which made provision for image rights exploitation by companies other than those in a contractual relationship with the Board; it had drafted that clause because it was very keen to avoid conflicts between commitments entered into by the players before signing those contracts and its own obligations to its commercial partners. It was specifically concerned to protect its relationship with Digicel, which was then a new and boisterous entrant to the Caribbean mobile phone market, and when negotiating its new commercial contact with Digicel, the Board had agreed that its players would not endorse any of Digicel's competitors while representing the West Indies team—an undertaking which it was not in a position to give.[8] However, while negotiations with Digicel were ongoing, several of the most high-profile players had signed personal sponsorship deals with Cable & Wireless (hereafter CW), a previous sponsor of West Indies cricket and the dominant player in the burgeoning Caribbean market. In addition to those contracts, CW had a longstanding image rights agreement with Brian Lara, the team captain and perhaps the most widely recognised player in West Indies cricket history. Despite the Board's endeavours, CW had secured the right to commercially exploit the images of the best West Indies players of the age.

The commercial rivalry between the two companies has played out across sporting and juridical fields in the Caribbean and beyond. In *Digicel (Barbados)* v. *Cable and Wireless (Barbados)*,[9] CW was found not to have abused its dominant position in the domestic mobile telecommunications market when refusing to allow its subscribers to vote via their CW lines

---

[8] ESPNcricinfo, *Board Asks Players Association to Back Down on Clause* (23 November 2004), http://www.espncricinfo.com/westindies/content/story/136045.html

[9] Digicel (Barbados) Ltd v. Cable and Wireless (Barbados) Ltd, Barbados S Ct No 974 of 2005.

in a phone-in competition run by Digicel; in *Digicel (St Lucia) and Others* v. *Cable and Wireless plc (and others)*,[10] the High Court in London held that CW had not unlawfully delayed the processes of interconnection that would allow Digicel to access the domestic markets in the wake of legislation to end monopoly practices in those markets; and in *Digicel (St Lucia) Ltd* v. *Cable and Wireless Ltd*,[11] the same court was concerned with the relationship between honest belief and the implied waiver of legal privilege. It was probably inevitable that the companies' mutually aggressive pursuance of West Indies cricketers would develop in the way it did—a proxy war with the strings of the WICB and WICA being pulled by Digicel and CW respectively, conducted at the same time that Digicel's strategy of litigation was gathering steam. Until late 2004, CW had been the principal sponsor of West Indies cricket, but by then the Board was in the late stage of negotiations with Digicel—which had taken the view that a close relationship with West Indies cricket would help raise its profile across the Caribbean (cricket being the only sport where the several Caribbean nations combine as an international representative side).[12] When CW became aware of those negotiations, it quietly took steps to sign those high-profile players onto individual endorsement contracts, doubtless with the knowledge and support of the WICA. Pursuant to its contract with CW, the Board gave it the opportunity to match the offer made by Digicel; but having secured personal contracts with the most high-profile players, it declined to do so. Securing the most high-profile players had doubtless diluted the value of Digicel's contract with the West Indies team, although it was already en route to penetrating the Caribbean market in mobile telecommunications, to the extent of securing a duopoly with

---

[10] Digicel (St Lucia) and Others v. Cable and Wireless plc (and others), (2010) EWHC 774.

[11] Digicel (St Lucia) Ltd v. Cable and Wireless Ltd, (2009) 2 All ER 1094, Ch Div.

[12] H. BECKLES, A NATION IMAGINED: THE FIRST WEST INDIES CRICKET TEAM (2004).

CW, 'with only a few smaller companies edging their way into these newly liberalised markets' by the time the player contract saga had come to an end.[13]

The biggest losers, then, were not the two telephone companies but West Indies cricket. Shortly before the Australia tour, the dispute was referred to Adrian Saunders, a judge from St Vincent and a member of the Caribbean Court of Justice, for mediation. Saunders' report was leaked by one of the parties; it intimated that he suggested distinguishing the players' individual endorsement contracts from those of the WICB, meaning the Board could not prevent the players from taking up, or acting upon, private endorsement deals and, for their part, the players could not use West Indies team logos or other branding in endorsements that arose in non-work contexts. That approach would have been entirely consistent with the courts' treatment of endorsement disputes in the USA[14] and (as explored further) across the EU, and for a time it seemed that the matter would be resolved on that basis.[15] However, the agreement floundered, partly on the parties' inability to conclude negotiations on retainer contracts and certain peripheral issues but mainly because WIPA advised the players not to submit their personal endorsement contracts to the Board for inspection. The Board, keen to ensure that 'it did not commit an involuntary breach of its sponsorship agreement with Digicel', wanted to satisfy itself that

> The personal endorsement contracts ... were unquestionably in the nature of individual contracts and contained no provisions which could be construed as passing off by the player of his connection

[13] Alton Worldwide, *Caribbean: Telecoms Market Overview and Statistics*, 2 (2006), *available at* http://www.altongp.com/previousprojects/Tellecommunications/CDMA%20Caribbean/Caribbean%20-%20Telecoms%20Market%20Overview%20&%20Statistics.pdf

[14] *See, e.g.,* Healan Laboratories v. Topps Chewing Gum 202 F.2d 866 (2nd Cir. 1963).

[15] ESPNcricinfo, *West Indies Board Seeks to Resolve Contracts Issue* (22 February 2005), *available at* http://www.espncricinfo.com/westindies/content/story/144751.html

with the West Indies team by attribution or by defining himself as a member of the team.[16]

The tour to Australia was only secured after Keith Mitchell, the prime minister of Grenada and chairman of the CARICOM group's cricket subcommittee, had received assurances from CW that, during the tour, 'it would do nothing to give the impression that the relationship between itself and (the players) is in their capacity as members of the West Indies cricket team'.[17]

However, the truce was short-lived. The Board was of the view that during the tour,

> As is clear to the Caribbean public, every opportunity has been taken to use the images of the Cable and Wireless contracted players in ways which trade on the membership of the West Indies Cricket Team, refer to them as members of a team and make many references to West Indies Cricket.[18]

Against this background, the Board reverted to its prior position—it would not consider the CW-contracted players for selection until it was satisfied that the contracts 'contain no provisions which could be construed as passing off'.[19] There was talk of CW having engaged not just in passing off but also in ambush marketing.[20] Digicel's own review of the Australia tour referred to the players' association as 'a terrorist organisation'[21] and there was a widely held view that its chief executive officer,

[16] T. Griffith, *The Background to the Dispute*, ESPNCRICINFO (5 March 2005), *available at* http://www.espncricinfo.com/westindies/content/story/208251.html

[17] *Id.*

[18] *Id.*

[19] *Id.*

[20] ESPNcricinfo, *Crucial Meeting Could Decide Dispute's Fate* (7 March 2005), *available at* http://www.espncricinfo.com/westindies/content/story/145896.html

[21] ESPNcricinfo, *WIPA Hit Out at Lara's Non-selection* (21 March 2005), *available at* http://www.espncricinfo.com/thestands/content/story/146343.html

Dinanath Ramnarine, had acted on behalf of the players in their ostensibly personal negotiations with CW.[22] For its part, WIPA condemned the Board for having 'direct contact' with the players about the ongoing negotiations rather than liaising with the association,[23] and for refusing to let it see the contract which the Board signed with Digicel.[24] In June 2005, the Board allowed the contract negotiations to be reviewed by an independent panel and, while it deliberated, a weakened side comprising only those players who were willing to sign the WICB contracts was selected for a tour of Sri Lanka.[25] The players were so polarised that they had to be housed in two separate hotels[26] and in the interim, the lead member of the review panel opined that the Digicel contract could be annulled because the secret negotiations breached the Board's contractual agreement with CW that any such negotiations would be carried out openly,[27] although the two other members distanced themselves from that finding.[28] The dispute finally entered its endgame in December 2005, six weeks after the two parties agreed to ask the international governing body, the ICC, and the Federation of International Cricketers' Associations to draft a new provision term dealing with retainer contracts

[22] M. Williamson, *Just Who Does Ramnarine Represent?* ESPNCRICINFO (1 April 2005), *available at* https://www.espncricinfo.com/westindies/content/story/143735.html

[23] ESPNcricinfo, *Ramnarine Condemns Board's Direct Contact with Players* (10 June 2005), *available at* http://www.espncricinfo.com/westindies/content/story/210821.html

[24] F. Mohammed, *We Ain't Know What WI Want,* ESPNCRICINFO (4 July 2005), *available at* http://www.espncricinfo.com/ttexpress/content/story/212546.html

[25] ESPNcricinfo, *West Indies Name Second-string Squad* (1 July 2005), *available at* http://www.espncricinfo.com/slvwi/content/story/212349.html

[26] ESPNcricinfo, *Solutions for a Sorry Mess* (11 August 2005), *available at* http://www.espncricinfo.com/pakistan/content/story/215722.html

[27] ESPNcricinfo, *Digicel Deal Can Be Declared 'Null and Void'* (22 August 2005), *available at* http://www.espncricinfo.com/westindies/content/story/216787.html

[28] ESPNcricinfo, *West Indies Sponsorship Review Committee Split* (26 August 2005), *available at* https://www.espncricinfo.com/westindies/content/story/217161.html

and appropriate player compensation for the use of their image rights. However, not until September 2006 were all aspects of the dispute finally resolved.[29]

Ten years later, the West Indies dispute seems an anomaly: full-blown confrontations between athletes and their employers or their governing bodies, in which both sides are pawns in a game played by big business, remain the exception. When image rights disputes do occur, they are more likely to see clubs and players on the same side, usually in dispute with tax authorities who perceive players' image rights arrangements as a subterfuge to avoid income tax obligations.[30] But the passage of time affords an opportunity to explore the concept of 'image rights' and their regulation from a wider standpoint, and perhaps to consider whether there is a need for image rights legislation in India and elsewhere—especially for the Caribbean nations which share many social, legal and political similarities but which, let us remember, are separate and independent states with their own laws and legal structures. It is doubtless the case that athletes' advisers, commercial organisations, governing bodies and employers should be alive to the damage that image rights disputes can cause, and the mutual mistrust which bedevilled West Indies cricket then remains a festering sore. Stakeholders would do well to avoid protracted disputes such as this, and maybe a clearer legal framework would prevent such disputes from arising or would, at least, provide a better basis for their resolution than was displayed by the various parties that professed a concern for West Indies cricket. Engagement with, and education of, players, their agents, legal advisers, governing body members and union representatives might be important means of underpinning whatever provisions a model law might contain, while

[29] ESPNcricinfo, *Windies Board and Players' Association Sign Agreements* (6 September 2006), *available at* http://phone.espncricinfo.com/ci/content/story/258763.html

[30] D. McArdle, *You Had Me at 'No Capital Gains Tax on a Disposal': Legal and Theoretical Aspects of Stand-alone Image Rights*, 36(4) LEGAL STUD. 639, 639–657 (2016).

the use of standard terms or collective agreements that can help prevent such disputes arising could be central to the model law itself because mandatory recourse to mediation and arbitration, at least at first instance, would be infinitely preferable to court action. The history of litigation in sports disputes globally shows that court-imposed solutions are unlikely to provide long-term solutions and quite likely to undermine the parties' future working relationship, and maybe the seemingly irreversible decline of West Indies cricket provides testament to this.

The European Context

Against that background, this chapter finally considers the provisions for avoiding, and if necessary resolving, image rights disputes involving athletes and other performers in jurisdictions with no recourse to a statutory framework. First, it is axiomatic that parties' rights and duties in respect of image rights should be clearly laid down in contracts—whether those contracts are the result of collective agreements, standard terms or individually negotiated—and remedies for when things go awry will thus lie in breach of contract rather than passing off or statutes of general application. However, in some EU member states, there are remedies which apply only to those working in the sports industry or in other celebrity fields. Although exceptional, these are an example of how actors in cultural fields like sports have been able to secure protections and remedies which are unique to one particular sphere of activity, and they might also provide for mandatory dispute resolution or recourse to 'sports courts' which, again, are not available to those in other walks of life. However, they are still national remedies—rooted in the legal norms of that particular jurisdiction and being reliant on that jurisdiction's capacity to create specific remedies for a particular industry, so rather than being a prime example of sports law, or as some would have it, a *lex sportiva*, as might first appear, maybe they are the antithesis of it: the existence of these provisions and the extent of the remedies available under them, even when they give power and authority to sports-specific bodies such as arbitral tribunals, are dependent on what national laws allow, and they have no application beyond the jurisdiction.

The starting point for considering these potential sources of image rights disputes resolution was a study of image rights in the EU, initially earmarked for (but eventually not incorporated into) the European Commission report on the Rights of Sport Event Organisers which came out in 2014.[31] Respondents in each of the 28 member states were asked to consider the following scenario.[32]

> Club A entered into an employment contract (or similar working relationship) with Player B. According to the contract, B is not entitled, either on his own behalf or with or through any third party, to commercially exploit his/her image in a club context. Some years ago, A entered into an exclusive sponsorship agreement with sportswear company B-DIDAS. When performing their services under the contract with A, all players must wear a kit manufactured by B-DIDAS.

[31] B. Hugenholdz et al., Study on Sports Organisers' Rights in the European Union (2014), *available at* http://www.ivir.nl/publicaties/download/1353

[32] The case study was informed by the decision of the Audacia Provincial de Barcelona, AC/2006/1955, May 2006. Here, Nike appealed against the rejection at first instance (by the Mercantile Court) of its application for precautionary measures—specifically, an order compelling a player to abide by a contractual clause which obliged him to exclusively use Nike footwear and other apparel, pursuant to a club contract, rather than using Adidas products in accordance with a personal endorsement contract he had signed with that company. Nike also sought an order preventing Adidas from executing the agreements it had signed with the player. The Mercantile Court had held, and the Superior Court agreed, that under Spanish law the player would be entitled to unilaterally revoke his contract with Adidas, subject to the statutory limitation periods on revocation and potentially damages. However, the Superior Court also said that the agreement reached between Nike and the player did not fulfil all the essential legal criteria: the 'contract' was nothing more than a preliminary agreement in an ongoing negotiation process and did not constitute a contract. That being the case, the absence of a contract meant it was impossible for Nike to argue that Adidas had engaged in unfair competition by inducing the player to enter into an agreement with it.

> Some time prior to signing with A, B had entered into a personal sponsorship and endorsement agreement with sportswear company NIEK to exploit B's image in advertisements for NIEK shoes. The agreement also foresaw the obligation for B to wear NIEK shoes during football games and in the public eye. This agreement still exists. Club A was aware of the agreement between Player B and NIEK.

The broad legal issues concerning image rights have received some academic and practitioner comment (notably on issues of taxation[33] and unauthorised use in computer games), but other than the Nike litigation on which the question was based, only three cases were discussed by national respondents (one involving badminton in the Netherlands, another involving skiing in Finland[34] and the third being *Irvine*[35]). While the dearth of case law does not necessarily mean that such conflicts rarely arise,

[33] *See also* R. Cloete, *The Taxation of Image Rights: A Comparative Analysis*, 45(3) DE JURE 556, 556–567 (2012).

[34] In the Netherlands, the national governing body for badminton had concluded an exclusive sponsorship contract with equipment manufacturer Yonex, but a number of national team members already had individual sponsorship contracts with other brands. The governing body exerted a great deal of pressure on the players with individual sponsorship contracts to use Yonex equipment despite their individual contractual obligations: they were threatened with being left out of the national team if they refused to breach their individual contracts. The Utrecht District Court found that by exerting this pressure, the governing body actively induced those players with individual sponsorship contracts to breach their individual contracts and had thus acted wrongfully both towards the players with individual sponsorship contracts and their respective sponsors. The governing body was held liable in damages as a consequence. Rechtbank Utrecht, 30 November 2011, 289895/HA ZA 10-1563, *available at* http://uitspraken.rechtspraak.nl/#sne lzoeken/?zoekterm=dunlop. In contrast, where similar personal sponsorship agreements held by two ski-jumpers in Finland conflicted with those held by the national federation the Competition Court found in favour of the federation. This was because the arrangement was a longstanding practice which benefited the sponsors that funded the sport domestically. However, the Finnish respondent stressed that the competition laws applicable to such situations would not apply to similar disputes arising in the context of employment relationships: Hautamski, 756/61/04, 11 November 2004.

[35] Irvine v. Talksport, (2002) I WLR 2355.

there was no evidence to suggest that image rights violations were a cause for concern within European sporting or celebrity culture. Maybe there are under-the-radar incidents or disputes that get settled away from the glare of litigation, but the emergence of sports acts was the single most interesting aspect of the case study. National respondents' answers suggested that if such incidents did come to pass, domestic laws provided remedies which were much the same in every member state—a distinction would be drawn between an athlete's obligations in a club or employment context and their right to pursue individual image exploitation opportunities outside of it. Indeed, this remedy reflects the one suggested by Justice Saunders in the West Indies cricket case, and both sports-specific remedies such as sports acts and more general legal norms made provision for it; outcomes tended not to change regardless of where the source of the remedy lie, and the extent of the players' rights and obligations depended on how far the concept of 'club context' extended and how it would be interpreted in the event of any ambiguity. Image rights disputes such as that in West Indies cricket can thus be avoided by careful and considered drafting of contract terms, ideally resulting in standard terms or implementation through a collective agreement, rather than the ad hoc shifting the goalposts that the WICB tried to engage in. Since *URBSFA* v. *Bosman*,[36] it has been generally accepted that any provisions which impact on athletes' economic interests should have their explicit consent,[37] so much so that it might now be regarded as a fundamental principle of global sports law,[38] and collective agreements are one way of signifying this, standard terms and sports acts might be others—but they still rely on judicial interpretation and, in the case of mediation or arbitration, a willingness on the part of both parties to play ball (such a willingness being noticeably absent in West Indies cricket). Perhaps that reliance on the potential vagaries of judicial interpretation may be seen as an argument in favour of sports acts of the kind that

---

[36] URBSFA v. Bosman, (1995) ECR I-4921.

[37] EUROPEAN COMMISSION, WHITE PAPER ON SPORT 391 (2007).

[38] K. Foster, *Is There a Global Sports Law?* 2(1) ENT. SPORTS L. J. (2003), *available at* https://www.entsportslawjournal.com/21/volume/2/issue/1/

currently exist in France, Greece, Hungary, Portugal, Romania, Spain and Poland, or for a statutory personality right of the kind that exists in Guernsey and a handful of other jurisdictions worldwide,[39] but there is no evidence that jurisdictions which relied on principles of contract construction or interpretation of the common law resolved the matter differently to those countries which had a statutory framework, sports-specific legislation or extensive collective agreements. Indeed, there is nothing to suggest that this is an extensive problem in dire need of an urgent solution. That said, the emergence of sports acts, Guernsey-type image rights databases and collective agreements are interesting and important features that are worth further exploration in the context of Indian sport and celebrity culture.

Conclusion

For the time being, the use of standard contract terms and the judicial interpretation of those terms will remain fundamental in preventing (or resolving) image disputes. This being the case, one would argue that any contract term which fetters a performer's image rights and freedoms should stipulate as a minimum:

1. The extent to which the performer is obliged to assign his/her rights: what specific rights are assigned and what specific rights are reserved for individual exploitation.
2. Whether or not this assignment of image rights is exclusive.
3. What remuneration shall be offered to the performer in consideration for him/her assigning those rights.

Key terms such as 'club context' or 'tournament context' should be clear and unambiguous.

When image rights disputes do arise, they are more likely to be a consequence of inadequate drafting and a consequent degree of

[39] R. Buchan & G. Grassie, *Personality Rights: A Brand New Species?* 49(5) J. L. Soc'y Scot. 48 (2004).

confusion rather than a deliberate violation of an existing contract or dishonest practice, perhaps motivated by perceived obligations to a third party but within which players are inadvertently caught in the middle rather than engaging in deliberately dishonest acts themselves. But some of the Indian cases mentioned previously seem to have their origins in sharp practice by third parties, and on those occasions the idea of a distinct statutory remedy has more to commend it. There is probably scope for exploring the potential of an Indian sports act, and there is certainly scope for asking whether India can learn anything from other jurisdictions' experience of image rights exploitation and protection as part of those explorations. And 10 years later, one is still left wondering what on earth the WICB and the WIPA were playing at.

Broadcasting of Sports in India

Saurabh Bhattacharjee

Introduction

Ever since the first ever radio broadcast of a sporting event took place on 11 April 1921 in the form of coverage of a boxing bout between Johnny Dundee and Johnny Ray at Pittsburgh,[1] broadcasting has been at the fulcrum of the growth of modern sports into gigantic, multinational and multibillion-dollars enterprise. Indeed, if the value of global sports market has been estimated to be around 1 per cent of the global GDP, approximately between US$600 and US$700 billion.[2] Buoyed by massive viewership that sporting events command and expansion of commercial television broadcasters, the need to fill their schedule and attract viewers, broadcasters are willing to spend incredibly large sums to acquire broadcasting rights.[3] For example, NBC Universal paid

---

[1] John McCoy, *Radio Sports Broadcasting in the United States, Britain and Australia 1920–1956 and Its Influence on the Olympic Games*, 5(1) J. OLYMPIC HIST. 20, 20 (1997).

[2] KPMG, *The Business of Sports: Playing to Win as the Game Unfurls* (September 2016), *available at* https://assets.kpmg.com/content/dam/kpmg/in/pdf/2016/09/the-business-of-sports.pdf

[3] *Id.*

US$1.226 billion for the Rio Olympic Games 2016.[4] Similarly, the National Football League (NFL) in the USA signed contracts pertaining to television rights of valuation of US$4.275 billion with Fox Sports between 2006 and 2012.[5] Not surprisingly, as observed by World Intellectual Property Organization (WIPO), 'the sale of broadcasting and media rights is now the biggest source of revenue, generating the funds needed to finance major sporting events, refurbish stadiums, and contribute to the development of sport at grassroots level'.[6] Indeed, a report by the global accounting firm, KPMG, estimated that broadcasting rights accounted for approximately 35 per cent of the global sports event market.[7] Television has also propelled the growth of sports through other indirect means such as increased exposure, rise in live attendance and gate revenues, and wider sale of merchandise.[8] The symbiotic interdependence of sports and television industry has become a central feature of modern sports. As an American court had commented with prescience, '[Sporting events] provide [ ] a magnificent spectacle for television programs and television provides an excellent outlet and market for [sporting events]. They both can use and indeed need each other.'[9]

[4] Jan Dawson, *Olympics TV Rights Costs Run Risk for NBC Universal*, VARIETY (12 July 2016), *available at* http://variety.com/2016/tv/news/nbcuniversal-olympics-2016-broadcast-costs-1201811506/

[5] GLENN M. WONG, ESSENTIALS OF SPORTS LAW 6 (2010).

[6] WORLD INTELLECTUAL PROPERTY ORGANISATION, *BROADCASTING AND MEDIA RIGHTS IN SPORTS*, *available at* http://www.wipo.int/ip-sport/en/broadcasting.html

[7] THOMAS HOEHN & ZAFEIRA KASTRINAKI, *Broadcasting and Sport: Value Drivers of TV Right Deals in European Football*, CITY (2012), *available at* https://www.city.ac.uk/__data/assets/pdf_file/0007/120130/Hoehn_Kastrinaki_Sports_Rights_Feb_2012.pdf

[8] Roger G. Noll, *Broadcasting and Team Sports*, 54 SCOT. J. POL. ECON. 400, 416 (2007).

[9] United States v. NFL, 116 F. Supp. 319, 325 (E.D. Pa. 1953) quoted in Lacie L. Kaiser, *Revisiting the Sports Broadcasting Act of 1961: A Call for Equitable Immunity from Section One of the Sherman Act for All Professional Sports Leagues*, 54 DEPAUL L. REV. 1237, 1238 (2005).

Even as the political economy of broadcasting has become inextricably linked with growth of sports, technological evolution and liberalisation of policy regimes have brought about tectonic shifts in the broadcasting sector itself. Growth of satellite television, proliferation of cable channels and digital transmission through the Internet have dramatically increased the demand for sports rights and globalised the business of broadcasting rights,[10] thereby causing considerable increase in revenue for major sports. Indeed, the contrast between the Reliance Cricket World Cup in 1987, where the total income from the tournament for the Board of Control for Cricket in India (BCCI) was about ₹6 lakh,[11] and Indian Premier League (IPL), whose TV rights were sold in 2008 to Sony Entertainment–World Sport Group for approximately US$1 billion,[12] illustrate the profound impact of the transformation in the television market on sports.

Ironically, while the expansion of sports broadcast market has provided increased income for sports-persons and larger amounts for sporting bodies to invest in development of sporting facilities and infrastructure, this phenomenon of universal access to sporting events is in danger of being eroded with the consequent commodification of broadcasting and rise of paid television channels.[13] Indeed, commodification of broadcasting has seen a steady marginalisation of free over-the-air public broadcasters from the sports market and their replacement by paid subscription-based networks.[14] In this process of what has been described as siphoning, public access to sports broadcast has diminished, even as the business of sports broadcasting has expanded meteorically.[15]

---

[10] Noll, *supra* note 8, at 416.

[11] GIDEON HAIGH, SPHERE OF INFLUENCE: WRITINGS ON CRICKET AND ITS DISCONTENTS 4 (2010).

[12] *Id.* at 30; *see also* Nagraj Gollapudi, *Will IPL Media Rights Cross the Billion Dollar Mark*, ESPNCRICINFO (2 September 2017), *available at* http://www.espncricinfo.com/india/content/story/1119060.html

[13] T. EVENS ET AL., THE POLITICAL ECONOMY OF TELEVISION SPORTS RIGHTS 6 (2013).

[14] Noll, *supra* note 8, at 416.

[15] Sriram Kilappakam, *Sports Broadcast Regulation in India*, IN INDIA AND INTERNATIONAL LAW 365, 367 (Bimal Patel ed., 2008).

In so far as sport is seen as a sociocultural activity that performs valuable public health function and integrative social function in building an inclusive society,[16] this paradox of reduced public access to sports broadcasting poses a profound regulatory challenge. The challenge is compounded by the scope for viewing access to sports as part of a person's right to information.[17]

Not surprisingly, several jurisdictions have sought to strike a balance between the commercial interests of broadcasters and sports federations and public interest of wider access to sports events through anti-siphoning statutes and administrative norms.[18] Indeed, according to one account, the UK attempted to introduce measures to guarantee access to events of national interest on television in the 1950s itself.[19] India has not been an exception to this global trend on anti-siphoning rules and the Parliament enacted the Sports Broadcasting Signals (Mandatory Sharing with Prasar Bharati) Act, 2007 (hereinafter SBSA), on 8 March 2007. This legislation introduced a statutory mechanism wherein the broadcasters are required to mandatorily share the broadcast signals with the public service broadcaster Prasar Bharati for major sporting events. As a result, a larger audience shall have access to major sporting events of national importance on the free-to-air Doordarshan. As a trade-off for such sharing of signals, the statute enjoins Prasar Bharati to share a part of its advertising revenue with the broadcaster, thereby harmonising the public interest embedded in wider access for sporting events with the commercial interests of the broadcasters.

However, this delicate balance between the competing interests that the Act seeks to manage has been, as shall be argued in this chapter, threatened by overzealous and expansive judicial

---

[16] R. Craufurd Smith & B. Bottcher, *Football and Fundamental Rights: Regulating Access to Major Sporting Events on Television*, 8(1) EUR. PUB. L. 107, 111 (2002).

[17] Richard Parrish & Samuli Miettinen, *Sports Broadcasting in Community Law*, IN TV RIGHTS AND SPORTS: LEGAL ASPECTS 24 (Ian Blackshaw ed., 2009).

[18] Kilappakam, *supra* note 15, at 366.

[19] Smith & Bottcher, *supra* note 16, at 112.

interpretation. In this chapter, I argue that Indian judiciary's interpretation of SBSA in *Star Sports India Private Limited v. Prasar Bharati*[20] (hereinafter *Star Sports* case) has led to imposition of very onerous obligations on the broadcasters. Such expansive reading of the rights of Prasar Bharati and obligations of the broadcasters not only constitute a subversion of the text and the spirt of SBSA but is also likely to prejudicially affect the growth of television broadcasting market in sports in India. To the extent that growth of some of sports in India is contingent on broadcast revenues, this chapter shall argue that judiciary's excessive deference to rights of Prasar Bharati may impede the further growth of sports in India.

In order to situate my central argument in its broader context, the chapter shall start with a discussion of the advent of broadcasting rights. Thereafter, the legal framework for anti-siphoning and broadcast sharing in India shall be examined. This shall be followed by a review of anti-siphoning laws in other jurisdictions. From this springboard, the chapter shall proceed to a critique of the *Star Sports* case and its impact on sports in India.

Emergence of Broadcasting Rights: An Overview

Invention of live transmission of events through relay of Hertzian waves and the consequent rise of live broadcasting of sports threw up several questions of intellectual property rights right from its inception. Even as sports organisers tried to monetise broadcast, the question of existence and ownership of property rights over the broadcast vexed the courts.[21] But the existence of proprietary rights in sports broadcast was recognised by the US District Court for the *Western District of Pennsylvania in Pittsburgh Athletic Co. v. KQV Broadcasting*[22] when it ruled that the sports teams and their leagues have an exclusive property

---

[20] Star Sports India Private Limited v. Prasar Bharati, (2016) 11 SCC 433.
[21] WONG, *supra* note 5, at 710.
[22] 24 F. Sup. 490 (W. D. Pa. 1938).

rights to the play-by-play broadcasts of their games and that any broadcaster shall have to obtain the consent before relaying an event.[23] Thereafter, as exemplified by the extension of copyright to television broadcast by the Copyright Act of 1956 in UK, rights of broadcasters slowly found recognition in intellectual property law.[24] Legal protection was considered to be necessary to safeguard the investment of the broadcaster in relaying sports events and to recognise the labour involved in the production and dissemination of broadcast.[25] Recognition of legal rights for broadcasters was also seen as essential for protecting broadcasting organisations against unfair competition and preventing unjust enrichment by third parties at the cost of the broadcasters.[26]

However, even as British law bracketed rights of broadcasters within the umbrella of copyright, the distinctiveness of such broadcasting rights posed certain problems, especially in the field of sports. One such point of uniqueness is the fact that the underlying material that constitutes the subject of the broadcast may not be a work of authorship protected by copyright or any other neighbouring right.[27] This is more so in the field of sports where, for example, the European Court of Justice held in *Premier League* v. *QC Leisure*[28] that sports events do not qualify as

---

[23] John T. Wolohan, *Sports Broadcasting Rights in the United States*, INT'L SPORTS L. J. 52, 53 (Winter 2007).

[24] LIONEL BENTLY & BRAD SHERMAN, INTELLECTUAL PROPERTY LAW 34 (2014).

[25] CATHERINE COLSTON & JONATHAN GALLOWAY, MODERN INTELLECTUAL PROPERTY LAW 313 (2010).

[26] Lucie Guibault & Roy Melzer, *The Legal Protection of Broadcast Signals*, 10 IRIS PL. 2, 2 (2004), *available at* https://www.ivir.nl/publicaties/download/768.pdf

[27] COLSTON & GALLOWAY, *supra* note 25.

[28] Joined Cases C 403/08 and 429/08—Football Association Premier League Ltd and Others v. QC Leisure and Others and Karen Murphy v. Media Protection Services Ltd (2011) ECR-I-9083, *available at* http://curia.europa.eu/juris/document/document.jsf;jsessionid=9ea7d0f130d5c7b1e0b6 5ea54d738b75d82f111ea4d4.e34KaxiLc3eQc40LaxqMbN4PaN4Me0?text=&docid=110361&pageIndex=0&doclang=EN&mode=lst&dir=&occ=first&part=1&cid=1197837

protected subject matter under European Union (EU) copyright law.[29] Further, broadcasts, unlike literary or musical works, do not involve protection of any fixed item but only pertain to communication of signals.[30] As such, broadcast rights conceptually differ from ordinary copyright in a significant way.

Thus, broadcasting rights were first endorsed in the international law in the form of neighbouring rights. The European Agreement on Protection of Television Broadcasts (EAT) 1960,[31] devoted exclusively to broadcasting, spoke of neighbouring rights.[32] Unlike this agreement which was regional in nature, the Rome Convention 1961 was the first global convention to recognise broadcasting rights in the form of neighbouring rights. The Rome Convention not only extended legal protection to broadcasting rights but also delineated the ambit of these rights.[33] The convention defined 'broadcasting' as the 'transmission by wireless means for public reception of sounds or of images and sounds'.[34] Article 13 of the convention affirmed that the

> Broadcasting organizations have the right to authorize or prohibit the re-broadcasting of their broadcasts, the fixation of their broadcasts, the reproduction of fixations of their broadcasts [and] the communication to the public of television broadcasts if such communication is made in places accessible to the public against payment of an entrance fee.[35]

---

[29] Thomas Margoni, *The Protection of Sports Events in the EU: Property, Intellectual Property, Unfair Competition and Special Forms of Protection*, 47 INT'L REV. INTELL. PROP. COMP. L. 386, 389 (2016).

[30] BENTLY & SHERMAN, *supra* note 24, at 87–88.

[31] European Agreement on the Protection of Television Broadcasts— COETS 2 (22 June 1960), *available at* http://www.wipo.int/edocs/lexdocs/treaties/en/ce-34ptb/trt_ce_34ptb_001en.pdf

[32] Guibault & Melzer, *supra* note 26, at 3.

[33] International Convention for the Protection of Performers, Producers of Phonograms and Broadcasting Organizations (Rome Convention) of 1961.

[34] Article 3(f), Rome Convention 1961.

[35] Article 13, Rome Convention 1961.

The convention also clarified that the term of protection for such right shall be 20 years from the end of the year in which the broadcast took place.[36]

The rights outlined in the Rome Convention have been supplemented by the Brussels or Satellites Convention 1974[37] which enjoined states to prevent the 'unauthorised distribution on or from its territory of any programme-carrying signal transmitted by satellite'[38] and later reiterated in the TRIPS Agreement. The agreement, which sought to lay down the global minimum standards with respect to intellectual property, stated that broadcasting organisations shall have 'the right to prohibit the unauthorized fixation, the reproduction of fixations, and the rebroadcasting by wireless means of broadcasts, as well as the communication to the public of their television broadcasts'.[39]

European regional law has also taken forward the scope of broadcast protection. Along with the EAT and the European Satellite Convention 1974[40] which reiterated the protection extend by the Rome Convention, the Rental and Lending Rights Directive[41] and the InfoSoc Directive[42] issued by the

[36] Article 14, Rome Convention 1961.

[37] The Brussels Convention Relating to the Distribution of Programme—Carrying Signals Transmitted by Satellite, 21 May 1974, 34 I.L.M 3.

[38] WIPO, Summary of the Brussels Convention Relating to the Distribution of Programme—Carrying Signals Transmitted by Satellite (1974), *available at* http://www.wipo.int/treaties/en/ip/brussels/summary_brussels.html

[39] Article 14(3), Agreement on the Trade-Related Aspects of Intellectual Property Rights, 1–4 April 1994, 33 I.L.M 1125.

[40] European Convention Relating to Questions on Copyright Law and Neighbouring Rights in the Framework of Transfrontier Broadcasting by Satellite 1974.

[41] EUR-Lex, *Council Directive 92/100/EEC of 19 November 1992 on Rental Right and Lending Right and on Certain Rights Related to Copyright in the Field of Intellectual Property*, 346 O. J. L. 0061, 0061 (27 November 1992), *available at* http://eur-lex.europa.eu/legal-content/EN/TXT/HTML/?uri=CELEX:31992L0100&from=EN

[42] EUR-Lex, *Directive 2001/29/EC of the European Parliament and of the Council of 22 May 2001 on the Harmonisation of Certain Aspects of*

European Commission have strengthened the scope of legal protection available for broadcasters. Indeed, it has been argued that the rights of broadcasting organisations under the European law are more extensive than those protected by the international law.[43]

In addition, there have been recent attempts by WIPO to adapt the content of broadcasting rights to recent technological changes through a new treaty.[44]

The recognition and expansion of broadcasting rights in the international law have been uneven and not bereft of controversy. Nonetheless, it is beyond doubt that the international instruments discussed in this section have cumulatively formed a normative basis for legal protection of rights of broadcasting organisations and have aided the gradual entrenchment of such rights within the municipal laws of several states.

Broadcasting Rights in India

The first two Indian legislations on copyright—the Copyright Act of 1914 and the Copyright Act of 1957—did not contain any provision on broadcasting rights. But with growing entrenchment of broadcasting rights in the international law, these rights were given normative endorsement in India too. With the TRIPS Agreement being negotiated under the aegis of the Uruguay Round of Trade Dialogue, amendments were made in 1994 to the Copyright Act of 1957 to introduce a chapter on the rights of broadcasting organisations which came into effect from 10 May

Copyright and Related Rights in the Information Society, 167 O. J. L. 0010, 0010 (22 June 2001), *available at* http://eur-lex.europa.eu/legal-content/EN/TXT/HTML/?uri=CELEX:32001L0029&from=EN

[43] Guibault & Melzer, *supra* note 26, at 4.

[44] Girish Kumar & Relfi Paul, *Rights of Broadcasting Organisation: Do We Need Legal Reform*, 2 IND. J. INTELL. PROP. L. 87, 91 (2009). *See*, generally, Tom Rivers, *A Broadcasters' Treaty*, IN COPYRIGHT LAW: A HANDBOOK OF CONTEMPORARY RESEARCH 483 (Paul Torremans ed., 2007).

1995.[45] These rights were further broadened through another set of amendments in 2012.[46]

Chapter VIII of the Copyright Act defines a broadcast and provides the scope of the broadcasting rights in India. Section 2(dd) of the Copyright Act of 1957 defines broadcast as 'communication to the public by means of any wireless diffusion, whether in one or more of the forms of signs, sounds or visual images or by wire and includes a rebroadcast'.[47] This definition is fairly inclusive in so far as it does not differentiate between the different kinds of broadcast. In other words, it is well-suited to adapt to technological changes since it embraces not only broadcast on television but also broadcast on the Internet, mobile and other digital platforms.

Section 37 acknowledges that whenever any programme is broadcast, the broadcasting organisation shall have a special right known as 'broadcast reproduction right' over such programme.[48] It also asserts that the broadcast reproduction right shall subsist in broadcasting organisation for a period of 25 years.

By spelling out the grounds for infringement, Section 37(2) also delineates the scope of such broadcasting right. It states that no person shall, without licence, (a) re-broadcast the broadcast; (b) cause the broadcast to be heard or seen by the public on payment of any charges; (c) make any sound recording or visual recording of the broadcast; (d) make any reproduction of such sound recording or visual recording where such initial recording was done without licence or, where it was licenced, for any purpose not envisaged by such licence; or (e) sell or give on commercial rental or offer for sale or for such rental any such sound recording or visual recording referred to in clause (c) or clause (d).

Pertinently, judicial interpretation of broadcasting right in India has consistently distinguished between broadcasting right

---

[45] Copyright (Amendment) Act 1994 (Act no. 38 of 1994).
[46] Copyright (Amendment) Act 2012 (Act no. 27 of 2012).
[47] Section 2 (dd), Copyright Act 1957.
[48] Section 37, Copyright Act 1957.

and copyright. The Madras High Court held in *Raj Video Vision* v. *M/s Sun TV* that satellite television broadcasting right is an independent right for which copyright could not be claimed.[49] This position was later reiterated by the Delhi High Court in *A. A. Associates* v. *Prem Goel*[50] and by the Bombay High Court in *M/s Video Masters* v. *M/s Nishi Productions*.[51] The most systematic exposition on this question was provided by the Delhi High Court in the case of *ESPN Star Sports* v. *Global Broadcast*[52] where the court affirmed the distinction between copyright and broadcasting right. The High Court held that:

> [T]he Legislature itself by terming broadcast rights as those akin to copyright clearly brought out the distinction between the nature of two rights in Indian Copyright Act, 1957. This was a clear manifestation of the legislative intent to treat copyright and broadcasting reproduction rights as distinct and separate rights.[53]

Thus, Chapter VIII of the Copyright Act of 1957 provides a statutory framework for vesting and protection of broadcasting rights as a set of neighbouring rights that are conceptually distinct and separate from copyright.

Nonetheless, the broadcasting rights enumerated in Section 37 have not been envisaged as absolute. In fact, Section 39 places explicit limitation with respect to use for bona fide teaching or research and reporting of current events. In addition, it also makes broadcasting rights subject to the same fair-dealing exceptions that copyright has been subject to through the provisions of Section 52 of the Act. These exceptions indicate the statutory intent of the Parliament to arrive at appropriate balance between the rights of the broadcasters and public interest embedded in wider access to broadcast. Indeed, such balancing of interests

---

[49] Raj Video Vision v. M/s Sun TV, 1994 SCC Online Mad 249.
[50] A.A. Associates v. Prem Goel, AIR 2002 Del 142.
[51] M/s. Video Masters v. M/s. Nishi Productions, 1998 (3) BomCR 782.
[52] ESPN Star Sports v. Global Broadcast, 2008 SCC Online Del 1385.
[53] *Id.* at para 17.

of individual and society is viewed as essential to all intellectual property laws.[54]

It is arguable in this context that such limitations on the rights of broadcasting organisations flow from the Constitution of India itself. Article 19(1)(a) of the Constitution which guarantees freedom of speech and expression has been interpreted to include the right to receive and impart information.[55] In fact, it has also been suggested that the right to information can also be derived from the fundamental right (FR) to life under Article 21.[56] More specifically in the context of broadcast, the Supreme Court in *Secretary, Ministry of Information and Broadcasting* v. *Cricket Association of Bengal (CAB)*[57] ruled that the right to communicate includes the right to communicate through any means available, whether print or electronic or audiovisual.[58] In a direct mandate that the Court imposed on the state to ensure wider access to broadcast, it said:

Air waves constitute public property and must be utilised for advancing public good. No individual has a right to utilise then at his choice and pleasure and for purposes of his choice including profit.... Airwaves being public property, it is the duty of the State to see that airwaves are so utilised as to advance the free speech right of the citizens which is served by ensuring plurality and diversity of views, opinions and ideas.[59]

In so far as the citizens have a FR to impart and receive information as part of the freedom of speech and expression and the state has a corresponding duty to ensure that airwaves are utilised to promote freedom of speech, it is reasonable to surmise

[54] N. S. GOPALKRISHNAN & T. G. AGITHA, PRINCIPLES OF INTELLECTUAL PROPERTY 362 (2014).

[55] Hamdard Dawakhana v. Union of India, AIR 1960 SC 554; PUCL v. Union of India, (2003) 4 SCC 399.

[56] R.P. Ltd v. Indian Express, AIR 1989 SC 190.

[57] Secretary, Ministry of Information and Broadcasting v. Cricket Association of Bengal, (1995) 2 SCC 161.

[58] *Id.* at para 120.

[59] *Id.* at 292, para 122.

that restrictions on broadcasting rights need not be limited to the express provisions embodied in Section 39 of the Copyright Act and the state has a duty to proactively ensure wider access to broadcast of events of public importance. This obligation of the state formed the constitutional justification for enactment of SBSA 2007 for ensuring public access on sporting events on public television.

Legislative Framework on Broadcast Sharing in India

The origin of SBSA lies in the popularity of cricket and the history of cricket broadcasting in India. Until 1993, the public broadcaster, Doordarshan, which had a monopoly in the television market, used to broadcast cricket matches organised in India and the BCCI used to pay a small sum in return for such broadcast.[60] With the advent of economic liberalisation, the CAB, a constituent of BCCI, awarded the broadcast rights for Hero Cup 1993, a tournament being organised to mark the diamond jubilee of the organisation, to Trans World International (TWI), a global sports television company.[61] Doordarshan and its parent body, the Ministry of Information and Broadcasting, claimed that the award of the rights to TWI was a violation of the Telegraph Act, 1885 and refused to provide uplinking facilities for the tournament.[62] CAB sought judicial redress and the dispute led to the landmark judgement in the *CAB* case discussed earlier in the chapter. The Supreme Court famously held that

> The right to telecast sporting event will therefore also include the right to educate and inform the present and the prospective sportsmen interested in the particular game and also to inform and entertain the lovers of the game. Hence, when a telecaster

---

[60] BORIA MAJUMDAR, TWENTY YARDS TO FREEDOM: A SOCIAL HISTORY OF INDIAN CRICKET 368 (2004).

[61] *Id.* at 371.

[62] HAIGH, *supra* note 11, at 9.

desires to telecast a sporting event, it is incorrect to say that the free-speech element is absent from his right.[63]

Justice Jeevan Reddy in a separate concurring judgement went on to hold that

> From the standpoint of Article 19(1)(a), what is paramount is the right of the listeners and viewers and not the right of the broadcaster—whether the broadcaster is the State, public corporation or a private individual or body. A monopoly over broadcasting, whether by Government or by anybody else, is inconsistent with the free speech right of the citizens.[64]

Thus, cricket became the proximate cause for Supreme Court to intervene and free not just sports broadcasting but also the broader television market from stranglehold of the state. Indeed, as Boria Majumdar wrote in his work *Twenty-two Yards to Freedom*, 'liberalisation of Indian media will forever remain a gift of Indian cricket to the Indian nation'.[65]

The *CAB* judgement opened up the cricket broadcast for several players such as ESPN, Star TV, Zee Television, Ten Sports and Nimbus Communications, and sale of broadcast rights to private television companies became the norm.[66] The royalties BCCI thus earned enable them to invest in the costly organisational and technical infrastructure involved in running the sport. Nonetheless, Doordarshan was able to strike commercial agreements with broadcasters and ensure telecast of major games on payment of royalty.[67] However, such negotiation with Ten Sports, the broadcast rights holder for the India's historic tour to Pakistan in 2004 (the first full tour by India to Pakistan in 15 years), got stuck in an impasse.

[63] *Supra* note 57, at 224, para 75.
[64] *Id.*, at 292, para 194.
[65] MAJUMDAR, *supra* note 60, at 405.
[66] HAIGH, *supra* note 11, at 9.
[67] Prashant Reddy, *The Broadcast of World Cup Cricket Matches and the SBS Act 2007—Did the Delhi HC Get it Right?* SPICYIP (21 February 2011), *available at* https://spicyip.com/2011/02/broadcast-of-world-cup-cricket-matches.html

With the prospect of the series not being broadcast on Doordarshan looming large, a public interest litigation (PIL) was filed in several High Courts, including the Madras High Court. The High Court observed that 'there is a prima facie case of fundamental rights of freedom and speech made out by the petitioners'[68] and directed Ten Sports to transmit the series in India through Doordarshan for payment to be worked out. On appeal, the Supreme Court continued with this arrangement and induced Doordarshan and Ten Sports to work out a revenue-sharing agreement so as to ensure broadcast on public television.[69]

While this was a one-off intervention, the approach of the judiciary categorically signalled that access to cricket broadcast may implicate FR of viewers and therefore may impose limits on the exclusive right of the broadcaster. This juxtaposition was evident in the rhetorical question posed by the Madras High Court in its interim order:

> But the airwave being a public property of 103 crores of Indians, can those primary rights be curtailed by allowing the third respondent to claim exclusivity even though it holds only second-ary rights to cater to the needs of only a specialized class of viewers through satellites and by pay channels?[70]

Even as the dust settled on the revenue-sharing agreement between Ten Sports and Doordarshan regarding India's tour of Pakistan, the Ministry of Information and Broadcasting issued the Policy Guideline for Downlinking of Television Channels 2005.[71] This policy guideline made it mandatory for sports

[68] Citizen Consumer & Civic Action Group v. Ten Sports, (2006) 5 Comp LJ 74 (Mad).

[69] *See*, for a description of litigation on this series, Kilappakam, *supra* note 15. *See also* Ten Sports v. Citizen Consumer & Civic Action Group, (2004) 5 SCC 351.

[70] *Supra* note 68.

[71] Policy Guideline for Downlinking of Television Channels 2005, F.No.13/2/2002–BP&L/BC-IV, Ministry of Information and Broadcasting, Government of India, 11 November 2005, *available at* http://cablequest. org/pdfs/broadcaters/DOWNLINKING-GUIDELINES.pdf

channels to share their feed with Prasar Bharati for national and international sporting events of national importance, held in India or abroad[72] with a revenue-sharing formula of 75:25 in the favour of the rights holders.[73] Immediately on its introduction, this policy was challenged by several broadcast companies before multiple forums.[74]

It was in this context that SBSA 2007 was enacted. It sought to enshrine the scheme outlined in the policy guideline in a statutory framework in order to guarantee access to sporting events of national importance on public television. It has been described as a statutory licence system.[75]

Section 3(1), which is the heart of the Act and is based on Paragraph 5.2 of the policy guideline, requires content rights owners, holders and broadcast service providers to simultaneously share the broadcast signal of sporting events of national importance, without its advertisements, to the Prasar Bharati.[76] The rules framed under the Act[77] supplement the obligation under Section 3(1) by stating that the signals shall include signals of the pre-live event and the post-live event coverage[78] and shall be the best feed, free from commercial advertisements.[79]

The trade-off for such mandatory sharing of signal is a continuation of the revenue-sharing formula laid down in Paragraph 5.2.5 of the policy guideline. Section 3(2) states that

[72] *Id.* at para 5.2.

[73] *Id.* at para 5.2.5.

[74] Kilappakam, *supra* note 15, at 379.

[75] Aparajita Lath & Prashant Reddy, *Is Prasar Bharati Having the Cake and Eating It Too: Star Sports v Prasar Bharati*, Spicy IP (9 August 2017), *available at* https://spicyip.com/2016/08/is-prasar-bharati-having-its-cake-and-eating-it-too-star-sports-v-prasar-bharati-supreme-court.html

[76] Section 3(1), SBSA.

[77] Sports Broadcast Signals (Mandatory Sharing with Prasar Bharati) Rules, 2007.

[78] Rule 3(4), Sports Broadcast Signals (Mandatory Sharing with Prasar Bharati) Rules, 2007.

[79] Rule 3(3), Sports Broadcast Signals (Mandatory Sharing with Prasar Bharati) Rules, 2007.

the advertising revenue earned by Prasar Bharati shall be shared in the ratio of 75:25 in favour of the rights holder in case of television broadcast and 50:50 for radio broadcast.

In pursuance of the Act, the Central government issued a notification in October 2007, designating sports of national importance.[80] While this notification was restricted to men's cricket,[81] a subsequent notification issued in 2012[82] designated Summer Olympics, Asian Games, Commonwealth Games, Paralympics, and few major tournaments in hockey, tennis and football as well. Special Olympics and a few more events have been added through a recent notification issued in January 2017.[83]

Thus, SBSA along with the rules and the notification cumulatively provides a statutory mechanism that seeks to ensure wider access to major sporting events on public television even as it respects the commercial imperatives of broadcaster by providing a formula for revenue-sharing. Admittedly, it has been argued that such anti-siphoning laws are unnecessary since sporting bodies are propelled by the imperative to popularise their sport and, therefore, they will strive to ensure wider access through their choice of broadcasters and terms of broadcast.[84] Some other

[80] Ministry of Information and Broadcasting, S.O. 1694(E), F. No. 16/8/2006/BP&1. Vol. III, 3 October 2007, *available at* http://www.mib.nic.in/sites/default/files/sbs1.pdf

[81] The notification designated as sporting events of national importance:

(1) All official One-Day and Twenty-20 matches played by the Indian Men's Cricket Team and Such Test matches as are considered to be of high public interest by the Central Government.
(2) Semi-finals and finals of Men's World Cup and International Cricket Council Championship Trophy.

[82] Ministry of Information and Broadcasting, S.O. 1489(E), F. No. 16/1/2012- BP&L, 4 July 2012, *available at* http://www.mib.nic.in/sites/default/files/sbs6.pdf

[83] Ministry of Information and Broadcasting, S.O. 302(E), F. No. 16/1/2012- BP&L, 27 January 2017, *available at* http://www.mib.nic.in/sites/default/files/Notification_dated_27.1.2017.pdf

[84] Parrish & Miettinen, *supra* note 17, at 22.

scholars assert that facilitating acquisition of broadcast rights by public broadcasters is more effective than governing the exercise of rights acquired by broadcasters.[85] Finally, it is also argued that since there is no objective mechanism for determination of free price for sharing of signals, any statutory scheme gives an unfair advantage to the public broadcaster.[86]

While there could be reasonable disagreement on the fairness of the revenue-sharing formula, it is undeniable that the scheme of SBSA gives effect to the public mandate of the state, as recognised by the judiciary, to protect the right to information of citizens through access to sporting events. This is particularly relevant for a country like India where paid television subscribers number less than 15 per cent of the population.[87] Moreover, SBSA also got rid of the contentious series-by-series negotiations between broadcasters and Prasar Bharati that preceded the legislation, thereby providing legislative clarity on the rights of broadcasters, an essential element for maturity of the broadcast market. In fact, as discussed earlier, SBSA followed a broader global trend of regulatory intervention to ensure sports broadcast on public free-to-air television.

Global Regime on Broadcast Sharing

In recognition of the social role of sports and of access to major sporting events being an integral component of the right to freedom of information, several jurisdictions have introduced measures to prevent siphoning or migration of sporting events to paid television from free television through award of exclusive rights

[85] *Id.*

[86] *Id.*

[87] Harvin Ahluwalia, *India's Pay TV Market to Touch $18 Billion by 2025: Report*, LIVEMINT (25 July 2016), *available at* http://www.livemint.com/Consumer/X9lwKpRLLf05gi4khHlFJN/Indias-payTV-market-to-touch-18-billion-by-2025-report.html. *See also* Statista, *Number of Pay TV Subscribers in India from 2016 to 2022*, *available at* https://www.statista.com/statistics/262013/number-of-pay-tv-subscribers-in-india/

to television broadcasters.[88] Indeed, the European Parliament established a regime through an amendment[89] to the Television Without Frontiers Directive in 1997[90] that allowed member states to use appropriate measures to ensure that broadcasters do not broadcast on an exclusive basis events of major importance and guarantee access to such events on free-to-air television.[91] Critically, the directive did not impose any mandate on the states nor did it specify the nature of measures that could be taken.[92] Nonetheless, it recognised the legitimacy of such anti-siphoning measures as long as they were in accordance with European community law.[93]

The non-committal approach of the directive on the nature of measures was prudent for the models of such anti-siphoning measures adopted in different jurisdictions in and beyond Europe have varied.

In the USA, the Federal Communications Commission (FCC) issued rules in 1975 which could be described as a model of anti-siphoning based on quantitative restrictions. The rules stated that cable channels could not devote more than 90 per cent of their time to film and sports.[94] Further, a complex scheme of

---

[88] Kilappakam, *supra* note 15, at 366.

[89] European Council Directive 97/36/EC, OJ L 202 of 30 July 1997.

[90] European Council Directive 89/552/EEC, OJ L 298 of 17 October 1989.

[91] Article 3(a), European Council Directive 97/36/EC.

[92] This directive has been replaced by a new directive in 2007 but the substance of Article 3(a) has been reproduced in Article 3(i) of the new directive. Directive 2007/65/EC, OJ L 332 of 18 December 2007.

[93] Article 3(a)(2) of the directive stated that

[M]ember States shall immediately notify to the Commission any measures taken or to be taken pursuant to paragraph 1. Within a period of three months from the notification, the Commission shall verify that such measures are compatible with Community law and communicate them to the other Member States.

[94] Home Box Office Inc. v. Federal Communications Commission, 567 F.2d 9 (D.C. Cir. 1977), 28.

prohibitions was introduced for broadcast of sporting events on cable television on the basis of coverage of such sports on free conventional television in the previous five years.[95]

The Broadcasting Services Act, 1992, passed by Australia introduced a first-rights model of anti-siphoning. Under this legislation, free-to-air broadcasters were given the first opportunity to bid for and obtain broadcast rights for sporting events that are listed as significant by the federal minister for communications.[96] Further, any commercial network can acquire the rights of a listed event only if it covers greater than 50 per cent of the Australian population.[97]

Part IV of the Broadcasting Act, 1996, enacted in UK mandates a regime wherein a broadcaster listed in the Pay TV category cannot broadcast designated sporting or other event of national importance without the consent of the Independent Television Commission (ITC) unless it is also broadcast by one channel categorised as a free-to-air television channel. While this regime does not guarantee the broadcast of major sporting events on free-to-air television, it does impose a major restriction on grant of exclusive broadcast rights to sporting events.

The Dutch model is closest to the Indian SBSA in its design. According to Article 5.1 of the Media Act, 2008, in the Netherlands,[98] broadcasters have to mandatorily share their feed for listed events, including sporting events with Nederlandse Omroep Stichting (NOS), the Dutch national broadcaster.[99] Thus, it envisages a mandatory sharing of feed model. But unlike SBSA, it also provides statutory guidance on principles that would govern classification of events into the list.

---

[95] *Id.*, 19.

[96] Paragraph 10(1)(e) of Schedule 2 to the Broadcasting Services Act 1992.

[97] *Id.* See Brendan Moylan, *Media Policy and Anti-Siphoning*, 16(3) COMM. L. BULLETIN 16, 17 (1997).

[98] WIPO, *Media Act 2008*, 29 December 2008, *available at* http://www.wipo.int/wipolex/en/details.jsp?id=9905

[99] *See*, generally, Vidushpat Singhania, *Sports Broadcasting Rights in India*, INT'L SPORTS L. J. 60, 62–64 (Winter 2007).

A cursory survey of anti-siphoning measures across these jurisdictions shows that such laws/administrative measures have become an integral part of regulatory landscape on sports and broadcast. While the anti-siphoning orders of the FCC in the USA were quashed by a court of appeals in the USA on jurisdictional and informational grounds[100] statutory norms on protection of public access to sports broadcast have been enforced by judiciary in several countries.

The House of Lords in UK in its decision in *R. (on the application of TV Danmark 1 Ltd)* v. *Independent Television Commission*[101] endorsed a refusal by the ITC to grant consent to TV Danmark 1, a satellite company in England which had obtained exclusive rights to a few football matches of the Denmark football team. The House of Lords referred to Article 3(a) of the Television Without Frontiers Directive and held:

> It is to prevent the exercise by broadcasters of exclusive rights in such a way that a substantial proportion of the public in another member state is deprived of the possibility of following a designated event. The obligation to achieve that result is in no way qualified by considerations of competition, free market economics, sanctity of contract and so forth.... Its terms represent a compromise between the policies in question and the interests of the general public in being able to watch sporting events for free.[102]

[100] *See* Home Box Office Inc. v. Federal Communications Commission, 567 F.2d 9 (D.C. Cir. 1977), where the court vacated the orders on the grounds that the commission had exceeded its jurisdiction, had not produced evidence to demonstrate the need for anti-siphoning rules and that restrictions on free speech were greater than what was essential for furthering the stated governmental interest. *See* James B. Perrine, *Constitutional Law Challenges to Anti-Siphoning Laws in the United States and Australia*, Legal Issues in Business, 3 SPORTS ADMIN. 21 (2001); Phillip M. Cox II, *Flag on the Play: The Siphoning Effect on Sports Television*, 47 FED. COMM. L. J. 571, 576–577 (1995); M. Agnes Siedlecki, *Sports Anti-Siphoning Rules for Pay-Cable Television: A Public Right to Free TV*, 53 IND. L. J. 821, 825–831 (1978) for analysis of the Home Box Office Inc. decision.

[101] R. (on the application of TV Danmark 1 Ltd) v. Independent Television Commission, (2001) 1 W.L.R. 1604.

[102] Lord Hoffman in para 33, at 1613.

The Court of Justice of European Communities also adjudicated on the anti-siphoning measures of UK in *Commission of the European Communities v. In front WM AG (France and Others, Intervening)*.[103] While it endorsed the challenge to the list drawn by UK on procedural grounds, the legitimacy of the anti-siphoning provisions in Part IV of the Broadcasting Act was not itself challenged.

Thus, anti-siphoning measures have been globally recognised as a legitimate instrument to balance the needs and concerns of public policy in promoting access to televised sports and the commercial imperatives of broadcasters and sports broadcast market in general. Enactment of SBSA by the Indian Parliament in 2007 therefore cannot be seen as exceptional and intrusive but a nuanced attempt to reconcile the competing interests of broadcasters and the viewing public. But as the next section of the chapter would aver, judicial interpretation of SBSA has imperilled this fine balance that the legislature has drawn.

Harming Sports by Protecting It: *Star Sports India Pvt. Limited v. Prasar Bharati*

With the growing monetary value of the television broadcast market in cricket in India, cricket has become the centrepiece of several disputes on the scope of broadcasting rights in India. Not surprisingly, the first major case, the *Star Sports* case,[104] to be adjudicated under SBSA also emerged out of cricket.

The case revolved around on-screen credits or the logos of sponsors provided on graphics and special features provided on the global feed of the cricket tournaments organised by the International Cricket Council (ICC). Star Sports India Private Ltd (hereinafter SSIPL), the rights holder, expressed to Prasar

---

[103] Commission of the European Communities v. Infront WM AG (France and Others, Intervening), (Case C-125/06 P), decided on 13 March 2008, (2008) 2 C.M.L.R. 28.

[104] *Supra* note 20.

214 / Saurabh Bhattacharjee

Bharati that the feed that would be shared with it would have the on-screen credits on them. Prasar Bharati, however, refused to accept such feed since Section 3 of SBSA required sharing of signals without advertisement. This impelled SSIPL to approach the Delhi High Court for a declaratory relief to the effect that

> Its obligation to share live broadcast signals of sporting events of national importance... is discharged by it sharing the live broadcast signal as per the feed made available to it by the organizer of the sporting event; with such commercial advertisements inserted by the organizer of the sporting event who is the principal 'content right owner' of the broadcast.[105]

The main basis of its petition was that the on-screen credits were inserted by the organiser and it had no control over these on-screen credits. Therefore, such credits arguable do not fall within the ambit of 'its advertisements', the phrase used in Section 3(1). The High Court, however, found no merit in the writ petition and held that 'Whosoever airs a live television broadcast of sporting events of national importance must share the same without any advertisements.'[106]

On appeal, the Supreme Court affirmed the findings of the High Court and agreed with Prasar Bharati's submission that Section 3 places obligations not just on broadcasting service but also on content rights owner and contents holder. Based on this premise, the Court observed:

> [E]xamined in this hue, it becomes clear that the words 'without its advertisements' which follow immediately after the words 'unless it simultaneously shares the live broadcasting signal' has to be given a meaning that such broadcasting signals are to be without advertisements, whether it is of the content rights owner, content holder or that of television or radio broadcasting service provider.[107]

---

[105] ESPN Software India Private Ltd v. Prasar Bharati, 2013 Indlaw DEL 2275, para 5.

[106] *Id.*, at para 27.

[107] *Supra* note 20, at 454, para 38.

Thus, the Court concluded that even if it is ICC which has inserted the on-screen credits, the feeds have to be without those logos/advertisements since it is plain that these advertisements have been placed by the content holder, that is, ICC. As a result, the appeal of SSPIL was dismissed by the Supreme Court.

More troublingly, the Court observed that 'If the advertisements are also to be included in the signals, there has to be sharing of the revenue.'[108] Thus, the Court appears to have indicated that on-screen credits may be allowed for payment of additional revenue. This reference to sharing of revenue seems to be predicated on the assertion that through broadcast on public television, such on-screen credits have a much larger viewership and the benefit of advertisement would accrue to those who have booked the advertisements and the service provider would be able to charge much more from the advertisers.[109]

It is submitted, however, that the Supreme Court's stance on on-screen credits as part of broadcast sharing in the *Star Sports India* case suffers from faulty assumptions and poor understanding of nature of sports broadcast, and an erroneous interpretation of the text of Section 3 of SBSA is contrary to the spirit of the statute and threatens to wreck the fine balance between the rights of broadcasters and interest of viewers.

First, Supreme Court's observation that the broadcaster must remove the on-screen credit, inserted on the global feed by the event organisers and not within their control, is based on an incomplete understanding of the nature of sports broadcast. Removal of on-screen credits may significantly increase the transmission cost for the broadcasters since these are not inserted by them but received on the global feed. Further, such on-screen credits pervade all aspects of modern sports viewing. These are visible on scorecards, additional statistical information, graphics, replays, etc.; removal of on-screen credits would substantially undermine the viewing experience as viewers may have to forego

[108] *Id.*, at 454, para 37.
[109] *Id.*, at 453–454, para 35.2.

such additional information which are essential for a complete understanding of ebbs and flows of the game in progress.[110]

Second, Supreme Court's observations that since Section 3(1) refers to content rights owner as well as broadcast service provider, the phrase 'its advertisement' would also encompass advertisements inserted by ICC, the content rights owner, flies against the face of logic and plain meaning of the text of the statute. A holistic reading of Section 3(1) would make it plain that the obligation to share the feed without advertisement falls on the entity sharing the feed with Prasar Bharati. Therefore, the words 'its advertisements' refer to advertisements added by such entity. In other words, if the feed is shared directly by the content rights owner with Prasar Bharati, then the prohibition would embrace advertisements added by the content rights owner. But where the feed is shared by a broadcasting service, the prohibition would apply only to the advertisements inserted by the broadcaster. Any other reading of this section would result in such impractical obligations being placed on the broadcaster as alluded to in the previous paragraph that would undermine the quality of the broadcast.

The Court's observation on revenue-sharing by the broadcaster with Prasar Bharati for on-screen credit is particularly troubling. As mentioned earlier, the Court based the economic justification for such revenue-sharing on the prospect of the broadcaster making a gain through such advertisements reaching a wider audience through Doordarshan. However, this contention ignores that the broadcaster does not make any money through on-screen credits.[111] Since they do not book the on-screen credits, broadcasters do not stand to monetise the prospect of these advertisements being extended to a wider viewership, and therefore this economic justification falls flat.

---

[110] Roshan Gopalkrishna, *Mandatory Sharing of Sports Broadcast Signals in India*, Part-I, LAW IN SPORTS (4 August 2016), *available at* https://www.lawinsport.com/articles/item/mandatory-sharing-of-sports-broadcast-signals-in-india-part-1-a-review-of-star-sports-v-prasar-bharati
[111] *Id.*

More worrisome is the normative justification offered for revenue-sharing in lieu of on-screen credits. Supreme Court observed that while sharing of signal must ordinarily be clean of advertisement,

> Exception is, however, made in sub-section (2) of section 3 which enables the broadcasting service provider to even share the contents along with advertisements, but subject to the condition that there has to be sharing of revenue in the proportion prescribed in sub-section (2) of Section 3.[112]

This is a gross inversion of the text and design of SBSA. As mentioned earlier, Section 3(2) provides the statutory formula for sharing of revenue by Prasar Bharati out of its revenue from such shared broadcast with the broadcaster as a trade-off for the compulsory sharing of feed. A plain reading would make it amply clear that this is a general norm to be applicable to very case of sharing of signal under Section 3.[113] Yet the preceding observation relegates it to the status of an exception. If Section 3(2) is to be read only as an exception to be applied in the case of feed with on-screen credits, would this imply that there is no obligation upon Prasar Bharati for sharing its revenue in case of routine application of Section 3(1)? The answer to the question is suggestive of the absurdity of the Court's position.

Further, since the broadcaster does not earn any revenue from on-screen credits, there is a huge cloud of confusion about how such on-screen credits would be valued and payment be operationalised.[114] Did the Court mean that the broadcaster must not only share its signal but also in addition pay 70 per cent of its revenue from broadcast on its network? An affirmative answer to this question would render SBSA an extractive legislation that not only restricts but also nullifies the proprietary rights of the broadcaster in its telecast, thus raising the spectre of unconstitutionality. Such payment of revenue would also lead to unjust

---

[112] *Supra* note 20, at 453, para 35.2.
[113] Lath & Reddy, *supra* note 75.
[114] *Id.*

enrichment of Prasar Bharati which would not only earn revenue of the broadcast on its network but also obtain a lion's share of the revenue earned by the broadcaster.[115]

Most perniciously, Supreme Court's reading of SBSA in the *Star Sports* case may impede the growth of television broadcast rights in sports. The restrictions imposed on the broadcasters by the Supreme Court on the basis of Section 3 of SBSA may deter entry of broadcasters into sports or lead to undervaluation of television rights for sporting events classified as events of national importance. Either way, it would have a deleterious impact on access to sports and growth of sports in the country. Reluctance among broadcasters to bid for sporting events may lead to decline in television coverage, on both paid and public television. Undervaluation of broadcast rights would leave sports bodies with less funds to invest in infrastructure, grass-roots programme and training of sports-persons, thus harming growth of sports in the country.

Conclusion

This chapter has traced the recognition of broadcasting rights as part of intellectual property rights law and the consequent symbiotic expansion of sports and television broadcast of sports into global businesses. Further, it has highlighted the paradox of siphoning of sports broadcast away from free-to-air television to paid television with expansion of the broadcast market and deleterious impact it has on the right to information of the public to access sports. In this context, anti-siphoning laws that impose some limitations on exclusive rights of broadcasters in order to promote broadcast of sports on public television, have been widely used across jurisdictions. While the nature of these regulations varies across jurisdictions, they are united in their attempt to strike a balance between the commercial interests of broadcasters and sports federations and public interest.

---

[115] Gopalkrishna, *supra* note 110.

SBSA 2007 is also one such attempt to combat siphoning of sports broadcast to private television network. The statute tries to harmonise the right to information of the public with the interests of broadcasters by minimal interference with exclusive rights of the broadcasters through obligation to share feed for a few select sporting events. Through a statutory formula for revenue-sharing, the Parliament sought to provide recompense for this minimal interference with broadcast rights.

However, this chapter avers that the maximalist approach of Prasar Bharati and the judiciary to broadcaster's obligation under SBSA jeopardises this statutory scheme. The judicial position on SBSA and on-screen credit, as reflected in *Star Sports India* case, betrays ignorance of the realities of sports broadcast, subverts the text, spirit and purpose of the statute, and imposes an impractically onerous obligation on the broadcaster. In doing so, the Court has created substantial hurdles for growth of sports broadcast market in India and given the close relationship between monetisation of broadcast rights and growth of sports, such hurdles may stem the expansion of sports in general in India. Admittedly, bigger and more lucrative sports such as cricket and football may be able to absorb the shock, but these concerns would be particularly pertinent in case of sports with a smaller fan base and relatively lower valuation. Therefore, there is a real danger of the very sustenance of sports in India being jeopardised by such maximalist position on broadcast sharing in the name of public access to sports.

It is averred that the subversion and ambiguity created as a result of this decision calls for urgent parliamentary intervention to clarify the legal position on on-screen credits and the obligation of the broadcasters to share signals of sporting events. The recent decision of the Supreme Court in *Union of India* v. *BCCI*[116] on re-telecast of feed shared with Prasar Bharati by cable operators, where a two-judge bench held Section 3 of SBSA to be expropriatory in nature and, therefore, requiring

---

[116] Union of India v. BCCI, 2017 SCC Online 991.

strict interpretation,[117] offers a partial corrective in this regard. Nonetheless, stability of law and clear articulation of rights and obligations of broadcasters and viewing public call for immediate statutory amendments clarifying that Section 3(2) is not an exception to Section 3(1) and that on-screen credits, not inserted by the broadcasters, do not fall under the prohibition on advertisements imposed by Section 3(1).

[117] *Id.*, at para 30.

Commercialisation of Sports and Indian Franchise Leagues

Shameek Sen

Introduction

'*Yeh Dus Saal Aap Key Naam*' (These 10 years are dedicated to you)—This was the title of the theme song for the tenth edition of the broadcast of the VIVO Indian Premier League (IPL) being carried out by Sony Entertainment Television in the summer of 2017.[1] Indeed, much has happened in these 10 years. The Indian domestic scenario has undergone massive transformation not only in terms of how respective sports are played but also in terms of how they are marketed. More significantly, many traditional sporting tournaments and leagues, and sporting clubs whose saga

---

[1] Of course, the tenth year of Sony has proved to be its last year. Star India Limited, the direct competitor of Sony, has managed to outbid Sony by getting the exclusive broadcasting rights of the IPL for the next five years for a record-breaking sum of Rs. 16,347.50 crore, which roughly translates to Rs. 54.50 crore per match. See generally, Gaurav Laghate, *Rs 54.5 Crore per Match Is Not Insane, Look at It in Right Context: Star India CEO Uday Shankar*, The Economic Times, 5 September 2017, available at http://economictimes.indiatimes.com/articleshow/60359780.cms?utm_source=contentofinterest&utm_medium=text&utm_campaign=cppst

of exploits date back to almost historical times, have borne the brunt of such onslaught of commercialisation. In some cases, this dialectic between tradition and modernity in sports has thrown up interesting issues of ethics. These ethical issues also translate into legal issues in some distinct cases. This chapter aims to flag a few of these ethico-legal concerns.

The chapter is divided into three parts. The first part generally highlights the phenomenon of commercialisation of Indian sports and seeks to flag the significant changes that have been brought about in the last 10 years with respect to different sports and sporting tournaments in India, with the advent of franchise leagues. Then, this chapter goes on to specifically focus on one specific instance—the Indian Super League (ISL)–I-League debate—in the context of Indian football, which gives rise to many interesting questions of law and ethics. Finally, this chapter seeks to explore questions of whether, and in what ways, law can help in self-preservation of traditional sporting tournaments and clubs, and make them competent to face up to the gregarious onslaught of consumerism and commercialisation.

Franchise Leagues and the Traditional Sporting Structures: An Interplay

The New Webster Dictionary of the English Language defines 'sports' as a 'diversion, amusement, recreation, a pleasant pastime, having an athletic character'.[2] However, in the contemporary times, sports have moved far away from being a 'pleasant pastime' and an 'amusement' or 'recreation' to being a highly commercialised discipline—a sophisticated business operation. Thus, the almost amateurishly organised sporting tournaments and sporting clubs have given way to, or have been pushed into virtual obscurity, by multimillion-dollar professional sporting leagues, also known as franchise leagues.

---

[2] *See* NEW WEBSTER DICTIONARY OF THE ENGLISH LANGUAGE 942 (1981), referred to in Gregor Lentze, *The Legal Concept of Professional Sports Leagues: The Commissioner and an Alternative Approach from a Corporate Perspective*, 6 MARQ. SPORTS L. J. 65 (1995).

Franchise leagues are primarily envisaged as competitions between city-based clubs which tend to represent the aspirations of certain geographical territories. Thus, the underlying economic assumption behind such city-based franchises is that such leagues consist of teams which have an immediately identifiable catchment area for their fan base and marketability potentials. This idea of city-based franchises is principally opposed to having multiple clubs representing the same city, which leads to an inevitable split of the fan base and is, therefore, strictly professionally speaking, economically inefficient as a business model.[3]

However, an immediate pitfall of this approach can be evident from the fact that if one considers the recreational nature of sports, then the mundane economic and statistical parameters are far often outweighed by emotive behavioural patterns, which may or may not offer justifications premised of sound rationality.

A case in point is in the way football is played in the city of Kolkata, a city often referred to in the popular cultural references as the 'Mecca of Indian Football'. Kolkata has, in addition to the hundreds of locality-based clubs that play the game of football on a competitive basis, three prominent football clubs—Mohun Bagan Athletic Club, East Bengal Club and the Mohammedan Sporting Club. All these clubs, often referred to as the 'Big Three' of Kolkata football, have a luminous history of more than 100 years,[4] and

[3] In fact, it works on the same assumptions which had once led to the formation of professional SAs in the USA in the 1990s, which, to echo the thoughts of the economic thinkers belonging to the Chicago School, 'enhances efficiency because it increases the marketability of the generic product that previously existed and marketing a product becomes more successful than without the integration'. *See* Robert H. Heidt, *Don't Talk of Fairness: The Chicago School's Approach Towards Disciplining Professional Athletes*, 61 IND. L. J. 53, 55–56 (1985).

[4] Mohun Bagan Athletic Club was founded in 1889, East Bengal Club in 1920 and Mohammedan Sporting Club in 1891. Among the three, Mohun Bagan found its place in the history first when in 1911, it defeated East Yorkshire Regiment 2–1 in the final of the IFA Shield. This victory before 60,000 boisterous Bengalis shouting 'Vande Mataram' from the stands was heralded as one of the major landmarks of the Indian National Movement. In fact, some historical accounts of the nationalistic euphoria that followed this victory credit the shift of the national capital of the British India from

have an extensive fan base within inside and outside India. The matches played between Mohun Bagan and East Bengal (and to a limited extent, Mohammedan Sporting) find their rightful place in the legendary league of Derby matches[5] and are widely followed throughout the world. In fact, the emotions of people surrounding the match can be seen in the streets of Kolkata during the match, which brings the city to a virtual standstill. Such intense emotional upheavals could hardly be matched by the franchise-owned, professionally managed side Atletico de Kolkata, when they appeared for the ISL, despite all the glitz and glamour, and the lure of watching marquee ex-World Cuppers representing Indian cities.

Naturally, therefore, to start with, it will be grossly improper to draw a direct cause–effect co-relation between professionalism or commercial potential and their eventual impact on the spectators. Moreover, even if we take into account professional leagues that are more impactful than their traditional counterparts, in some cases, pure sporting logic demands that they are played in a manner that is at best supplementary, and definitely

---

Calcutta to Delhi, to a realisation of the British after this victory of Mohun Bagan that it would not be safe to continue with Calcutta, a city whose ultra-nationalistic tendencies got a definite boost after this victory, as the national capital. Far-fetched as it may be, this phenomenon definitely indicates the kind of impact a single football match and a single football club had created in the minds of the people of a subjugated country. *See*, generally, Arjun Wadhwa, *History of Football in India*, THE SPORTS CAMPUS (2008), *available at* http://www.thesportscampus.com/200805197/introduction-to-football/history-indian-football. *See also*, Subroto Sarkar, *Of the First Red-Letter Day in Indian Sports*, The Hindu, 21 July 2001, *available at* http://www.thehindu.com/2001/07/21/stories/0721096e.htm

[5] In fact, parallels are drawn between the Kolkata Derby and the Scottish Old Firm Derby played between Rangers F.C. and Celtic F.C., inasmuch as it is looked at as a cross-ethnic fight between the 'Nativists' (Mohun Bagan) and the 'Immigrants' (East Bengal), much like its Scottish counterpart. *See*, generally, Sarthak Dubey, *Mohun Bagan Vs. East Bengal—The Deadly Derby Awaits—Please Fasten Your Seat Belts*, GOAL (2011), *available at* http://www.goal.com/en-india/news/1064/i-league/2011/11/19/2762641/mohun-bagan-vs-east-bengal-the-deadly-derby-awaits-please-fasten. FIFA has also referred to this match as a 'Classic Rivalry'. *See* FIFA, *India's All-Consuming Rivalry* (2011), *available at* http://www.fifa.com/news/y=2011/m=4/news=india-all-consuming-rivalry-1414458.html

not substitutive of one another. To illustrate, one can look at the game of cricket. Although several domestic tournaments such as the Ranji Trophy, Duleep Trophy and Deodhar Trophy continue to be played (in most cases, before a sparsely populated stadium), it will be absolutely naive to assume that they have an identical, or even comparable, status to the IPL. In most of the domestic tournaments, there is hardly any television coverage of the matches. More often than not, a stellar performance in such matches goes absolutely unnoticed and virtually unreported. Quite obviously, it acts as a disincentive to the players participating in such matches, and it would not be improper to submit that it may adversely affect their levels of commitment and seriousness while playing these matches.

It is not only these logistic challenges that are faced by the domestic tournaments. Sometimes, the challenges are existential in nature. An example of such existential crisis can be seen in the way the Duleep Trophy, a traditional domestic season-opener, was almost removed from the cricket calendar of the Board of Control for Cricket in India (BCCI), but was restored in the last moment owing to a timely intervention of Mr Sourav Ganguly, himself a former cricketing legend and currently an able administrator of the game.[6] Similarly, the NKP Salve Challenger Trophy, which was an important List-A tournament in the late 1990s and the early 2000s, has simply been discontinued since 2014,

---

[6] However, despite the best intentions of the former cricketing legend, one thing is for sure—the Duleep Trophy, once a premier cricket tournament that had catapulted many players into national reckoning, is going to be an absolute low-key, insignificant affair. To quote a media report,

'The top Indian players will be gearing up for the Australia limited overs series and the second rung will be preparing for the New Zealand A series. You won't have the top 30–32 players playing. The players available will be the next 30, who will not remotely be in contention for national call-up', [an] official [of the BCCI] said.

See Express Web Desk, *Duleep Trophy Back after Sourav Ganguly's Letter to CoA, The Indian Express*, 29 August 2017, *available at* http://indianexpress.com/article/sports/cricket/duleep-trophy-back-after-sourav-ganguly-letter-to-coa-4819762/

arguably because of the packed calendar, which includes a clear window of more than a month reserved for the IPL, the proverbial cash cow of BCCI.

This tragic saga of Indian domestic cricket has obvious repercussions on the way the game is played in India. The virtual absence of the national players from the domestic cricketing scene, except during the IPL, implies that junior cricketers who break into the state ranks after a lot of blood and sweat miss the opportunity of rubbing shoulders with the greats of the game and learn the nuances of professional cricket from the Kohlis and the Ashwins. Moreover, the insatiable urge to get noticed and to earn some quick bucks from the game are luring them away from focusing on technique and put more emphasis on the IPL variety of hara-kiri cricket. The sufferer in the whole process is definitely the game of cricket.

The advent of franchise leagues has not missed the individual sporting disciplines also. India today has two such franchise tennis leagues,[7] a Premier Badminton League (PBL)[8] and a similar league involving the game of table tennis.[9] In addition, of course, there are leagues dealing with sports such as hockey,

---

[7] The Indian Premier Tennis League (IPTL) was started in 2014 by former player Mahesh Bhupathi, involving city-based teams from different parts of Asia. Its rival, the Champions Tennis League (CTL), was started in 2015 by another former tennis great Vijay Amritraj. Unlike the IPTL which has a pan-Asian presence, the CTL is confined to teams representing different Indian cities. See, generally, Ronny Rear, *IPTL and CTL: The Conflicting Reality of Want and Need*, Tennis World (2015), *available at* http://www.tennisworldusa.org/tennis/news/Editors_Thoughts/28843/iptl-and-ctl-the-conflicting-duality-of-want-and-need/

[8] It was first named the Indian Badminton League (IBL) when it was launched by the Badminton Association of India (BAI) in the year 2013. It was re-launched in 2016 as the PBL. It has teams representing Indian cities, fighting against each other in what has been called as 'The Highest Prize Money Badminton Tournament in the World'. See, generally, http://www.pbl-india.com/news

[9] The Ultimate Table Tennis (UTT) is the newest entrant in the franchise Leagues, having been launched in 2017. What is interesting to note with respect to this league is that unlike similar leagues in other sports, the teams in this table tennis league do not have a distinct city-based identity. They

wrestling and kabaddi, each of which is a highly successful commercial venture owing to prime-time television coverage, team ownerships by sporting and Bollywood personalities, and the city-based format in most cases. It would not be an overstatement to assert that with the advent of these glitzy and glamorous sporting leagues, the difference between competitive sports and reality television has got significantly blurred. It is also true that many sports-persons, whose dexterity in their sport would have otherwise gone completely unnoticed, are brought to the centre stage of public attention as a result of participation in these widely followed franchise leagues.

However, as much as these leagues could potentially bring about developments in certain sports, what goes unnoticed amidst all the frenzy surrounding these leagues is that many traditional domestic tournaments are undergoing a gradual journey towards ultimate extinction, simply because they cannot by any means match up to the franchise leagues in terms of either coverage or marketing. A good example of such direct conflict between a franchise league and a traditional league can be witnessed in the context of a recent fiasco involving the game of football, which shall be the focus of discussion in the forthcoming section.

The ISL–I-League Fiasco: A Saga of the Inevitable?

If one looks at the history of the game of football in India, it can be seen that until the 1996–1997 season, football used to be largely confined to specific centres such as Kolkata, Goa and Kerala, with the local football clubs competing among themselves for the local leagues (like the Calcutta Football League), and some premier domestic tournaments such as the Durand Cup, the Rovers Cup and the Federation Cup. In addition, the individual states used to compete for the Santosh Trophy. Overall, it was seen that there was no single national football league that could be played on a home-and-away basis like the English Premier

---

are rather known by corporate brand names. *See*, generally, https://www.ultimatetabletennis.in/

League of the Spanish La Liga. With the aim of having such a professionally run national football tournament, the National Football League (NFL) was started in 1996, which later got rechristened to be called the I-League in 2007.[10]

In the last 10 years, the I-League has had a mixed impact on the game. While prominent clubs such as Mohun Bagan, East Bengal and others which have a dedicated fan base have definitely benefited from the league, the same does not hold true for many other legendary clubs, which were forced to close down, either due to management issues or because of other reasons.[11] On the other hand, the I-League has definitely been instrumental in reaching the game out to centres which had hitherto been in the penumbral zone of Indian football. The biggest testament to the growing influence of the I-League to non-traditional centres can be witnessed from the fact that the I-League in the year 2016 was won by Aizawl FC, a relatively lesser known club from the north-eastern part of the country.[12]

In the year 2013, the All India Football Federation (AIFF) joined hands with IMG Reliance and Star Sports to launch the ISL, the city-based franchise league, with the clear intention of making the game of football the 'Second Sport' of India after cricket and to 'create a movement around football' and 'putting India on the global map'.[13]

However, the point to be noted here is that at least in its formative years, the ISL was never looked at as a substitute of

[10] *See*, generally, I-League, *History*, *available at* http://ileague.in/history/

[11] The first champions of the NFL, the JCT Football Club of Ludhiana (a club that had been serving Indian football since 1971), was one such legendary club which was forced to disband their football operations in 2011. Similarly, teams such as Mahindra United and FC Kochi were also forced to shut down due to various reasons. *Id.*

[12] *See*, generally, http://www.aizawlfc.com/

[13] *See* IMG, *Reliance, IMG Worldwide and Star India, Launch 'Indian Super League' for Football* (2013), *available at* https://web.archive.org/web/20160313201118/; http://img.com/news/news/2013/october/reliance,-img-worldwide-and-star-india,-launch-%60in.aspx

the I-League. In fact, the Fédération Internationale de Football Association (FIFA) General Secretary Jerome Valcke, on his visit to India during the inauguration of the ISL, had remarked,

> We will not call ISL a league. For us, there is one league and it is the I-League. ISL is a tournament and helps in the recognition of the sport, because it brings a lot of attention not only in India, but also outside. But then again, you cannot have two leagues in a country—it doesn't work. So, for us, there is one league under the aegis of the federation and that's the I-League.[14]

In the last three years of its existence, the ISL definitely created its imprint over the Indian footballing milieu, and this prompted the AIFF to take this 'revolution' to its logical next step—merging the I-League with the ISL and giving to the ISL the recognition of the only national football league in India.

While some of the I-League clubs like the Bengaluru FC, a corporate club managed by the JSW Group which has done remarkably well in the I-League in the few years that it participated in it, immediately decided to join the ISL, there was serious resentment from the traditional Kolkata giants—Mohun Bagan and East Bengal—and they were joined in their protests by Aizawl FC and several other clubs.[15] Among the reasons of their objections, one of the primary concerns expressed was about the fact that the clubs would have to give out the intellectual property rights of the clubs, including club names, emblems, jersey colours, etc. to the promoters of the merged league for a period of 30 years.[16] Moreover, since the ISL principally operates on a city-based franchise model, the clubs such as Mohun Bagan and East Bengal

---

[14] See Mihir Vasavda, *I-League, ISL Situation Explained: New Proposal Shakes Old Wedding, The Indian Express*, 16 May 2017, *available at* http://indianexpress.com/article/sports/football/indian-super-league-bengaluru-fc-mohun-bagan-isl-bigwigs-likely-to-jump-aboard-4657431/

[15] See, generally, Amitabha Das Sharma, *Objections Raised on I-League–ISL Merger, The Hindu*, 29 March 2017, *available at* http://www.thehindu.com/todays-paper/tp-sports/objections-raised-on-i-league-isl-merger/article17718235.ece

[16] *Id.*

would be required to move out of Kolkata, their traditional fortress for the last century, because Kolkata already had a team in the ISL—the Atletico de Kolkata. In addition, there were concerns expressed about the payment of licensing fees, sharing of profits, etc. Due to all of these reasons (and obviously many more), these two doyens of Indian football refused to join the ISL, and, as a result, the merger was pushed back, at least by a year.[17]

The story does not end here though. Although the ISL and the I-League will coexist at least for one more season, it is a well-acknowledged fact that all the prominent Indian players have signed up for different ISL franchises instead of the I-League counterparts, obviously because it makes sound professional sense in doing so, considering the much higher incentives offered by the ISL franchises than their I-League counterparts. Thus, the I-League clubs are mostly left with largely the second-category Indian players who have not found favour with any of the ISL franchises or virtual rookies who are yet to make their mark. Of course, an eternal optimist would look at this situation as an opportunity for youngsters to prove their mettle before scores of expectant supporters; one cannot deny the fact that no matter what, the I-League has been relegated to the status of a Second Division of the ISL. Moreover, as opposed to when it had been made clear that the winners of the I-League and the Federation Cup, the two premier national championships despite the ISL, would get to represent India in the continental championships (such as the AFC Champions League and the AFC Cup tournaments), that status of representing India in the AFC Cup has now formally passed on to the champions of the ISL, thus making the priorities of the football satraps crystal clear. Not only does that make the Federation Cup virtually defunct, but this also indicates giving an official recognition to a private tournament.[18]

[17] *See* Abhranil Roy, *5 Reasons Why the I-League–ISL Merger Will Be Harder than It Sounds* SPORTSKEEDA (20 March 2017), *available at* https://www.sportskeeda.com/football/5-reasons-why-the-i-league-isl-merger-will-be-harder-than-it-sounds/5

[18] *See*, generally, Goal, *AFC Slot Confirmed for ISL Winner*, GOAL (2017), *available at* http://www.goal.com/en-in/news/indian-football-afc-slot-confirmed-for-isl-winner/wqroz2bug3ru173di6ozp383f

This relegation of the traditional clubs and tournaments into a virtual obscurity can be looked at as symptomatic of a larger malaise. While it is not disputed that in today's times of commercialisation and cut-throat competition, survival of the fittest is the name of the game in any professionally managed corporate exercise, one cannot lose sight of the fact that sports, by their very nature, cannot be divorced from extra-commercial reasons such as emotions and aspirations. In fact, one can venture an extension of this argument to claim that there exists an ethico-legal need to preserve the traditional clubs and tournaments. The forthcoming section seeks to explore such possibilities, relying on examples from the West.

Legal Protection to Traditional Clubs and Tournaments: How Far Feasible?

Any possibility of envisaging any safeguard to traditional sporting clubs and tournaments is premised on a basic understanding of the 'specific' nature of sports—a realisation that sports management and regulation is different from regulating any other commercial venture, because of its specific cultural and social contexts.[19] In the context of the policy spaces, one can witness this element of specificity of sports being specifically highlighted in the European Union (EU). The Helsinki Report on Sport was one such report from the European Commission to the European Council (of heads of state and government) drafted 'with a view to safeguarding current sports structures and maintaining the social function of sport within the Community framework'.[20]

---

[19] For a detailed account of the specificity of sports and how the EU Law seeks to preserve this specificity, *see*, generally, Robert Siekmann, *Is Sport 'Special' in EU Law and Policy?* IN THE FUTURE OF SPORTS LAW IN THE EUROPEAN UNION—BEYOND THE EU REFORM TREATY AND THE WHITE PAPER 37–49 (Roger Blanpain et al. eds, 2008).

[20] COM (1999) 644, *available at* http://eur-lex.europa.eu/legal-content/EN/TXT/PDF/?uri=CELEX:51999DC0644&from=EN

In the introduction, the report, while acknowledging the social functions of sports, states:

> This social function of sport, which is in the general interest, has for some years been affected by the emergence of new phenomena which sometimes call into question the ethics of sport and the principles on which it is organised, be they violence in the stadiums, the increase in doping practices or *the search for quick profits to the detriment of a more balanced development of sport.* This report gives pointers for reconciling the economic dimension of sport with its popular, educational, social and cultural dimensions. (Emphasis added)

Drawing reference to the Declaration on Sports attached to the Treaty of Amsterdam amending the Treaty on European Union, the treaties establishing the European communities and certain related Acts, 1997,[21] the observation by the Council of Europe that sports is 'an ideal platform for social democracy'[22] and the conclusions of the EU Conference on Sport organised by the Commission in Olympia in May 1999, 'sport must be able to assimilate the new commercial framework in which it must develop, *without at the same time losing its identity and autonomy, which underpin the functions it performs in the social, cultural, health and educational areas*' (emphasis added);[23] the report focuses on the need for a convergent endeavour, where the

---

[21] The declaration states:

The Conference emphasises the social significance of sport, in particular its role in forging identity and bringing people together. The Conference therefore calls on the bodies of the European Union to listen to sports associations when important questions affecting sport are at issue. In this connection, special consideration should be given to the particular characteristics of amateur sport. (emphasis added)

See 11997D/AFI/DCL/29, *available at* http://eur-lex.europa.eu/legal-content/EN/TXT/?uri=CELEX%3A11997D%2FAFI%2FDCL%2F29

[22] 'Social cohesion and sport' Clearing House, Sport Division of the Council of Europe, Committee for the Development of Sport, Strasbourg, March 1999, referred to in *supra* note 20.

[23] *Id.*

commercialisation of sports does not completely obliterate sports of its traditional and cultural contexts. It states:[24]

> *This new approach involves preserving the traditional values of sport, while at the same time assimilating a changing economic and legal environment.* It is designed to view sport globally and coherently. This overall vision assumes greater consultation between the various protagonists (sporting movement, Member States and European Community) at each level. (Emphasis added)

Acknowledging the need to promote both amateur and professional sports and integrating all sections of the society (young, disabled, etc.) into sports, the report specifically deals with the economic dimensions when it observes:

> Operations with an economic dimension should be founded on the principles of transparency and balanced access to the market, effective and proven redistribution and clarification of contracts, while prominence is given to the 'specific nature of sport'.[25]

Similar thoughts are echoed by the Nice Declaration on 'the specific characteristics of sport and its social function in Europe, of which account should be taken in implementing common policies', 2000.[26] The declaration, which is largely premised on the Helsinki model, states:

> Sporting organisations and the Member States have a primary responsibility in the conduct of sporting affairs. Even though not having any direct powers in this area, *the Community must, in its action under the various Treaty provisions, take account of the social, educational and cultural functions inherent in sport and making it special, in order that the code of ethics and the solidarity essential to the preservation of its social role may be respected and nurtured.*[27] (Emphasis added)

[24] *Id.* at Section 4.1.
[25] *Id.* at Section 4.2.3.
[26] This declaration can be found online at http://www.europarl.europa.eu/summits/nice2_en.htm#an4
[27] *Id.* at Section 1.

Like the Helsinki Report, the Nice Declaration too discusses the societal benefits accruing out of sports, when it observes:[28]

> Sport is a human activity resting on fundamental social, educational and cultural values. It is a factor making for integration, involvement in social life, tolerance, acceptance of differences and playing by the rules.

From all these documents, one fact clearly emerges—considering the enormous significance that sports has on the society, it will not be wise to subject sports to the same grinds of a corporate boardroom that completely denudes it of its recreational facet. The recurrent refrain of 'preservation of identity', deemed to be of paramount necessity in all these documents, is definitely a matter of utmost importance, so far as the regulation of sports is concerned.

This element of identity preservation, especially in sporting events that have assumed national importance either due to reasons of antiquity or because of genuine spectator interest or both, can be seen in the UK, where certain sporting events are lined up as 'listed events'[29] for the purposes of free-to-air live broadcasting by broadcasters who have at least 95 per cent access to the viewers in the UK, as per the terms of the Broadcasting Act,

---

[28] *Id.* at Section 3.

[29] According to the Department for Digital, Culture, Media and Sport (DCMS) Broadcasting Policy Division leaflet, a

> Listed Event is one which has 'national resonance'. It should contain an element that serves to unite the nation and not only be of significance to people who normally follow the sport in question. The Government recognises the importance of a national identity within the sporting arena, for example the shared pride and expectation of watching our representatives compete in and perform well at the Olympic Games, and it is for this reason that such events are protected by inclusion in the list.

This document can be accessed online at http://webarchive.nationalarchives. gov.uk/+/; http:/www.culture.gov.uk/PDF/sport_on_television.pdf

1996.[30] It is interesting to note that in the list of such protected events, the tournaments whose full live coverage is protected include the Olympics, the FIFA World Cup Finals, the European Championship Finals, the Wimbledon Finals and several other sporting events of 'national resonance'.[31] However, interestingly enough, this list, even if it has the FA Cup Final and the Scottish FA Cup Final (in Scotland only), does not have any of the matches of the English Premier League in it. In a FAQ on the coverage of individual sports on television, the DCMS, while answering a question on why Premier League matches are not listed, states:[32]

> The list must include only those events which have national importance and are of real interest to people who do not usually follow the sports concerned. Although the Premier League is of great interest to football fans, it does not strike a chord with the

[30] *Id.* The same list has also been adopted by the Ofcom Code on Sports and Other Listed & Designated Events. However, this 95 per cent viewership criteria can be amended by the secretary of state, under Section 97 of the Digital Economy Act, 2017. This is primarily aimed at 'future proofing' the listed events regime, in line with the ever-decreasing number of television sets in the UK. This 'future proofing' is an absolute necessity in order to safeguard the interests of the listed events. In the words of Barbara Slater, the director of BBC Sports,

> But the future of listed events is far from certain. The legislation on which broadcasters qualify was written many years ago in an analogue era and must be updated to avoid it becoming defunct. Rather than risk the abolition of listed events 'by the back door', Government and Parliament should act to deliver a regime fit for the digital era and ensure that our great sporting moments continue to be available to everyone.

See Barbara Slater, *An Uncertain Future for Listed Events*, BBC (2017), *available at* http://www.bbc.co.uk/blogs/aboutthebbc/entries/f0237cf9-cf6c-4d68-8576-048992a8fcde. *See also* John Woodhouse, *Listed Sporting Events* (Briefing Paper No. 00802, House of Commons Library, 9 June 2017) *available at* http://researchbriefings.files.parliament.uk/documents/SN00802/SN00802.pdf

[31] *See supra* note 29.

[32] *Id.*

general viewer in the same way as the World Cup or the European Championships—both of which are listed.

Although the answer does not directly refer to the FA Cup, the fact that it also finds its place in the list would naturally extend the 'national importance' criteria to the FA Cup as well. This formulation is very significant, if one looks at the nature of the two tournaments. The English Premier League was founded in 1992 (much in the same manner as the ISL) as a commercial venture by breaking away from the Football League First Division, with the tacit support of the Football Association (FA), and several broadcasting magnates.[33] On the other hand, the FA Cup is the world's oldest surviving football tournament, being played from 1871–1872. It is a knockout tournament involving not only the teams from the Premier Leagues but lower division teams as well. Although the stakes and the average viewership of the Premier League far outweigh the FA Cup, still the historical significance and universal appeal of the FA Cup make it an event of 'national importance', unlike its more glamorous counterpart.

The lesson that one can learn from this demarcation, if one looks for parallels in the Indian context, is that considering the unique specificities of sports, it would be absolutely naive to suggest that just because a tournament is not commercially beneficial, it should be pushed to the brink of extinction, by an almost wilful disregard shown towards them. Instead, quite like it is observed in the UK, the State should provide specific targeted incentives to such sporting tournaments (even if it be to the exclusion of the more profitable ventures), such that sporting history, traditions and cultures are adequately preserved and protected.

At this juncture, it is to be mentioned that India too has its list of sporting events of national importance. According to two recent gazette notifications, live TV signals of all official

---

[33] *See*, generally, Jason Rodrigues, *Premier League Football at 20: The Start of a Whole New Ball Game, The Guardian*, 2 February 2012, *available at* https://www.theguardian.com/football/from-the-archive-blog/2012/feb/02/20-years-premier-league-football-1992

one-day international, Twenty20 and test matches played by the Indian men's cricket team, semi-finals and finals of the men's World Cup and International Cricket Council Championship Trophy, all matches of Davis Cup and Grand Slam tournaments (men's and women's singles finals, all quarter-finals onwards matches featuring Indian players and all matches featuring Indian players in men's, women's doubles or mixed doubles from quarter-finals onwards), the Hockey World Cup (all matches featuring India, semi-finals and finals), Champions Trophy (all matches featuring India and finals) and Indira Gandhi Gold Cup (women semi-finals and finals), the Football World Cup (opening match, semi-finals and finals), Asia Cup (all matches featuring India and semi-finals and finals) and Santosh Trophy (semi-finals and finals), in addition to the Commonwealth Games, Asian Games, Summer and Special Olympics and Paralympics, have to be mandatory shared with Prasar Bharati, the public broadcaster.[34]

Inasmuch as this is definitely a noteworthy step in ensuring the viewers' rights to view such important sporting events through the free-to-air public broadcasters, it is submitted that it does precious little to salvage the fortunes of the marginalised sporting leagues and tournaments. The reasons for this assertion are two-fold. First, many tournaments of historical prominence, such as the Durand Cup and the IFA Shield, Beighton Cup, Ranji Trophy and other domestic cricket tournaments continue to, unlike the English FA Cup, lie in the same twilight zone of public oblivion. Moreover, even if any of those tournaments were to feature in

---

[34] *See*, generally, Harveen Ahluwalia, *Govt Lists Cricket Events Whose Broadcast Feeds Must Be Shared with Prasar Bharati*, *Livemint*, 26 October 2016, *available at* http://www.livemint.com/Consumer/GL0TKqz7ijmXLTV10a33rJ/Govt-lists-cricket-events-whose-broadcast-feeds-must-be-shar.html. *See also*, generally, Harveen Ahluwalia, *Govt Lists Non-cricket Sporting Events of National Importance*, *Livemint*, 3 March 2017, *available at* http://www.livemint.com/Sports/9au73qn1qtCjUEwg96tSUO/Govt-lists-noncricket-sporting-events-of-national-importanc.html

any such list, the list only provides for mandatory sharing of signals—it cannot force a broadcaster to broadcast an event. Therefore, decisions as to whether or not to broadcast, timeslots and platforms of such broadcasting, etc. continue to remain determined by market forces, and the neglect to the traditional sporting tourneys and clubs continue to persist.

However, the panacea to the ailment lies not only in ensuring better broadcasting platforms to the traditional sports tournaments. In fact, it is just a perfunctory remedy to the main problem. The primary concern lies in the systematic marginalisation of the traditional sporting clubs and tournaments, whose interests are to be safeguarded. One way to do it is to look at the issue through the prism of the fundamental rights (FRs) discourse.

In a number of cases, the courts have decided that sporting federations, even if they are not 'State' within the meaning of Article 12 of the Constitution, not being 'financially, functionally and administratively' dominated by or under the control of the government,[35] are nonetheless amenable to the writ jurisdiction of the High Courts under Article 226 of the Constitution.[36] The reasoning behind this position is essentially premised on the assumption that this approach looks at the increased scope for horizontal application of fundamental rights, by placing reliance on the 'Public Functions' test.[37] According to this approach, the

---

[35] *See* the new, nuanced description of state given by the Supreme Court in the case of Pradeep Kumar Biswas v. Indian Institute of Chemical Biology, (2002) 5 SCC 111.

[36] *See, e.g.,* BCCI v. Cricket Association of Bihar, (2015) 3 SCC 251. *See also* Ajay Jadeja v. Union of India, (2001) SCC OnLine Del 1024; Rahul Mehra v. Union of India, (2004) SCC OnLine Del 837; Narinder Batra v. Union of India, (2009) SCC OnLine Del 480; Amit Kumar Dhankhar v. Union of India, (2014) SCC OnLine Del 3451.

[37] The Court rightly observed:

Any organization or entity that has such pervasive control over the game and its affairs and such powers... cannot be said to be undertaking private functions... if the Government not only allows

sporting federations, even if they may not be considered to be 'State' as per the constitutive definition that is contingent upon the pervasive control exercised by the government,[38] could nevertheless be amenable to Article 226 for breaches of fundamental rights. The fundamental rights violations that can immediately attract judicial attention with respect to the issue in hand would include Articles 14, 15, 19(1)(g) and 21.

Apart from the obvious issues of discrimination that is concomitant to the violation of the tenets of equality, the writ remedies can also be invoked for the deprivation of the players' rights to trade, business and occupation, as enshrined in Article 19(1)(g). In addition, the expansive attributes of the terms 'life' and 'personal liberty' in Article 21 are definitely elastic enough to encompass within their widened ambit existential concerns of the sportsmen, sporting clubs and federations, and the spectators alike.

Of course, such a purported enforcement of a writ remedy under Article 226 does by no means act as an absolute safeguard against commercially motivated systematic marginalisation of the form that is noticed in the Indian sporting scenario in the recent times. The State is definitely empowered to impose reasonable restrictions upon the enjoyment of any of the rights thus claimed. Nevertheless, by allowing for the opportunity of a strict judicial scrutiny, there will be definitely an enormous pressure upon the sports federations to satisfy the threshold enquiries, before going ahead with indiscriminate obliterations of such events of cultural and traditional significance.

---

an autonomous/private body to discharge functions which it could in law take over or regulate but even lends its assistance to such non-government body to undertake such functions which by their very nature are public functions, it cannot be said that the functions are not public functions or that entity discharging the same is not answerable on the standards generally applicable to judicial review of State action. *See id.*

[38] *See supra* note 35.

Conclusion

Nelson Mandela, the former president of South Africa and an icon of the struggle against colonialism and apartheid, had once famously remarked:[39]

> Sport has the power to change the world. It has the power to inspire. It has the power to unite people in a way that little else does. It speaks to youth in a language they understand. Sport can create hope where once there was only despair. It is more powerful than government in breaking down racial barriers.

Sports do indeed have the power to change the world. However, the converse is also unfortunately true. The indiscriminate urge for making more moolahs has led the organisers of sporting events and sporting federations to go for a rampant, indiscriminate spree of commercialisation. As much as it could in some areas help in more systematic and efficient management of certain sports and games, the fact remains that it can also force clubs, tournaments and, in some cases, even games and their formats towards an ultimate, irrevocable extinction. Such extinction of cultures and traditions is not only an ethical concern, there are legal ramifications as well. What is required of the legal system is to appreciate the specificities of the discipline of sports, much like the EU and the UK. Providing for a specific broadcasting regime by demarcating more of such traditional matches as events of 'national importance', providing for writ remedies for violation of any of the constitutionally guaranteed rights and protections while managing and regulating the 'public functions' of sports and otherwise ensuring a legal protection regime for these events which may be lowly in terms of their economic worth but rank enormously high in terms of their emotive appeal are some of the legal and policy protections that may be envisaged in order to make sports more equitable, broad-based and responsive to the respective sociocultural contexts.

---

[39] *See* https://sportforpeace.wordpress.com/tag/nelson-mandela-quotes/

Way Forward for Sports in India

Lovely Dasgupta

The discussion in this book so far has clarified a lot about sports law within India. Sport has grown from being just an activity for leisure to an activity that is treated as an industry. And like all industries, there are innumerable issues that are cropping up day in and day out. Importantly, in the Indian context, sport has transformed from a mere pastime to a professional activity. It now involves livelihood of millions youth. Burdened with the problem of a developing country, sports provide a way out for youths across the spectrum. India, therefore, needs to deliberate seriously about regulating sports. Leaving it to the whims and fancies of the sports governing bodies is not adequate, for there are potentials of exploitation and rampant violations of the rights of the sports-persons. The book, as discussed in the introduction, aimed to map out all the relevant issues within the field of sports in India. The theme is India and its sports-persons. The dedication to the book, as indicated in the introduction, is about the integral role sports played in India's freedom struggle, though the book is not an account of the socio-historical role of sports in India. Nonetheless, such reference highlights the role sports play in national development. All the authors have accordingly highlighted the importance of developmental aspects of sports. In India, where sports-persons largely come from rural or semi-urban background, the need for legal regulation is of paramount importance. And the developments at the global level do help lawyers and policymakers to reflect on the kind of regulation that Indian should adopt for sports. Added to this aspect is the gross commercialisation of sports in India. That too requires application of different laws across the spectrum. Importantly, the State needs to ensure that commercialised sports do not dilute the essence of sports. Importantly, the commercialisation of sports cannot be an excuse for the sports governing bodies to become opaque and non-accountable.

As seen in the first chapter, the Constitution of India can be an important tool in instilling transparency within the sports governing bodies. Especially, the use of Article 226 is an important development insofar as sports governance is concerned. Livelihood issues of thousands of sports-persons cannot be left at the whims and fancies of the private sports bodies. Hence, by characterising the sports governing bodies as public authority, a great degree of judicial scrutiny is exercised. One can always argue that it is time-consuming, and what about enormous backlog of cases? However, in an environment of regulatory void and uncertainty, Article 226 remedy appears to be the most viable option available. However, in order to regulate the sports governing bodies, litigation under Article 226 need not be the first option. On the contrary, an effective regulatory framework needs to be put in place. In this regard, the various facets of non-profit organisations (NPO) law can be utilised, as is explained in the second chapter. Thus, for example, society registration law, not for profit companies and specific tax exemption are some of the legislative tools which are currently applied to sports governing bodies. These legislative tools can be used to instil accountability and ensure a level playing field. Accountability would also lessen the chances of corruption and abuse. In turn, the ultimate beneficiary will be the talented athletes. Merit, and not connection, will be the key to selection. However, for this to happen, the tools of the NPO law will have to be effectively used by the State.

Sports governing bodies cannot be let off on the ground that they are autonomous. A strong State's role is key to protect the interests of all the stakeholders. In the garb of autonomy, sports governing bodies have the ability to be arbitrary. The recent spate of controversies, be it the match-fixing at Indian Premier League (IPL) or the Commonwealth scam or the rampant abuse of performance enhancing drugs, all paint a grim picture. With sports in India generating millions in terms of revenue, there is a lot at stake for all. Hence, the necessity for a better legal framework is being argued in the third chapter. One way of bringing about better governance in sports is to amend the National Sports Code, 2011. And the present government has attempted to do the same by forming a nine-member committee to draft a comprehensive National Sports Code. The work (hopefully) is in progress since the committee was constituted in January 2017. As we are writing, there is nothing on paper yet. There are news reports about the committee having submitted its report to the Ministry of Youth Affairs and Sports. The ministry, in turn, has submitted the recommendation to the Delhi High Court.[1] Only time will tell as to what, if at all, the National Sports Code will be. As of now, the principle legislation is the National Sports Code, 2011, which provides a framework of governance. However, legal framework notwithstanding, the role of the public-spirited citizen cannot be belittled. This is evident from the manner in which public interest litigation (PIL) is being used to counter the dominance of sports governing bodies. As has been explained in the fourth chapter, PIL is an important tool for better governance of sports. The different cases where PIL has been used show how the larger interest of public can override the power of sports governing bodies. Further, PIL can be used to counter abuse of public infrastructure by the sports governing bodies.

A larger concern for the sportsperson is the observance of human rights. In the context of anti-doping programme, this

[1] PTI, Vijay Goel Clarifies Stand on Sports Code, The Times of India, 19 July 2017, *available at* https://timesofindia.indiatimes.com/sports/more-sports/others/vijay-goel-clarifies-stand-on-sports-code/articleshow/59669218.cms

concern is relevant. The sports governing bodies, being the anti-doping agencies, are responsible for observing the same. One key area of debate in the execution of anti-doping programme is privacy. The debate is succinctly highlighted in the fifth chapter. The World Anti-Doping Code (WADC) requires compliances such as blood testing, whereabouts filing, urine testing and blood profiling which infringes on the privacy rights of the athlete. The compliances are mandatory and the athletes are left with no choice. The sports governing bodies are the custodian of the data generated through the sample testing and compliance measures. Accordingly, they are equally responsible to strictly comply with the data protection laws. Importantly, they are expected to ensure that identity of an athlete, accused of anti-doping rule violation, is protected. WADC does specify the measures aimed at protecting the privacy of athletes. The State, however, should play a proactive role in ensuring compliance by sports governing bodies with the privacy protection norms. Associated with the privacy concerns under WADC is the requirement of an effective anti-doping education programme. The sixth chapter highlights the need for the same by pinpointing the measures to be taken. Use of vernacular language as well as interesting and engaging pedagogy are some of the ways, for in the absence of an effective anti-doping education programme, athletes are likely to commit inadvertent doping offences. And with strict liability principle being the key to WADC, inadvertent doping leads to consequences of anti-doping rule violation. Here again, one is looking for the State to put in place measures as well as adequate infrastructure support for enabling an effective anti-doping education programme.

Increasing commercialisation has positioned sport in the category of a viable profession. Hence, athletes seek equal access to sports not only to participate but also to practise it like any other trade/profession. In this context, an important issue is discrimination, for instance, on the basis of religion. This issue is discussed in the context of basketball in the seventh chapter. Religious discrimination through the rules of the game create barriers to accessibility. Understandably, domestic anti-discrimination laws are not applicable to international federations. However, a

State, like India, can play a proactive role to create opinion at the international level against such discrimination. A strong political stand on the part of the State can go a long way in addressing all kind of discrimination, be it religious or gender. An effective way of ensuring accountability within the sports governing bodies is faster resolution of disputes. And arbitration of sports dispute is the most viable way of quick resolution of such disputes. The eighth chapter delves into sports arbitration by pointing out the pros as well as cons of the existing arbitral system. Importantly, under the existing sports arbitration system, the athletes are forced to agree to arbitration. The absence of free consent does challenge the legitimacy of the existing sports arbitration. Additionally, the closed list of arbitrators and multi-layered arbitration agreement are some of the problems associated with sports arbitration. Importantly, there is an urgent need of an independent sports arbitral body in India. Indian courts will then have jurisdiction in case of any challenge to the awards of this body. Thus, the athlete will be saved the trouble of going to Court of Arbitration for Sport (CAS) for each and every dispute. Importantly, the athletes will be protected under the domestic arbitration law, namely the Arbitration and Conciliation Act of 1996. A fallout of commercialisation of sports is the dispute over athletes' image rights. Across the world, there are numerous cases pertaining to athletes' image rights, and the ninth chapter deals with the same. Interestingly, though India has not yet witnessed excessive disputes over athletes' image rights, there is lot to learn from the global developments. And the important point is customising the existing intellectual property law like trademark to protect athletes' image rights. Another aspect of commercialised sport is the contest over sports broadcast. The tenth chapter highlights the issues. Importantly, in India, the tussle is primarily based on allowing the free-to-air service provider compulsory access to paid broadcasts. This sharing of signal by the paid broadcaster has raised question on its nature of obligation. The extent to which the paid broadcaster has to remove on-screen credit is the subject of current debate. The concern is that if the obligations on paid broadcaster become more onerous, they will refrain from bidding for low-key sporting events. Since signal sharing impinges on the revenue base of the paid broadcaster, their decision to bid or not will be dictated by concerns of profitability. And sports with lower valuation will suffer the most. Here, the State has an important role in clarifying the legal position and not leave it to the whims of judicial interpretation.

Finally, as the eleventh chapter underlines, sport is not only about commercialisation and commodification. In the Indian context, there is more to sport than just money. And it is the sociocultural aspect of sport that is threatened in the current environment of corporatised sport. With commercial leagues, sponsored by large media houses and corporate backing, growing at a rapid pace, traditional clubs are under threat. The cultural aspect of sports in India is under strain, and its existence is threatened. Hence, the need is for the State to intervene and take measures to uphold the cultural aspect of sport. Sport needs money and cannot be stopped from changing its format. However, the traditional clubs such as Mohun Bagan and East Bengal, which have contributed to the growth of football in India, need to be given State aid. Similar other clubs or tournaments in other sports too should be given State protection. On the whole, commercialisation of sports is a private act where State has no role and is equally incapable of stopping the process. State though has a major role to play in developing a sound policy on sports which is comprehensive enough to cover all aspects of good governance. Additionally, the State also needs to come up with legal framework that can be used to adequately regulate sports and provide effective solutions in case of disputes.

More so, with the current attitude of powerful sports governing bodies like Board of Control for Cricket in India (BCCI), to defy State dictates, the time has come to regulate sports. Thus, for example, BCCI can be barred from using the word India for its team. That BCCI is openly defying to comply with both WADA and NADA mandate is worrying. Unless the State uses measures stringent enough to make the sports governing fall in line, there is bound to be anarchy. Additionally, powerful sports governing bodies, if allowed to act arbitrary, will sell away all that is recognised as sports. State is in an enviable position to preserve both the cultural and the functional aspects of sport, without hindering the process of commercialisation. To force the sports governing bodies to be transparent and accountable to the Indian public, commercialisation has to be used by the State, which needs to ensure that commercialisation promotes and furthers the cause of all the stakeholders involved. An example of such an intervention has been the mandatory sharing of broadcast signals by the private broadcasters with Prasar Bharati. This ensures that the public service broadcaster is in a position to provide signals to areas where paid channels are not accessible. Although there are problems with the manner in which the signals are shared and the strictures on private broadcasters, it still is a step in the right direction. Unless the State sends a message to the sports governing bodies that they need to be accountable and transparent, athletes and other stakeholders' interest cannot be protected.

Additionally, the State can facilitate the institutionalisation of a merit-based system that produces champions. With litigation galore on selection of athletes for national as well as international competitions, there has to be a merit-based selection process. Importantly, the State has to ensure that sports governing bodies face minimal political interference. Further, one has to ensure that selection is done in strict compliance with the norms laid down by the international federations. In addition, the National Sports Code, 2011, should also be strictly complied with. The need for a domestic dispute settlement body, cutting down on the dependency on traditional court, is equally important. As noted previously, a quick resolution of disputes ensures better protection of athletes' right. Importantly though, it also ensures that the sports governing bodies are more sensitive to the issues facing the athletes. In this respect, the State has to be equally proactive to the protection of athletes against sexual harassment. And it is not only about bringing in a law specific to sportsperson, but it is also about effective implementation of the same. The Indian government will have to ensure that its organisations like the Sports Authority of India seriously monitor the ground situation. Be it the coaches or other support personnel, everyone should be closely watched over to ensure that they do not harass the athletes.

Finally, the Central government has to coordinate with the state governments to help build infrastructure for developing grass-roots-level sports. It is not enough to regulate sports at the professional level. It is equally important that accessibility is provided to athletes both at the junior and the sub-junior levels. Leaving the entire process of training and grooming to private sector cannot ensure that India produces champions. A programme similar to the National Collegiate Athletic Association (NCAA) needs to be set up in India. The need is to tap in talent from schools and colleges and channel them systematically. Parents juggling around for the best training for their wards is not essentially the most effective way to groom and produce champions. India needs to have a collective effort from all the governments, irrespective of their political ideology, to have an effective athlete-grooming programme. The NCAA, though a US model, is effective to harness the talent in the schools and colleges. This ensures that the parents do not have to run around to train their wards. Further, students can be incentivised to play sports without getting burdened with the load of studies. Finally, it will enable students who are not interested in studies to take up sports as an alternate career choice. India needs to use innovative efforts to not only bring in an effective regulatory structure for sports but also ensure a continuous source of champions. State governments have to build in safety checks that help millions of athletes across India to access the best of infrastructure. This includes providing the best of training facility as well as best of education programme. The education programme can be designed by the State to make the athletes aware of their rights. Further, the education programme also needs to sensitise the sports administrators and other stakeholders to the issues of accountability and transparency. For Indian athletes to be world champions, the key is an effective sports policy and regulatory system dealing with the vagaries of commercialised sport.

ABOUT THE EDITORS AND CONTRIBUTORS

Editors

Lovely Dasgupta has been teaching sports law for the last 13 years. She did her LLM, MPhil and PhD from W.B. National University of Juridical Sciences (NUJS), Kolkata. She is associated with other subjects such as contract, commercial law, legal education and consumer law. She has published in both national and international journals.

Shameek Sen is an Assistant Professor (Law) at NUJS. He specialises in public law disciplines such as constitutional law and media law. He also takes keen interest in human rights, public health law, water law and environmental law. After graduating from NUJS in 2005 as a part of the very first graduating batch of the university and finishing his LLM in 2007 (where he won the prestigious Nani Palkhivala Gold Medal for securing the highest marks in his batch), Sen joined as an Assistant Professor in NUJS. He completed his MPhil in the year 2008 and PhD in the year 2017. His doctoral thesis was titled 'Right to Freedom of Speech and Expression with Special Reference to Decency and Morality'. He has published journal articles and book chapters on many areas of law, and is presently writing a casebook on constitutional law. He has also been invited to several international and national conferences as a resource person on media and constitutional law issues.

Contributors

Akhilendra P. Singh is Research Associate, Centre for Comparative Law, NLU, Delhi, and holds LLM (NLU, Delhi) and LLB (Banaras Hindu University [BHU], Varanasi) degrees.

Agnidipto Tarafder is a PhD scholar and a Lecturer at NUJS, Kolkata. His primary area of interest is privacy law and data protection, and his PhD topic is about the dimensions of the law of privacy. Additionally, he teaches courses in law of privacy, legal methods and international investment law. His other areas of interest are constitutional law, international criminal law and privacy and data protection.

Carmel Sharma is a budding advocate and has interest in sports and other rights-related issues.

Daniel Mathew completed his LLM programme from the National Law University of India (NLSIU), Bengaluru, in 2009 and secured the first rank in the university, for which he was awarded the Nani Palkhivala Memorial Gold Medal. He received his LLB from Faculty of Law, University of Delhi, and BA (Hons) in Economics from St Stephens College, University of Delhi. From 2009 to 2013, he worked as Assistant Professor at NUJS wherein he was engaged in teaching and researching in dispute resolution, constitutional law, human rights and legal methods. Since 2014, he has been an Assistant Professor at NLU, Delhi, where he teaches courses on alternate dispute resolution, international commercial arbitration, intentional investment arbitration, human rights and jurisprudence. He is an editor of the *Journal of National Law University, Delhi.*

David McArdle is the author of *Dispute Resolution in Sport* (2015) and is a Senior Lecturer at the School of Law, University of Stirling in Scotland. He holds an LLB from the University of Wales, Aberystwyth, and a PhD from Manchester Metropolitan

University, England. He teaches sports law, employment law and trade union law. His current research is concerned with medico-legal issues in sports, particularly statutory responses to concussion and the rights of transgender and pregnant athletes, and he has also written extensively on the wider issues of employment and discrimination law, participant safety and alternative dispute resolution in the sports context. He has worked with athletes on the development of players' associations and is currently working with a governing body on drafting contract terms and employment agreements for a range of staff ranging from professional players to volunteer administrators and officials. He has been the sole applicant, or a contributor, to bids which have yielded over £700,000 in grant income from the European Commission, the Scottish government and others. He has authored over 30 government reports and academic publications in quality legal journals including *Legal Studies* and *Social and Legal Studies*. He was formerly a visiting fellow in international sports law at Texas A&M University and is an advisory board member at the Gujarat National Law University.

Gautam Karhadkar is part of the sports and gaming and litigation practice at Krida Legal. He has represented leading sportsmen, government authorities and private organisations and clients in these domains of law.

Mahendra Pal Singh is a stalwart in the field of constitutional law. He is Chair Professor, Centre for Comparative Law, NLU, Delhi; Chancellor, Central University of Haryana; former Chairperson and Head, Delhi Judicial Academy; former Vice-Chancellor, NUJS, Kolkata; and former Head, Dean and Professor of Law at Faculty of Law, University of Delhi.

Nitin Mittal is a part of the sports and gaming practice at Krida Legal. He has represented sportsmen and government authorities and advised private organisations on implementation of sports leagues, online gaming platforms, etc.

P. Ishwara Bhat, MA, LLM, PhD (Mysore), is currently the Vice-Chancellor of the NUJS, Kolkata. Earlier, he taught at the University of Mysore from 1984 to November 2011 and was Dean of Faculty of Law for three terms and Acting Vice-Chancellor for four months. He has specialisation in constitutional law. He was Fulbright-Nehru Visiting Professor in 2010 and involved in co-teaching non-profit organisations (NPOs) law at Columbus Law School of Catholic University of America, Washington, DC. In 2009, he was a Visiting Professor to Queen's University, Kingston, Canada, to handle a course on comparative legal traditions. He researched on NPOs law and made presentations at Trisakti University, Jakarta (2008), Peking University, Beijing (2005) and ISTR regional conference at Bangkok (2006). He had attended Salzburg Seminar in 1997. He was recipient of Shastri Visiting Research Fellowship in 1992 and researched on comparative study of language rights in India and Canada in the universities of York, Toronto and Ottawa. He has delivered special lectures in various Indian universities and national law schools. He presented papers on 'Language Rights and Education in SAARC Countries' at the USIEF Conference in Kathmandu (2012), 'NPO Law and Tax Exemption' in Seoul (2013) and 'Public Trust Law' in Tokyo (2015). He has published a wide range of books and 105 articles in national and international journals. He has drafted legislative bills and university statutes.

Richa R. Mulchandani is a historian as well as sports educator. She is working as Senior Assistant Professor of History and Director of Centre for Sports and Entertainment Law at Gujarat National Law University (GNLU), Gandhinagar, Gujarat. She is also the Convener, Legal History Museum, GNLU, which is one of the top three NLUs of India and she feels proud to be a part of it.

Her areas of research are legal and constitutional history, modernisation of law in Asia, sports law and history of medicines, maritime history and cultural heritage. She has presented and published number of articles and papers in national and international journals. She was former Dean, Student Welfare Organisation. She has also served as researcher for Sarva Shiksha Abhiyan in 2006 and headed the research project in 2011–2012, and is currently undertaking the '5% Sample Checking of U-DISE 2016–2017 of Gujarat' as a co-investigator.

Since 2015, she is researching with Osaka University on modernisation of law in Asia, and presently she is appointed as Visiting Professor, Pantheon-Sorbonne University, Paris 1, France, for the year 2017. She was invited twice as Visiting Associate Professor at Osaka University, Osaka, Japan, in 2015–2016 and 2016–2017.

Presently, she is also pursuing *Shastry* course in *Dharmashastras* from Baroda Sanskrit Mahavidyalaya.

Saurabh Bhattacharjee is an Assistant Professor at NUJS, Kolkata, where he teaches courses on legal methods, labour law, law and impoverishment, and adjudication of socio-economic rights. He has also taught sports law as a Visiting Faculty at the National Academy of Legal Studies and Research (NALSAR), Hyderabad, and he is pursuing his doctoral research on juridification of sports in India. He completed his undergraduate law degree at NALSAR, Hyderabad, in 2005 where he was awarded with several medals for academic proficiency and the gold medal for 'Best All-Round Male Student'. Subsequently, he obtained an LLM degree at the University of Michigan Law School where he was awarded the Grotius Fellowship for the year 2008–2009. He has also taught at the National Law University (NLU) of Jodhpur as an Assistant Professor and has been invited to teach as guest lecturer at Indian Institute of Social Work and Business Management (IISWBM), Kolkata; Administrative Training Institute, Government of West Bengal; and West Bengal State Judicial Academy. Before joining academia, Saurabh worked with The Other Media, New Delhi, on campaigns on issues of conflict and human rights, corporate accountability and refugee rights. Apart from teaching, Saurabh has done research projects for organisations such as United

Nations Conference on Trade and Development (UNCTAD) and Indira Gandhi National Open University (IGNOU). He has authored several legislative reports submitted before parliamentary standing committees including the Committee on Agriculture and Committee on Labour and Welfare, and ministries of Union government including the Ministry of Rural Development and Ministry of Labour and Employment. He is also a member of the Committee to Review Vagrancy Laws, constituted by the Government of West Bengal.

Shreeyash Uday Lalit is an LLM candidate at the University of Cambridge for the year 2017–2018, for which he also secured the Narotam Sekhsaria Scholarship and the J. N. Tata Scholarship. He pursued his LLB degree from the Faculty of Law, University of Delhi, after having completed the BTech degree from Indian Institute of Technology, Guwahati. During his LLB candidature, he interned with a Supreme Court judge, Union law officer and several firms of outstanding repute while also participating in extra-curricular activities in the form of moots, debates, publications and conferences. He was the Student Editor of the *Delhi Law Review*, Convenor of the Moot Court Society and Editor-in-Chief of the college newsletter. At University of Cambridge, Shreeyash is preparing to study courses in the field of constitutional law and theory.

Saurabh Mishra is a qualified lawyer working as a Senior Executive for Star India Pvt. Ltd, as a legal and regulatory expert. He is an Advisor for the Football Players' Association of India (FPAI) and a Project Manager for Slum Soccer on a pro bono basis. He did his BA LLB from NUJS, Kolkata, and was a recipient of the Eastern Book Company Gold Medal in Alternative Dispute Resolution. He also received the Graduate Scholar Award at the Fifth International Conference on Sport and Society in July 2014. He has previously worked with organisations such as Adidas and Atletico de Kolkata, a franchise in the Hero Indian Super League. He regularly writes on contemporary developments in sports law, and his work has been well received internationally.

Shreya Mishra is an Assistant Professor of Law at Maharashtra National Law University (MNLU), Nagpur. She completed her LLM (International and Comparative Law) from NUJS, Kolkata, in 2015, post completion of her BA LLB (Hons) from Rajiv Gandhi National University of Law (RGNUL), Punjab, in 2014. A gold medallist in her chosen specialisation of constitutional laws, Shreya cleared UGC-NET in 2015. Her varied areas of interest include maritime law, air and space law, environmental law, energy law, jurisprudence, comparative constitutional law and public policy. In relation to these fields, she holds a few publications in reputed journals and has been invited to speak at prestigious international conferences.

Shivam Singh is a practising lawyer at the Supreme Court of India and Delhi High Court. In addition to being an alumnus of NLSIU, Bengaluru, he holds an LLM from Columbia Law School and was a Sports Law Research Fellow at Harvard Law School. He has also been invited as a visiting faculty for sports law at Columbia University and regularly lectures at several law schools in India. Shivam has multiple reported judgements in the Supreme Court to his credit and has also published widely on sports-related topics in national as well as international journals.

Vidushpat Singhania is an advocate registered with the Delhi Bar Council. He has been Secretary of the Indian Premier League Probe Committee and a member of the British Association for Sport and Law, International Association of Sports Law, FICCI National Sports Committee and the Governing Body of the Sports Authority of India. He is a member of the Gaming and Leisure Group of UK–India Business Council, Regulatory Commission of the Indian Super League, International Association of Gaming Advisors, All India Sports Council and ASSOCHAM's Sports Committee. He has represented the wrestler Narsingh Yadav, the Commonwealth Games Federation and the Athletic Federation of India before Court of Arbitration for Sports; a renowned cricketer before the BCCI's Anti-Doping Disciplinary Panel; and a few sports-persons before the National Anti-Doping Panel.

Vidushpat is the co-author of the book *Law and Sports in India*, and he has written articles for the *International Sports Law Journal*, *World Sports Law Report*, online sport portals and various national dailies. He was involved in drafting the National Sports Development Bill and the Prevention of Sporting Fraud Bill for Ministry of Youth Affairs and Sports and has assisted the Justice Mudgal Doping Probe Committee and the National Sports Development Code Committee.

INDEX

abuse of dominant position, 42
anti-doping
  ADRV, regulation, 136
  Article 10 after WADA,
    changes, 71
  Article 10 of WADC, 71
  Article 10.4, 74
  Article 10.5, 73
  Article 2 of WADC, 70
  Charline Van Snick v.
    Fédération Internationale
    de Judo, 75–77
  defences in, 72
  education programmes
    Access Control Programme in
      China, 133
    ADRV violation, 132
    Australia, 130
    China tools, 134
    combat drug issues in UK,
      130
    doping organisation or sports
      institution, 133
    empirical study in India, 139
    France, 132
    higher education institutions,
      133
    India, 135
    outreach programme in
      China, 134
    pilot study in India, 136
    public or private laboratory
      in France, 133
    research analysis in India,
      136
    responsibility of education in
      India, 139
  training courses in China,
    134
  UK, 128
  USA, 126, 127
  UKAD v. *Gareth Warburton*
    and Rhys Williams, 74
Appeals Arbitration Division
  (AAD), 172
appearance and advertising con-
    tracts, 65
appointment of arbitrators, 170
  AAD, 172
  CAS, 170
  I-CAS, 172
  OAD, 172
  RAC, 173
  SFT, 175
arbitration agreement, 160
  IOA rules, 161
Arbitration and Conciliation Act of
    1996, 158, 165, 245
arbitration commission (AC), 164,
    170
Article 4.4.2 of the FIBA
    Regulations, 143
  Statute, 145
Asia Cup in China, 142
Australian Sports Anti-Doping
    Authority (ASADA), 130,
    132

Bill of 2013, 58
Board of Control for Cricket in
    India (BCCI), 23, 194
Bombay Public Trusts Act, 1950,
    37
broadcasting contracts, 66

Broadcasting Services Act, 1992, 211

cases
  A. A. Associates v. *Prem Goel*, 202
  Ajay Hasia v. *Khalid Mujib Sehravardi*, 6, 9
  Ajay Jadeja v. Union of India, 17
  Ajay Jadeja v. UOI and Ors, 49
  Amit Kumar Dhankhar v. Union of India, 17
  BCCI v. Cricket Association of Bihar, 50
  Board of Control for Cricket in India & Anr. v. Netaji Cricket Club and Ors, 48
  Booz Allen v. SBI Home Finance, 159
  Consumer Education and Research Centre v. Union of India, 14
  Danilova and Lazuntina v. IOC and FIS, 171
  Deccan Chronical Holding Limited (DCHL) v. BCCI, 68
  Fertilizer Corporation Kamgar v. Union of India, 85
  Githa Hariharan v. Reserve Bank of India, 14
  Irvine v. *Talksport*, 178
  M/s Centrotrade Minerals v. Hindustan Copper Ltd, 165
  M/s Video Masters v. M/s Nishi Productions, 202
  Mohini Jain v. State of Karnataka, 15
  Mumbai Cricket Association v. DIT (Exemption), 40
  Mumbai Kamagar Sabha v. Abdul Thai, 84

  Narinder Batra v. Union of India, 17
  Parmanand Katara v. Union of India, 13
  People's Union for Democratic Rights & Others v. Union of India & Others, 85
  People's Union of Democratic Rights v. Union of India, 13
  Pradeep Kumar Biswas v. Indian Institute of Chemical Biology, 7
  Pradeep Kumar Biswas v. Indian Institute of Chemical Biology and Ors, 49
  R. Rajagopal v. State of Tamil Nadu, 14, 178
  Rahul Mehra v. Union of India, 17
  Raj Video Vision v. M/s Sun TV, 202
  Rajasthan State Electricity Board v. *Mohan Lal*, 5
  Ramsharan Autyanuprasi & Another v. Union of India & Others, 85
  S. M. Ilyas v. Indian Council of Agricultural Research, 9
  S. P. Gupta v. Union of India, 85
  Sabhajit Tewary v. Union of India, 7
  Sarita Devi case, 86–89
  Secretary, Ministry of Information and Broadcasting v. Cricket Association of Bengal, 203
  Star Sports India Private Limited v. Prasar Bharati, 196
  Sukhdev Singh v. Bhagatram Sardar Singh Raghuvanshi, 5
  Titan Industries Ltd v. *Ramkumar Jewellers*, 178

UKAD v. Gareth Warburton
  and Rhys Williams
  (UKAD—2015), 74
Zee Telefilms v. Union of
  India, 8
Centrotrade, 166
China Anti-Doping Agency
  (CHINADA), 133
Code of 2011
  Bill of 2013, 59
  equal voting rights, 57
  NSFs, 57
  vision and mission, 56
commercialisation, 247
Companies Act of 2013, 38
  section 135(1), 42
Competition Appellate Tribunal,
  42
Competition Commission of India
  (CCI), 41
corporate social responsibility
  (CSR)
  sports associations (SAs), 42
Court of Arbitration for Sports
  (CAS), 156
Cricket Association of Bihar Case,
  89–95

doping-free sport
  basic principle and primary
    goal, 123
  professional codes of conduct,
    124
  programs and activities, 123

ejusdem generis rule, 5
Ethics Commission and
  Independent Code of
  Ethics, 58

Federation Internationale de
  Hockey (FIH) in 1924, 23

Fertilizer Corporation case, 85
FIFA, 154
First Civil Division of the Swiss
  Federal Tribunal (SFT),
  170
Football Association (FA), 236
fundamental rights (FRs), 3
  constitutional provisions, 11
  horizontal application, 11
  judiciary approach, 12–15
  SC engagement, 13
  sports bodies and judicial
    review, 15–17
  vertical application, 10
  violations, 239

gender discrimination
  India, 60
  case studies, 63
good governance principles, 47
  checks and balances, 55
  democratic process, 53
    clear organisational frame-
      work, 54
    decision-making bodies, 54
    members, role and rights, 54
    stakeholders, role and rights,
      54
  solidarity, 55
  transparency and public com-
    munication, 48
    accountability standards,
      establishment, 52
    cases, 48
    confidentiality, 53
    disbursement and allocation
      of funds, 53
    financial reporting, 52
    internal control, measures, 52
    performance indicators, iden-
      tification, 52
    risk management, 53

Hindu Minority and Guardianship Act, 1956, 14
Hockey India, 3

Indian Constitution, 10, 15
architects of, 11
the State, definition in Article 12, 4–10
Indian Contract Act, 1872, 161
Section 10, 163
Indian Hockey Federation, 24
Indian Olympic Association (IOA), 3
founded in 1927, 23
Indian Premier League (IPL), 92
Drought Case, 95–97
Indian scenario of sports, 3
Indian Super League (ISL), 224
Indian Trusts Act, 37
Information and Education Committee (IEC), 136
intellectual property law, 245
International Cricket Council establishment of, 23
international federations, 144
International Football Association Board (IFAB), 154
International Olympic Association, 68
International Olympic Committee (IOC), 143

Kerala Sports Act, 2000, 43

law of non-profit companies impact of, 38–39
liberal economic policy, 3
locus standi, 84

match-fixing and spot-fixing, 77–79
Pakistan cricket spot-fixing scandal in 2010, 80

Sporting Fraud Bill, 2013, prevention, 79
Memorandum and Articles of Association, 54
Memorandum and Rules and Regulations of Indian Olympic Association, 159
Ministry of Youth Affairs and Sports (MYAS), 88
post 2001, 56

naming rights contracts, 66
National Anti-Doping Agency (NADA), 72, 103, 135
National Anti-Doping Code 2015, 73
National Collegiate Athletic Association (NCAA), 248
National Dope Testing Laboratory (NDTL), 136
National Sports Code, 2011, 243, 247
National Sports Development Bill of 2013, 58
National Sports Development Code of India, 2011 (NSDCI), 56
national sports federations (NSFs), 56

Ordinary Arbitration Division (OAD), 172

Pakistan cricket spot-fixing scandal in 2010, 80
personal appearance contract, 65
procedural relaxations, 38
professional services contracts, 64
Programme for Education and Awareness on Anti-Doping in Sports (PEADS), 136

Public Interest Litigation (PIL), 83
Jurisprudence vis-à-vis Indian
Sports Law, 86
Cricket Association of Bihar
Case, 89–95
IPL Drought Case, 95–97
Sachin Tendulkar Bharat
Ratna Case, 97–99
Sarita Devi case, 87, 89
sports law, concept, 84–86
public trust law
Bombay model, 37
impact of, 37–38

Regional Anti-Doping
Organizations (RADOs),
122
Registration of Societies Act
Suffice, 51
religious dictates and sports in
India
FIBA
Central Board, 152
FIBA
championship cups, 155
FIFA, 153
remedial steps, 150
rule amended, 154
SALDEF, 151
sports and human rights, 147
Article 4.4.2, 148
NCAA Rulebook, 148
Universal Declaration of
Human Rights (UDHR),
149
Right to Information (RTI) Act,
2005, 58
rules arbitration commission
(RAC), 160
rules of the sporting federation
and the Arbitration and
Conciliation Act 1996,
160

Sachin Tendulkar Bharat Ratna
Case, 97–99
Sikh American Legal Defense
and Education Fund
(SALDEF), 151
Societies Registration Act, 1860,
7, 34
sponsorships and endorsement
contracts, 64
Sporting Fraud Bill, 2013
key provisions, 80
objectives, 79
sports administration, 47
checks and balances, 55
democratic process, 53
clear organisational framework, 54
decision-making bodies, 54
members, role and rights, 54
stakeholders, role and rights,
54
parameters of human rights,
26–28
solidarity, 55
transparency and public communication, 48
accountability standards,
establishment, 52
cases, 48
confidentiality, 53
disbursement and allocation
of funds, 53
financial reporting, 52
internal control, measures, 52
performance indicators, identification, 52
risk management, 53
sports associations (SAs), 19
communitarian base, 26
communitarian forum, 20
Competition Act, control, 41
constitutional law, impact,
28–34

contribution of organisations, 23
corporate social responsibility (CSR), 42
cultures, 21
flow of funds, 25
Kerala Sports Act, 2000, 43
National Sports Policy, 2001, 24
post-Industrial Revolution, 24
sports activities, economic dimensions, 25
tax exemption and deduction laws, impact, 39–41
Sports Authority of India (SAI), 57, 136
sports bodies, 3
Sports Broadcasting Signals (Mandatory Sharing with Prasar Bharati) Act, 2007, 195
sports contracts, 63
  categories, 67
  importance of, 69
  peculiarity in, 67
  termination of, 68
sports federations, 53
sports governing bodies, 243
sports jurisprudence in India, 4
Sports Recreation Alliance (SRA), 24
Stakeholders, 52
standard player contracts See professional services contracts, 64

state laws, 36

Tamil Nadu Societies Registration Act, 23
The Board of Control for Cricket in India, 3
the State in Article 12, 4–10
Therapeutic use exemption (TUE), 136
tiered arbitration clauses, 164
Trans World International (TWI), 204
Travancore–Cochin Act, 1955, 34

UK Anti-Doping Agency (UKADA), 128
US Anti-Doping Agency (USADA), 126

World Anti-Doping Agency (WADA), 70, 101
  anti-doping programmes
    privacy and data protection, implications, 110–116
  defamation and journalistic responsibility
    disclosers, implications, 116–119
  personal liberty and bodily integrity
    implications, 103–110
World Anti-Doping Code (WADC), 70
writ remedy under Article 226, 239

Other titles in this series:

Law of Business Contracts in India, Sairam Bhat (ed.)

Water and the Laws in India, Ramaswamy R. Iyer (ed.)

Protection of Himalayan Biodiversity: International Environmental Law and a Regional Legal Framework, Ananda Mohan Bhattarai

Social Justice and Labour Jurisprudence, Sharath Babu and Rashmi Shetty

Social Legislation of the East India Company: Public Justice versus Public Instruction, Nancy Gardner Cassels

Natural Resources Conservation Law, Sairam Bhat

Business and Human Rights, Manoj Kumar Sinha (ed.)

Crime and Justice in India, N. Prabha Unnithan (ed.)

In Custody: Law, Impunity and Prisoner Abuse in South Asia, Nitya Ramakrishnan

Law and Economics (Volume I: Theory and Volume II: Practice), Subhashis Gangopadhyay and V. Santhakumar (eds)

Separated and Divorced Women in India: Economic Rights and Entitlements, Kirti Singh

Women and Law: Critical Feminist Perspectives, Kalpana Kannabiran (ed.)

The Protection of Geographical Indications in India: A New Perspective on the French and European Experience, Delphine Marie-Vivien

Child Sexual Abuse and Protection Laws in India, Debarati Halder